DANTE IN DEUTSCHLAND

New Studies in the Age of Goethe

New Studies in the Age of Goethe, sponsored by the Goethe Society of North America, aims to publish innovative research that contextualizes the "Age of Goethe," whether within the fields of literature, history (including art history and history of science), philosophy, art, music, or politics. Though the series editors welcome all approaches and perspectives, they are especially interested in interdisciplinary projects, creative approaches to archival or original source materials, theoretically informed scholarship, work that introduces previously undiscovered materials, and projects that re-examine traditional epochal boundaries or open new channels of interpretations.

Recent titles in the series:

Dante in Deutschland: An Itinerary of Romantic Myth
Daniel DiMassa

Play in the Age of Goethe: Theories, Narratives, and Practices of Play around 1800
Edgar Landgraf and Elliott Schreiber, eds.

Pretexts for Writing: German Romantic Prefaces, Literature, and Philosophy
Seán Williams

Odysseys of Recognition: Performing Intersubjectivity in Homer, Aristotle, Shakespeare, Goethe, and Kleist
Ellwood Wiggins

A Pedagogy of Observation: Nineteenth-Century Panoramas, German Literature, and Reading Culture
Vance Byrd

Romanticism, Origins, and the History of Heredity
Christine Lehleiter

Aesthetics as Secular Millennialism: Its Trail from Baumgarten and Kant to Walt Disney and Hitler
Benjamin Bennett

The Mask and the Quill: Actress-Writers in Germany from Enlightenment to Romanticism
Mary Helen Dupree

After Jena: Goethe's Elective Affinities and the End of the Old Regime
Peter J. Schwartz

Reading Riddles: Rhetorics of Obscurity from Romanticism to Freud
Brian Tucker

For more information about the series, please visit www.bucknelluniversitypress.org.

DANTE IN DEUTSCHLAND

An Itinerary of Romantic Myth

Daniel DiMassa

Bucknell University | University Press

Lewisburg, Pennsylvania

Library of Congress Cataloging-in-Publication Data
Names: DiMassa, Daniel, author.
Title: Dante in Deutschland : an itinerary of Romantic myth / Daniel DiMassa.
Description: Lewisburg, Pennsylvania : Bucknell University Press, [2022] | Series: New studies in the age of Goethe | Includes bibliographical references and index.
Identifiers: LCCN 2021046801 | ISBN 9781684484188 (paperback ; alk. paper) | ISBN 9781684484195 (hardback ; alk. paper) | ISBN 9781684484201 (epub) | ISBN 9781684484218 (mobi) | ISBN 9781684484225 (pdf)
Subjects: LCSH: Dante Alighieri, 1265–1321—Appreciation—Germany. | Dante Alighieri, 1265–1321. Divina commedia—Influence. | German literature—19th century—History and criticism. | Romanticism—Germany. | Mythology in literature. | LCGFT: Literary criticism.
Classification: LCC PQ4385.G4 D56 2022 | DDC 851/.1—dc23/eng/20211124
LC record available at https://lccn.loc.gov/2021046801

A British Cataloging-in-Publication record for this book is available from the British Library.

∞ The paper used in this publication meets the requirements of the American National Standard for Information Sciences—Permanence of Paper for Printed Library Materials, ANSI Z39.48-1992.

www.bucknelluniversitypress.org

Distributed worldwide by Rutgers University Press

Manufactured in the United States of America

For Victoria and Teddy

CONTENTS

FIGURES

ABBREVIATIONS

AWSW	*August Wilhelm von Schlegel's Sämmtliche Werke*. Edited by Eduard Böcking. 12 vols. Leipzig: Weidmann, 1846–1847.
CA	Gerhart Hauptmann, *Sämtliche Werke*. Edited by Hans-Egon Hass. Centenar-Ausgabe. 11 vols. Berlin: Propyläen, 1962–1974 (Sonderausgabe 1996).
FA	Johann Wolfgang Goethe, *Sämtliche Werke: Briefe, Tagebücher und Gespräche*. Edited by Dieter Borchmeyer et al. 40 vols. Frankfurt: Deutscher Klassiker, 1985–.
GkFA	Thomas Mann, *Große kommentierte Frankfurter Ausgabe: Werke—Briefe—Tagebücher*. Edited by Heinrich Detering et al. 23 vols. Frankfurt: S. Fischer, 2002–.
GW	Rudolf Borchardt, *Gesammelte Werke in Einzelbänden*. Edited by Marie Luise Borchardt. 14 vols. Stuttgart: Ernst Klett, 1955–.
HkA	Friedrich Wilhelm Joseph Schelling, *Historisch-kritische Ausgabe*. Edited by Hans Michael Baumgartner et al. 35 vols. Stuttgart: Frommann-Holzboog, 1976–.
Inf./ Purg./ Par.	Dante, *The Divine Comedy of Dante Alighieri*. Edited and translated by Robert M. Durling and Ronald L. Martinez. 3 vols. New York: Oxford University Press, 1996–2013.
KAV	August Wilhelm Schlegel, *Kritische Ausgabe der Vorlesungen*. Edited by Ernst Behler and Frank Jolles. 6 vols. Paderborn: F. Schöningh, 1989–.
KFSA	Friedrich von Schlegel, *Kritische Friedrich-Schlegel-Ausgabe*. Edited by Ernst Behler, Jean Jacques Anstett, and Hans Eichner. 35 vols. Munich: F. Schöningh, 1958–.

MA	Johann Wolfgang Goethe, *Sämtliche Werke nach Epochen seines Schaffens*. Edited by Karl Richter, Herbert Göpfert, Norbert Miller, and Gerhard Sauder. 21 vols. Munich: Hanser, 1985–.
SBD	Friedrich Wilhelm Joseph Schelling, *Briefe und Dokumente*. Edited by Horst Fuhrmans. 3 vols. Bonn: Bouvier, 1962–1965.
Schriften	*Novalis Schriften: Die Werke Friedrich von Hardenbergs*. Edited by Richard Samuel, with Hans-Joachim Mähl, Heinz Ritter, and Gerhard Schulz. 6 vols. Stuttgart: Kohlhammer, 1960–.
SGSW	Stefan George, *Sämtliche Werke*. 18 vols. Stuttgart: Klett-Cotta, 1982–2013.
SW	*Friedrich Wilhelm Joseph von Schellings Sämmtliche Werke*. Edited by Karl Friedrich August Schelling. 14 vols. Stuttgart: Cotta, 1856–1861.
VN	Dante, *Vita nuova*. In *Opere minori di Dante Alighieri*, edited by Giorgio Bárberi Squarotti, vol. 1. Torino: Unione tipografico-editrice torinese, 1983.
WA	*Goethes Werke*. 133 vols. Weimar: Böhlau, 1887–1919.

A NOTE ON TRANSLATION

Translations are my own unless otherwise noted. Translations from the *Commedia* are those of Robert M. Durling and Ronald L. Martinez (Oxford University Press, 1996–2011), except for those otherwise noted.

DANTE IN DEUTSCHLAND

Introduction

Orienting Romanticism

IN 1787, in a report from Naples, Goethe described the vexation that came of discussing national poets with literati in Italy. Did he favor Ariosto or Tasso, they wanted to know. It would not suffice to answer that Italy had been blessed with two first-class poets: he was expected to exalt one poet and compensate for his excellence by denigrating the other. Irritating though this was, the affair became dreadful when talk turned to Dante. Goethe once found that his words of praise for the great Florentine were, by virtue of sheer principle, unacceptable to his Italian interlocutor, who explained that "jeder Ausländer müsse Verzicht tun auf das Verständnis eines so außerordentlichen Geistes" (foreigners must give up trying to understand such an extraordinary spirit). After some back-and-forth, Goethe threw up his hands in frustration: surely he never understood the *Commedia*, for he found the *Inferno* "abscheulich" (abominable), the *Purgatorio* "zweideutig" (ambiguous), and the *Paradiso* simply "langweilig" (boring) (MA 15:461).

Over two centuries later, the notion that the *Commedia* should be illegible to all but Dante's countrymen strikes us as a comedy of its own sort. So, too, does Goethe's criticism. Precious few texts have found more readers in more languages. Neither the cultural stature of the *Commedia*, nor the herculean feat of rendering its 14,233 lines of *endecasillabo* into another language, have thwarted translators from undertaking the task. Every couple of years, or sometimes more than once in the same year, we celebrate these translators for what seems a "fiendishly difficult" feat, akin perhaps to summiting Mount Everest.[1] Special honors are reserved for the brave souls who remain faithful to the *terza rima* of the original, as well as for the unflagging wayfarers who render full translations of all three canticles. "The perfect translation of Dante's 'Divine Comedy' remains one of literature's holiest grails," as Joseph Luzzi has written.[2] No doubt this is true, but it is not just literary folk who venerate the poem and its poet. Artists from Botticelli to Dalí have given visual expression to the poem, whose panoply of images has likewise inspired creators of Japanese anime and American video games. Fittingly enough, the poet who wrote of "l'amor che move il sole e l'altre stelle" (the love that moves the sun and the other stars) has an asteroid named in his honor. Understanding for the *Commedia*, in other words, is anything but an Italian affair; it borders on the otherworldly.

This has not always been the case, nor would the notion have been conceivable to Goethe that modern European literatures, as one German poet wrote in 1908, owed their progress to Germans' discovery of Dante.[3] For in 1787, the mention of Dante was likely to conjure images of a gothic poet of the Church, not the rival of Homer. To most educated Europeans, the *Commedia* was reducible to two cantos, *Inferno* 5 and *Inferno* 33, which had come to represent extremes of human experience. The former, in which Paolo and Francesca recount how reading romances led them to adultery, became a touchstone for reflections on the depths of pathos. The latter, in which Ugolino intimates that starvation led him to eat his children's corpses, was a benchmark for the macabre. Goethe merely reflected contemporary standards, then, when he confessed to the Neapolitan his aversion to the *Commedia*.

Much has changed since Goethe, and the seeds of that change were planted in the years just after his return from Italy. It is no secret that Dante, whose bust is now perched opposite that of Goethe in the Rococo Hall of Weimar's Anna-Amalia Bibliothek, owes his diffusion among Germans to Romantic readers. Ironically, the first significant translation of the *Commedia* into German—a series of translations by the budding philologist August Wilhelm Schlegel—appeared alongside a novella of Goethe in Friedrich Schiller's otherwise classicizing journal, *Die Horen* (*The Horae*). Schlegel, who went on to publish the founding journal of German Romanticism, the *Athenaeum*, relinquished his translation project in favor of an edition of Shakespeare; it was nearly three decades until Karl Ludwig Kannegießer completed the first translation of the entire *Commedia* into German verse. But the ground for Dante had been prepared. Schlegel's translations led to the formation of a fervent reading circle devoted to the *Commedia* in the university town of Jena, just outside Weimar. In the winter of 1799, at Leutragasse 5, a group of friends, rivals, and lovers wended their way through the Italian of Dante's poem. With the discipline of monks they gathered in the evening, plied their Italian on Dante's tercets, and retreated to their cells. The exercises became a daily office. By New Year's, 1800, the troupe had coursed through Hell and climbed to the third of Mount Purgatory's seven terraces, which is to say, they had covered some 50 percent of the poem.

The members of this "first avant-garde group in history" regarded Dante as an inflection point in history.[4] A. W. Schlegel, despite relinquishing his translation, described Dante as one of the "riesenhaften Schatten der Vorwelt, für die es jetzt an der Zeit ist, wieder aufzuerstehen" (gigantic shades of the primeval world, for whom the hour of resurrection has now come) (KAV 2/1:148). His younger brother, Friedrich Schlegel, who came to be the unofficial mouthpiece of Early German Romanticism (*Frühromantik*), was no less enamored. In his words, Dante was the "heilige[r] Stifter und Vater der modernen Poesie" (sacred founder and father of modern poetry) (KFSA 2:297). Their partners, Caroline and Dorothea, who were also writers, participated in these readings, as did the precocious philosopher of Idealism, Friedrich Schelling, who at the age of twenty-three had just been appointed a professor with the support of Goethe. It was Schelling who voiced the most superlative characterization of Dante's poem: the *Commedia* amounted not to a single poem but to the "ganze Gattung der neueren Poesie" (entire genre of modern poetry). As a world unto itself, he opined, it demanded its own theory (SW 5:152–153).

The present book traces the emergence and realization of that theory, arguing that to the Romantics, the *Commedia* was more than a touchstone—it was a lodestar, its author no less vital to them than Shakespeare had been to the Sturm und Drang. The Romantics' pursuit of the *Commedia* as a paradigmatic aesthetic object did more than popularize the poem among German readers: for many of their readers, it rendered the *Commedia* indistinguishable from the *Romantik*. In extreme cases, the poem resembled a national treasure bequeathed to Germans at the behest of its Romantic archaeologists.

There are ostensibly persuasive reasons to doubt such claims. Anyone who has leafed through the fragments and notes of the early Romantics, for example, has read statements like the ones above. They were not uncommon among the Schlegels, who often heaped similarly exuberant adulation upon other writers—notably Shakespeare, Calderón, and Goethe. Effusive praise of this sort is virtually synonymous with Romanticism, to the point that it rarely holds our attention. Consider, for example, that the Dantist, Robert Hollander, wrote off Romantic adaptations of the poem as a bit of

Goethean Sturm und Drang, while the Romanticist Ernst Behler mustered mostly platitudes when describing the Romantics' engagement with Dante.[5] In 2009, the organizers of a conference on the topic of "Metamorphosing Dante" indicated their interest in twentieth- and twenty-first-century adaptations of the *Commedia* by dismissing Romantic approaches to the poet as "a-critical . . . Kitsch tribute."[6] Such views presuppose that Romantic rhetoric could amount only to naivete, to idiocy, or to the ballyhoo of cultural propagandists. Some of that is valid, to be sure, but it ought not circumscribe the view of the Romantics' Dante. Their enthusiasm may be off-putting, but that does not make it uniformly vacuous. Kitschy or not, their engagement with the *Commedia* carried critical weight.

More perspicacious deliberation might still yield skepticism: perhaps the preoccupation with Dante was not internal to the project in Jena, but an untimely harbinger of the Romantics' conservative turn—their conversions to Catholicism, embrace of orthodoxy, rehabilitation of medieval Christian art, and rapprochement with imperial power. The *Commedia*, by this view, is not intrinsic to Romanticism so much as it is anticipatory of the puzzling emergence of conservatism from a cradle of radicality. There is something to be said for such a view. As this book shows, Dante came to figure in Germans' nationalistic and fascist recuperations of Romanticism in the first decades of the twentieth century. In 1800, however, that trajectory would have been difficult to surmise. In the very winter when the early Romantics read the *Commedia*, Friedrich Schlegel had just published a salacious and experimental novel; Schelling was putting the finishing touches on his seminal tracts in *Naturphilosophie*; their friend, Friedrich Schleiermacher, was preaching a gospel of Spinoza in his speeches on religion; and J. G. Fichte, the erstwhile philosophical idol of them all, had embroiled Jena in the "Atheism Controversy." The Romantics' reception of the *Commedia*, portend though it did a turn to conservatism, was contiguous with the literary and philosophical radicality that marked the pivotal early years in Jena.

Venerated neither for its Catholicism nor its canonicity, the *Commedia* represented a model for the realization of the most ambitious program of Romanticism, the so-called *neue Mythologie* (new mythology). The amorphous notion was born of disillusionment that came from the inability of the Enlightenment to approach the utopia that its stock in reason had underwritten. In this way, as Nicholas Halmi has written, the project of a new mythology aimed to "continue the emancipatory work of enlightenment by the very means from which the Enlightenment had imagined itself to have been emancipated."[7] Apodictic language was a hallmark of Romantic rhetoric, but the project was basically aspirational and speculative, and thus visible primarily in inchoate forms. It was a project with no end in sight. Conceived as a feat of aesthetic engineering on the grandest scale, it would hasten the advent of social harmony by uniting people in art; by educating the *Volk* and eliminating the barriers between them and the *Philosophen*; and by mediating the rift between materialists and idealists. Without exaggerating too much, one might regard the whole of Romanticism as an effort to summon the new mythology into being. Predictably, though, the logistics did not exist, and from the more explicitly deliberate attempts at a mythology, there remains a mélange of fragments—novels, poems, lecture notes, encyclopedias, and a range of chaotic plans in letters and journals. In the chapters that follow, I gather, sort, and piece together a network of these fragments, showing that, as they formulated their plans for the new mythology, the early German Romantics envisioned it taking the form of a new *Commedia*. Hardly just a *divertimento di notte*, the communal reading of the poem in 1799 shaped how German poets, theorists, and philosophers anticipated the advent of modern literature.

Situated at the imbrication of theory and practice, the project of a new mythology focuses our attention on a governing postulate of Romantic poetics: that theory instantiate itself as literature. To use Friedrich Schlegel's formulation, an adequate theory of the novel would have to be a novel (KFSA 2:337). This conviction found decisive scholarly articulation in Philippe Lacoue-Labarthe and Jean-Luc Nancy's *The Literary Absolute* (1988), which helped to popularize the notion of early German Romanticism as a precursor to twentieth-century theory. It continues to animate our understanding of Romanticism, resonating, for example, in Leif Weatherby's gnome that "Romanticism means the risk that theory is real."[8] It echoes in Halmi's study of the Romantic symbol, wherein Romanticism materializes as a form of theory that often complicates its own realization.[9] I point to these articulations neither to challenge them nor to bask in the triumph over our "naivete,"[10] but because they point to the Romantic omphalos that this book investigates. The project of a Dantean mythology resides at the nexus of theory and literature.

By examining not just the Romantics' attempt at a mythology, but their attempt at a *Dantean* mythology, the present study works from a place of advantage. The instruments of philology, hermeneutics, and history can be leveraged, if not to render the strange corpus of Romanticism familiar, then at least to triangulate that corpus with a familiar object. Beyond opening new interpretations of Romantic works, this operation allows us to trace an itinerary of Romantic myth, highlighting the waystations of a path that has remained in obscurity. Mapping that itinerary yields unexpected insight, for in the effort to perform just such a triangulation—to survey Romanticism with respect to Dante and the *Commedia*—we come upon a disconnect in the effort of Romanticism to realize theory as literature. It manifests itself already in my uncertainty whether to speak of a Romantic debt to Dante, on the one hand, or to the *Commedia*, on the other. That ambiguity illuminates a misalignment in the theorization and the realization of the new mythology. The waystations on the itinerary reveal that, having summoned the shadow of Dante, Romantic myth became fixated on the legitimation of its own *auctoritas*.

For a project that had endorsed a collective impulse, this was an unforeseen preoccupation. Its utopian aspirations, after all, epitomized the "kollektiv Verpflichtendes" (collectively binding force) of myth.[11] Yet the literature at hand reckons as much with the person of Dante as it seeks to appropriate the structures of the *Commedia*. There is a perceptible attempt to shore up the authority of the poet from whom myth originates. Schelling and Novalis, for example, beyond imitating the *Commedia*, generated Dantean myths of their authorial personae. These myths led to their comparison with Dante throughout the nineteenth century. The Schlegel brothers, who would have induced Goethe to anoint the project in his name, construed him at various points as a new Dante. Neo-Romantic projects of myth, too, focused on strategies of legitimation that were rooted in the authority of the poet. This authority—as in the cases of Gerhart Hauptmann, Rudolf Borchardt, and Stefan George—was invariably conditioned by the person of Dante. By adopting a poetic model whose hero was its author, the Romantics rendered the new mythology inseparable from the person who generated it.

That inseparability was consequential not just for the self-understanding of the early Romantics but also for how Romanticism was received, transformed, and renewed. Some of the earliest chroniclers of the period—Henrik Steffens and Heinrich Heine—detected a Dantean dynamic in the *Frühromantik*. It likely contributed to Heine's bleak view of the period's infatuation with Catholicism. For others, like Karl Immermann, the association with Dante was salutary.[12] To some, the Florentine poet became an emblem of German Romanticism. This was quite literally true of the *Lukasbund* (Brotherhood of St. Luke), a collective of Romantic German painters. They identified Saint Luke as their patron, but they stamped their works with a seal in which the evangelist bore the visage of Dante (figure I.1).[13] Many of these painters lived and worked in Rome, where nearly every one of them attended German lectures on the *Commedia*.[14] Several of them, including

fig. I.1. Friedrich Overbeck, *Emblem of the Lukasbund*, 1809. Bibliothek der Hansestadt Lübeck.

Philipp Veit, the stepson of Friedrich Schlegel, completed a series of frescoes of the *Commedia* in the Villa Massimo.[15] The frescoes ought not be understood under the rubric of the new mythology—many of the painters were orthodox Catholics.[16] Yet the centrality of Dante to the *Lukasbund*, and the national implications of their art, demonstrate how the prospect of a Dantean mythology stretched like a thread and wove together successive manifestations of the Romantic. So infused with national meaning had the reception of Dante become that, by the early twentieth century, two German historians lamented that the incompletion of the initial draft of the frescoes marked one of the "größten Verlusten nicht nur der Kunstgeschichte des 19. Jahrhunderts, sondern der deutschen Kulturgeschichte überhaupt" (greatest losses not only of art history of the nineteenth century, but of German cultural history at all) (figure I.2).[17]

fig. I.2. Adam Eberle after Peter Cornelius, *St. Bernard of Clairvaux and Dante before the Trinity*, 1830. Reproduced from J. Doellinger, *Umrisse zu Dante's Paradies, von Peter von Cornelius*. Leipzig: Boerner, 1830.

Picking up the thread at its source, Jena in 1799, the present book traces its course over the next century and a half. It focuses on the moments in that span when Dante's presence authorizes the generation of a new mythology. In brief, these moments encompass the theorization of and first attempts at a Dantean mythology, ca. 1800; Goethe's deployment of Dante in myths of the self and of the world, ca. 1830; Neo-Romantics' attempts at a new golden age, ca. 1900–1945; and finally, Thomas Mann's efforts at demythologization, ca. 1920–1947. The goal in tracing such a thread is not just to assert the significance of Dante for German readers—that speaks for itself—but to illuminate a narrative of Romantic poetics that has lain in obscurity. This obscurity is particularly curious given myth's status as a timeworn object of Romantic historiography. At the start of the last century, Fritz Strich identified myth as determinative of the German canon from Klopstock to Wagner. In the time since, that assessment has been advanced and refined. Manfred Frank investigated the philosophical roots of Romantic myth and traced its Dionysian valences across two centuries. More recently, George Williamson has charted an intellectual history of the debates around myth that roiled a wider German audience in the nineteenth century. There is no shortage of scholarship on Romantic myth, but I enumerate these seminal texts because they highlight something fundamental about the phenomenon: myth is a privileged object of interest in Romanticism, but Romantic myth eludes tidy periodization.[18]

The diachronic twists of the study at hand have their advantage: they focus our attention on a familiar yet puzzling trajectory of Romanticism—its move from radicality and revolution to Catholicism and conservatism. It is not the straight line from Schelling to Hitler that Lukács drew,[19] and yet a glance at the narrative shows that a myth inflected by Dante culminates in a trio of figures who embodied one form of fascism or another—Hauptmann, Borchardt, and George. To contest that trajectory would not only be futile, it would be irresponsible. There must be some reckoning with the course of this history. That does not entail, however, the dismissal of readings like those of Manfred Frank, Frederick Beiser, and Stefan Matuschek—each of whom contests the assertion of an irrational, reactionary Romanticism.[20] In fact, I agree with them: there was nothing intrinsically irrational or reactionary about the *Frühromantik*. It emerged from the height of the German Enlightenment and, with its new veneration of art, aspired to realize the goals of Enlightenment. Admittedly, such a positive view of the *Frühromantik* results in the apparent double bind of professing the irrational fate of a rational Romanticism.

The present book attempts, if not a resolution of that conundrum, then at least the start of one. It emerges from an attention to that inconsistency already observed in Romantic theory and poetry. Romantic theory suggested that in its scope, its arrangement, and its forms the *Commedia* demonstrated how to realize a new mythology; yet Romantic poetry fixated on the person and life of Dante. The result was a practice that discloses, particularly in Schelling and Novalis, an effort to legitimate itself as mythological by virtue of its authorship. That effort, combined with the attempts to align Goethe with Dante, reconfigured the new mythology: theorized as an enlightening religion of the senses, its assumption of poetic form was plagued by that perennial ordeal of traditional religion, the quest for legitimation. To be sure, this impulse was nascent in the furor of Romantic theory. Friedrich Schlegel and Novalis, for example, stylized themselves as evangelists of a new religion, and all the while that the *Commedia* figured in the talk of a mythology, Dante was never far off. Yet the decisive factor was the poetry. Its preoccupation with authorial legitimacy, visible in the imitation of a Dantean poetic subjectivity, displaced the locus of myth from poetry to poet.

There was a new mythology, after all, but its object was not nature, or spirit, or the absolute, it was Romanticism itself. The later chapters of this book show how the Dantean mythologization of Romantic *auctoritas* lent itself to nationalism, fascism, and irrationalism.

In short, the present book contends with Early German Romanticism and its legacy, arguing that the figure of Dante is crucial for that endeavor. Its trajectory, therefore, takes seriously the dynamic of reception that Hans Robert Jauss outlined: the following chapters trace a literary history that is intent not just on individual receptions of an autonomous object, but instead on a history wherein the reception of that object accrues its own agency and determines in turn the process of reception.[21] In this sense, the endeavor is not a traditional reception history of a poet, though many such histories help orient it. The most valuable among them are those by Arturo Farinelli, Werner Friederich, Michael Caesar, and Eva Hölter.[22] Mirjam Mansen, meanwhile, has written an important study of Dante's German reception in the first half of the twentieth century.[23] Fewer such reception histories concentrate on the position of Dante in early German Romanticism.[24] Noteworthy in this respect, then, is an early report by Clara Charlotte Fuchs, a student of Erich Auerbach, whose inaugural address in Marburg also took up the matter.[25] At that time, though, the Romantics' Dante was just finding new life among poets whose texts now merit an inquiry of their own. Indeed, the time is ripe for just such a reassessment.[26]

We would do well, however, before undertaking this endeavor, to revisit the *Commedia* and some of the perennial problems in its interpretation. They are an important propaedeutic in approaching the Romantics' reckoning with Dante.

By the time he began to write it, in the first decade of the fourteenth century, Dante was a poet of repute. With Guido Guinizelli and Guido Cavalcanti, he had refashioned the song tradition of the Provençal troubadours and codified it in a new style of love poetry, which he called the *dolce stil novo* (sweet new style) (*Purg.* 24.57). It was on display in his *Vita nuova*, where in ecstatic and religious terms he celebrated his love for Beatrice, a woman who had died several years earlier. From one angle, the *Commedia* is a fantastical resumption of this poetic-biographical material: from her place in heaven, Beatrice observes Dante's troubles among the living and sends a guide, Virgil, to lead him to her in Heaven. Thus the journey through the serpentine pit of Hell, up the terraces of Mount Purgatory, and—accompanied no longer by Virgil, but by Beatrice—into the spheres of Paradise where he witnesses a vision of God—the *Commedia* in a nutshell.

The apparent simplicity of the journey belies the complexity of the poetry. Schelling's inclination to read the poem as an all-encompassing genre gets at the unique multisidedness of the *Commedia*. Consider, for example, how its genres are interwoven. The poem has the elements of a romance, but the romance is part of a conversion narrative: the long-sought encounter with Beatrice yields purgation, compunction, and beatitude. If this makes the poem a fusion of, say, Provençal love poetry and Augustine's *Confessions*, then its encyclopedic ambitions—its didacticizing synthesis of diverse branches of knowledge—render it akin to Thomas Aquinas's *Summa theologica*. Yet Dante's incorporation of pagan deities, his invocation of the muses and of Apollo, and the scope of the poem suggest an affinity to the classical epic. So, too, does his being guided by Virgil. Dante is like Aeneas and Odysseus, after all, in that he visits the underworld. But as he notes, this also renders him analogous to Saint Paul (*Inf.* 2.32). Like Paul, who was rapt up to heaven, as well as John and Ezekiel, Dante witnesses cosmic spectacles on his pilgrimage. Thus the *Commedia* shares similarities, too, with the visionary literature of the Bible. This is to say nothing yet of Dante's designation of the poem as a comedy. The form and pretensions of the poem present unusual challenges of interpretation and classification.

No less daunting are its techniques of narration. When I wrote some handful of lines ago, for example, that "Dante is like Aeneas and Odysseus," I was not as careful as I might have been, or as careful as the poem sometimes demands. Occasionally, one must distinguish between Dante the pilgrim (i.e., the protagonist of the poem) and Dante the poet (its lyrical subject). One might even append Dante Alighieri (1265–1321), the historical figure, as a third Dante. The distinctions seem hairsplitting, more suited to Boccaccio's tale of women in Verona who, when they saw Dante, noted how his beard had been singed by the fires of Hell.[27] But these distinctions are consequences of the poem's insistence on its own reality. That insistence, as Erich Auerbach pointed out, found voice in an innovative technique of narration: the extended direct address to the reader.[28] Many of these addresses, like the one below, where Dante describes the arrival of a monster (Geryon), press for faith in the veracity of the poet's incredible claims:

> Sempre a quel ver c'ha faccia di menzogna
> de' l'uom chiuder le labbra fin ch'el puote,
> però che sanza colpa fa vergogna;
> ma qui tacer nol posso, e per le note
> di questa comedìa, lettor, ti giuro,

s'elle non sien di lunga grazia vòte,
    ch'i' vidi per quell' aere grosso e scuro
venir notando una figura in suso,
maravigliosa ad ogne cor sicuro.

(Always to that truth which has the face of
falsehood one should close one's lips as long as one
can, for without any guilt it brings shame;
    but here I cannot conceal it, and by the notes of
this comedy, reader, I swear to you, so may they not
fail to find long favor,
    that I saw, through that thick dark air, a figure
come swimming upward, fearful to the most
confident heart.) (*Inf.* 16.124–132)

The frequency and intensity of such addresses leave the impression that, whether readers grant the truth of the poem or not, Dante is convinced by it. Yet there is rarely not some ambiguity that haunts the status of such claims: in the address above, for example, it is not to be overlooked that the monster whose arrival Dante describes is a monster of fraud. The poet's tenacity demands a reckoning with the veracity of his claims, his artistry with their artifice.

Indeed, the status of the poem's truth and fiction has been vital since the earliest days of its reception, when to grant its literal truth was tantamount to heresy. In 1335, for example, a Dominican chapter house in Florence banned the text on grounds of heresy. Some defended the poem, as Teodolinda Barolini has explained, by distinguishing its author's poetic fictions from the theological truths behind them: the narrative was chalked up to fantasy, its allegorical meaning the stuff of real value.[29] Interpretations of this variety belong to the "allegory of the poets," a mode of interpretation that Dante described in the *Convivio*. Charles Singleton argued that this form of interpretation subordinates the text at every turn to some hidden allegorical meaning.[30] It is a "this for that," the text a hurdle to be got past. Singleton's distaste for the allegory of the poets was not new. Among its critics was Benedetto Croce, who bemoaned that the allegorical hunt debased the letter of the text.[31] He proposed an aesthetic exposition that would rely on philological exegesis: the *Commedia* would be treated like any other poetic text. It sounds sensible, to be sure, but its failure to think through the poem's claims to realism led Singleton to advocate a different approach—the "allegory of the theologians." This hermeneutic, also outlined in the *Convivio*, develops out of biblical exegesis. It postulates that the literal level of the text has a truth that, on occasion, yields an allegorical meaning. Instead of a "this for that," it is a "this *and* that." Ironically, the allegory of the theologians vouchsafes the poetry, whereas the allegory of the poets neglects the poetry. The conflict between the two centers on the status of literal truth.

In recent decades, Teodolinda Barolini has argued that to grant the dichotomy of poem-as-theology / poem-as-artifice is a misprision.[32] Those who would read the *Commedia* as theology dressed in poetry have struggled to reconcile its religious pretensions and its poetic self-consciousness, as if prophets were by necessity naive, bequeathing their testaments without the aid of literary devices. On the other hand, those who would read the poem to the exclusion of its religious ambitions, hell-bent on not falling prey to the author's fiction, have "revealed themselves to be the more fully duped by an author whose cunning they had not begun to penetrate" (20). The poem's literary force is intertwined with its claims to sacred truth; its poetry stands in the service of the vision. When that relationship is severed, Barolini argues, we lose purchase on Dante's "hall of mirrors." He must be confronted as *theologus-poeta*.

There are three modern *dantisti*, by Barolini's reckoning, who manage to "look at the *Commedia* not through a glass darkly but face to face" (3). The first is Bruno Nardi, an ex-seminarian whose essay "Dante profeta" takes seriously Dante's self-understanding as a prophet; even if he had not "been" to the afterlife, Dante believed it to have been revealed to him. The second is Charles Singleton. His insistence on the allegory of the theologians demands that the literal level of the poem be taken seriously. The last of the three is Erich Auerbach, who argued that the poem uses a religious hermeneutic, typology, in representing a secular vision. By this reading, the figures whom Dante encounters in the poem are the fulfillment of the same figures' earthly versions of themselves: their identities emerge with a crystalline intensity on the stage of eternity. Inasmuch as Nardi had reckoned with the poem's prophecies; Singleton with the literal level of its narrative; and Auerbach with its theologico-historical representations, Barolini sees all three as part of a modern school that confronts the poem's pretensions to truth.

The terms of these debates bear on the course of the present study in two respects, one more germane than the other. First, as chapter one shows, Barolini's preferred reader of the *Commedia*, Erich Auerbach, adopts an approach that has its roots in Romanticism. For all the abuse they have suffered, the early Romantics were arguably the first modern readers of the poem. That insight, though, is secondary to the matters of why and how the Romantics adopted Dante and the *Commedia*. It is in that respect, especially, that the debates over the poem's claims to truth are significant. In short, Dante purported and represented something qualitatively different from every other figure in the Romantic canon. The absoluteness of the difference enables Albert Ascoli to write that "it seems obvious that no single work and no writer in the Western canon possesses more authority . . . than Dante Alighieri and the 'poema sacro.'"[33] The Romantic attempts at myth betray the need for just such an authority. At this point, then, let us preview our course—which begins when Dante's authority was not universally accepted.

Before taking up the matter of myth, I examine how Dante came to the Romantics' attention in the first place. Chapter one thus sketches how A. W. Schlegel—traditionally regarded as the most prosaic of the Early Romantics—excavated the *Commedia* from its reputation of gothic barbarism. That excavation provides useful background. More importantly, though, it disabuses us of the notion, propagated by Hegel, that the Romantics belonged to the school of riddle-cracking, allegory-splitting mystifiers (i.e., those who endorsed the allegory of the poets). It shows instead that Schlegel, trained by philologists in Göttingen, treated the *Commedia* as an object worthy of rigorous philological scrutiny. The distinction merits attention, for the approachability of the poem as an object of philology signaled its assimilability to the Romantic project of myth. I turn to that project by inquiring briefly after the origins of Early German Romanticism. It is a detour that accomplishes two ends: it accounts for the theory of the *neue Mythologie* and it sheds light on how Early German Romanticism became a fecund ground for the *Commedia*. On that note, the first chapter concludes by returning to Dante with a heuristic summary of how and why his poem harmonized with the Romantic theory of myth.

Chapter two sees the Romantics' project of Dantean myth ramify. Early on, Schelling and Goethe were poised to realize a grand, didactic poem of nature. When the latter abandoned it, the former undertook a Dantean reinterpretation. Novalis, meanwhile, was at work on the seminal novel of Romanticism, using Dante's poetics of dreams to render a poetic myth of absolute idealism. These undertakings represented distinctive gestures at realizing the Romantic project. *Heinrich von Ofterdingen*, in particular, engages in genuinely inventive ways with the *Commedia*. Nevertheless, there were obstacles with which to reckon. In Schelling and Novalis, one witnesses approximations—subtle *and* egregious, impressive *and* pathetic—of Dante's person. Not mere imitations of the man, they are attempts to conjure his magic; they are efforts to manifest his authority and thereby legitimate the revelations to which their poetry lays claim. The impulse to do so can only have been magnified, meanwhile, by the Schlegel brothers, who at this time had laid the mantle of Dante before the feet of Goethe. Conceived as an aesthetic project with equalizing force, the new mythology soon became enthralled to matters of poetic subjectivity, authority, and legitimacy.

This shift rendered Dante's position in the Romantic project ambivalent. He possessed unique authority and exercised it with unique force, but no Romantic poet could accrue such authority by slavishly imitating him. In the wake of the project's theorization, then, Dante remained a paradigmatic model of Romantic myth, albeit from a distance. Despite molding his identity on Dante, for example, Novalis does not utter the name *Dante* once in his entire corpus. Chapter three reveals similar equivocations in the case of Goethe. To be sure, Goethe did not belong to the *Romantik* proper, nor did he envision the advent of a utopian new mythology. Yet he is an essential figure in this narrative, because in their quest to realize a new mythology, the Romantics regarded Goethe as their most important ally. As Schelling opined, the only modern equivalent of the *Commedia* was Goethe's *Faust* (SW 5:156). But Goethe, too, reckoned as much with the poet as with his poetry.

Chapter three locates the roots of Goethe's engagement with Dante in a common tendency toward "automythology," a practice of self-inscription wherein mythic patterns of signification serve to absolutize the contingency of a life. With an eye to Goethe's lyrics, we witness how he uses the iconography of Dante's automythology to codify the obstacles, crises, and failures of his genius. The phenomenon is all the more interesting because, eventually, Dante slips the bounds of Goethe's automythological texts. In a belated fulfilment of Romantic wishes, his presence registers itself across the entirety of *Faust II*. The juxtaposition of Dante's role in the lyrics and the drama yields unexpected insight. The latter turns out not to be an abandonment of the automythological project; it is a displacement, abstraction, and ultimately a resolution of the crises that haunted that project. Dante's iconography once symbolized the end of Goethe's Promethean youth. In *Faust II*, it sanctions his striving and supplies the imagistic lexicon by which he conceives of salvation. Goethe reckons with the poetry and the poet.

The later stations on our itinerary reveal how preoccupations with authority result in a transmogrification of Romantic myth. These stations, to be clear, are no longer in the historical domain of Romanticism. Yet each of them figures as a resumption of the Dantean mythological project, and in the cases of Hauptmann and Borchardt, these are explicit efforts to rehabilitate it as a Romantic project.[34] Our domain, then, is Neo-Romanticism, from whose purview the *Romantik* had become a lost golden age. Chapter four examines how Gerhart Hauptmann—known today mostly for his Naturalist dramas and his Nobel Prize—divorces myth from reason and yokes it instead to language and rhetoric. It is no Romantic maneuver, but rather a by-product of the glorification of that age. It reveals an ominous effect of Romantic self-mythologizations. Myth had been decoupled from normative principles and wed to the contingencies of the German past: linguistic style, poetic habitus, historic filiations, among others. The result was a mad quest, in the decades between the world wars, to supersede the Romantics' Dante and to become a spiritual-poetic *Führer.*

No less troubling are the cases of the poets Rudolf Borchardt and Stefan George, covered in chapter five. Though they did not work together—they were enemies—the juxtaposition of these conservative Modernists is illuminating. Like Hauptmann, their endeavors depended in unique ways on the formal structures and rhetorical shapes of language. In fact, each was a translator of the *Commedia*, who in a subversion of history, deployed Dante's forms to instantiate a new age of myth. For a time, Borchardt even envisioned George as a Dantean figure whose Romantic heritage would bring about the advent of that age. His expectations were no less audacious than those of George. Stylizing himself after Dante, George—arguably the most important German poet of the twentieth century—adopted a complex system of esotericism from the *Commedia*. With it, he granted the foundational myth of his cultic "Kreis" (circle) a hermetic seal. Dante, it turns out, is a key to unlocking the homocentric secrets of George's "secret Germany." Shut out of the circle, however, Borchardt undertook his own Dantean venture. He completed a translation of the *Commedia*, which he conceived as a recommencement of A. W. Schlegel's project. In doing so, Borchardt believed he would awaken the slumbering German tongue and restore the nation to its medieval glory.

Our itinerary concludes with chapter six, and Thomas Mann, who represents—as far as I can tell—the first and only figure to reject the project of Dantean myth. His novels *Der Zauberberg* (*The Magic Mountain*) and *Doktor Faustus* represent subversions of that project as it took shape in and around the George-Kreis. Well before Horkheimer and Adorno and Cassirer recognized the part of myth in the catastrophes of the century, Mann saw its deleterious potential to mystify and absolutize authority.[35]

Few of the junctures on this course are unfamiliar, but *Dante in Deutschland* trains our eyes on them as waystations along an otherwise unfamiliar path through the old terrain of German Romanticism. The result, besides recasting canonical texts in a new light, is a re-reading of the advent and attempted reincarnation of that movement whose meaning for the German twentieth century was so fatal. As an itinerary, though, this book is less invested in deciding questions of culpability than it is in tracing the path by which Romanticism participated in the dialectic of Enlightenment. No one who lived through the historical Enlightenment could have imagined the towering influence of Dante in the formation of German modernity.

Part I

Romanticism

CHAPTER ONE

Discovering Dante and Theorizing Myth

The Schlegel Brothers and the Origins of the Romantic Project

AS HE ASCENDS THE TERRACES of Mount Purgatory, Dante shudders at the penance inflicted on the envious: their eyes have been sewn shut because they ogled the goods of others. Terrible though the sight is, it worries him less than the "tormento di sotto" (torment below) (*Purg.* 13.133–138). There, on a lower terrace, the prideful bear such heavy stones that their backs are hunched to the ground. Already, Dante can feel the weight of humility. In a poem that stretches credulity, it is an unusually credible confession.

Pride is intrinsic to the enterprise of the *Commedia*. Like Aeneas and Saint Paul, Dante purports to have been elected to experience the afterlife. Upon learning this, he seeks confirmation: "Ma io?" (But I?) (*Inf.* 2.31). It is an expression of humility, colored by a tincture of feigned surprise: "Who, me?" Readers soon become inured to Dante's ambitious self-representation, as, for example, when he disputes biblical revelation that diverges from the content of his vision (*Purg.* 29.104–105). Do we even wince upon reading that he has little reason to fear his eyes being sewn shut? After all, it is a claim to virtue as well as a sign of his not needing to envy anyone in the first place. So pervasive is Dante's pride that the poem's expositions of humility usually underscore his deficit of it. On the terrace of pride, he sees that God has carved into the marble face of the mountain a depiction of the Annunciation (*Purg.* 10.28–45); Mary's humility is an example to those who repent of their pride. To record this image of humility, however, the ekphrasis requires that Dante play God by conjuring the Creator's artwork. To catalog such moments would seem ungenerous, were it not for the unusual pretensions of the poem. They illuminate the rhetorical strategies that ensure the reception Dante planned for the poem.

The irony of which Dante could not have been aware is that his poem was savaged at the hands of its heirs—not for the entirety of its reception, but certainly in the centuries prior to its rediscovery by Romantics. The seventeenth and eighteenth centuries were, in a manner of speaking, a period of purgatorial suffering for the reputation of Dante. The poet's reputation was divine, according to Voltaire, but only because it was mysterious—no one read him. "Il y a de lui une vingtaine de traits qu'on sait par cœur: cela suffit pour s'épargner la peine d'examiner la reste" (There are some twenty things one knows of him by heart, which suffices to spare the trouble of reading the rest).[1] Notwithstanding such disdain, Voltaire had a point: midway through the eighteenth century, Dante was hidden in the dark wood of European letters. His Latin treatise on church–state relations, *De Monarchia*, had been translated into German in 1559, for example, but it took far longer for the *Commedia* to find a German readership.[2] Since his death, around 1321, Dante had been brought low.

The eighteenth century was his nadir. As Joseph Luzzi has written, "the age of light was truly obscure" for Dante.[3] The incompatibility of the *Commedia* with the Enlightenment's rules of taste rendered it a Gothic monstrosity.[4] This rankled Johann Jakob Bodmer, a Swiss critic who had chafed at how Milton was spurned by enlightened rationalists. Displeasure over seeing Dante suffer similar criticism drove him to defend the *Commedia*.[5] Critics had applied contemporary standards of taste and morals to vastly different peoples and ages, he lamented. In their estimation, "übler Geschmack" (awful taste) supplied the *Commedia* its order; "gotische Kühnheit" (gothic audacity) governed its ornamentation (283–284). Dante may have been able to arouse passion, they admitted, but he was a naive genius whose poem lacked classical arrangement. It was a fair summary of his peers' criticism.

Condemned on grounds of taste, Dante was celebrated only as a genius of pathos. His cantos on Paolo and Francesca and Count Ugolino became touchstones for heroic and tragic literary productions. Heinrich Wilhelm von Gerstenberg adapted the grisly Ugolino material into a tragedy of the same name (1768). Josef Alois Gleich, an Austrian dramatist, and Casimir Boehlendorff, a friend of Friedrich Hölderlin, wrote dramas using the same material. Poets and painters in England—most prominently, Joshua Reynolds, Henry Fuseli (a former student of Bodmer), and Lord Byron—adapted, illustrated, and translated the same scenes with equal vigor. Even Bodmer incorporated Ugolino in a heroic drama, *Der Hungerthurm zu Pisa* (The Pisan tower of hunger, 1769). Episodic approaches like these reinforced the prevailing wisdom that Dante's genius, stifled by the weight of his gothic edifice, sparkled only intermittently in moments of pathos.

Bodmer may not have reversed Dante's fortune, but he anticipated the criticism that provided for the eventual reception of the *Commedia* by Romantics. A new historicism enabled Herder to rely on cultural and anthropological arguments to validate the excellence of Shakespeare's un-Aristotelian dramas. Herder's forays beyond classical territory shifted the standards by which good taste had been determined and led to revisionist accounts of long maligned schools and periods. Goethe published alongside Herder's Shakespeare essay a positive reassessment of gothic architecture. It sketched new reasons for considering the national and aesthetic dimensions of medieval art forms. *Von deutscher Baukunst* (*On German Architecture*, 1773) describes how visits to the Strasbourg Cathedral overturned Goethe's prejudices against *das Gotische* (the gothic), which had become a catchall for anything that challenged prevailing standards. Much like the Greek use of *barbarisch* (barbaric) to describe anything foreign, Goethe says, he had relied on a concept of the gothic that lacked nuance (MA 1/2:418). The conflation of the gothic and the barbaric, which Goethe's essay helped to overcome, had long plagued the *Commedia*. Johann Nicolaus Meinhard regarded the *Commedia* as the misshapen product of a "barbarischen Jahrhunderts" (barbaric century).[6] Before he was won over to the *Commedia*, Friedrich Schlegel described the Middle Ages as "das große barbarische Intermezzo" (the great barbaric intermezzo) and characterized Dante's poem as beholden to the "gotischen Begriffen des Barbaren" (gothic concepts of the barbarian) (KFSA 1:233–235). By the end of the eighteenth century, however, Bodmer, Herder, Goethe, and others had tilled the soil for a new reception of long neglected "barbarians" like Dante. Soon, he was no longer the victim of his century, but its luminary—a Luciferian figure, as Percy Shelley wrote, who had created a new language "out of a chaos of inharmonious barbarisms."[7] The poetry of this Luciferian figure was guided out of obscurity and into the light of modern criticism—not by Virgil, but by a Romantic scholar of philology. August Wilhelm Schlegel's recuperation of the *Commedia* helped to configure the poem as an aesthetic template for confronting the spiritual crises of European modernity.

MAKING DANTE MODERN

As a student in Göttingen (1786–1791), A. W. Schlegel undertook the most sympathetic assessment of Dante in German since Bodmer. There he met the historian of Romance literature Friedrich Bouterwek, studied under Gottfried August Bürger, a Sturm und Drang poet and revolutionary, and cultivated scholarly habits under the mentorship of Christian Gottlob Heyne, the classicist whose historicism paved the way from the Enlightenment's interest in fable to the later study of myth. Schlegel leveraged the historicism of the latter in a maneuver that helped to rehabilitate Dante. Schlegel acknowledged the barbarism of the fourteenth century, but in a twist he analogized it to the barbarism of the eighteenth. After all, Europe ca. 1790 no longer looked like *le meilleur des mondes possibles*, as the rationalist credo had it. The threat of violence loomed in France, where the proliferation of clubs and parties resembled a world mired in the factionalism of Guelphs and Ghibellines. It was not the affective intensity of the Sturm und Drang, in other words, with its adaptations of Ugolino, that brought about an appraisal of Dante in the German nineteenth century. It was a philologist's shrewd historicization.[8]

Schlegel's 1791 essay on Dante announces a new critical approach. It accepts his foreignness, the "männliche Klang seiner barbarischen Verse" (the manly tone of his barbaric verses), and seeks to translate his grandeur into the present (AWSW 3:200). That act of translation relies on a bivalent account of medieval Italy: first as the historical survey one expects of a commentary, second as an account of medieval Italy that reflects the contemporary moment, the age of revolution. The cancer on Dante's Italy, Schlegel writes, was factionalism (201–203).[9] But from the vantage point of modernity, such factionalism was only incipient. By the time of the French Revolution, it had metastasized and given structure to European society. Thus, no matter how full of *Barbarei* the thirteenth century, it had an indeterminacy that was preferable to the hardened enmity of the eighteenth century (201). The claim is hyperbolic, but it registers aspects of revolutionary France that later haunted the German supporters of the Revolution.[10] There could be no denying the threats of violence and barbarism, come though they did from the land of good taste.[11] By the light of Schlegel's comparison, Dante looked a shade less barbaric.

The historic parallels rendered Dante's voice timely. His anxiety over the diffusion of the empire's power, for example, rendered him an unlikely prophet among modern Germans. "Herrenlos war [Dantes] Land und fast jeder kleine Theil desselben von mannichfaltiger Unterdrückung gequält" (Dante's land was without leaders and nearly every small portion of it was tormented by diverse oppression), Schlegel wrote (203). Was this not the status quo of eighteenth-century Germans? Months before the sack of Mainz, and not long before the collapse of the empire, Schlegel's observations highlight the void of leadership that thwarted Germans from confronting the crises of revolution. Conflict between Frederick the Great and Maria Theresa had precluded any dreams of pan-Germanic unity. Their deaths blew gaps in German governance, and the reigns of their successors culminated only in disappointment. In short, Germans' political fate lay in the hands of a scattered host of minor princes and governors. There was thus a reflexive gesture inherent in the observation that Dante knew of no *Vaterland* (204). It was not uncommon for Schlegel's contemporaries to write as much. Schlegel was just uncommonly original in using such parallels to justify the excavation of medieval texts. It enabled him to make Dante and his world intelligible.

Comprehension gave way to admiration. With his world laid bare, Dante shone forth more brightly. Schlegel portrayed him as a man of action who, in an age devoid of political leadership, had drafted a poetry teeming with manliness and vitality. His view emerged from a reading of the thirteenth century, which he deemed riven by the gap between a heroic knightly culture and a pedantic monastic culture. Dante had channeled the former and developed it into a grand poetics of life, action, and experience. From the darkness of an exile imposed by pedants, Schlegel writes, Dante would one day shine forth (222). Though no poet of the Enlightenment, he was a luminary after all—albeit one of a new mark, the kind whom Shelley would later describe as a "Lucifer of that starry flock." In ringing the alarm at the real barbarism of Europe, Schlegel suggested that such poets might transform and transcend it. His celebration of Dante, in other words, augured the imminent programs of Weimar Classicism and Jena Romanticism.[12]

It is fitting, then, that Schlegel secured a publication of Dante in *Die Horen* (*The Horae*), the founding journal of German Classicism. It was a small coup owing to his emergence from the shadow of his mentors in Göttingen, according to his brother, Friedrich; they may even have been holding him back. Twin passions for Caroline Michaelis and Dante had elevated A. W. Schlegel's taste to new heights; surely, Friedrich Schiller would be a stalwart new patron (KFSA 23, 166). Friedrich Schlegel was not wrong, but there is irony in his optimism: just three years later, Schiller disavowed the brothers entirely. But not before A. W. Schlegel could place translations from and commentary on *Inferno* in Schiller's eminent journal.[13] Dante, that erstwhile barbarian, was now perched among the leading voices of German classicism.

Criticism had changed in the short span since Voltaire dismissed Dante. Schlegel's publication found impressive acclaim, from various corners.

Schiller's publisher deemed the translation a "Meisterstük" (masterpiece).[14] Herder, by this point an *éminence grise* in the recuperation of old texts, learned new things from Schlegel's commentary. He commended Schiller for its publication (145–146). Schiller, for his part, lavished praise on the contribution.[15] Wilhelm von Humboldt found it unremarkable, but better than the texts by Goethe and Herder with which it was paired.[16] The harshest criticism came from Friedrich Schlegel, who thought Schiller's editorial mismanagement had marred the translation's overall impression (KFSA 23:246–247). Friedrich Klopstock, meanwhile, by this point an aging poet of yesteryear, boasted curmudgeonly that he had known Dante "seit langer Zeit, vielleicht vor Schl.[egels] Geburt" (for a long while, perhaps before Schlegel's birth).[17] Schlegel may have looked like an upstart to Klopstock, but after centuries of neglect, Dante was getting his due.

ALLEGORY AND HISTORY IN ROMANTIC PHILOLOGY

For much of the life of the *Commedia*, there had prevailed the view that it was a document of deepest mysticism. Perceived to be a trove of allegorical riddles, it stood in apparent need of decipherment. Modern *dantisti* have lamented the degree to which such views governed the early exegesis of the poem. In the wake of the Romantic age, L. Mariotti wrote most colorfully of the problem:

> No sooner was his sacred poem rescued from oblivion than it fell into the hands of a swarm of commentators, who seized upon it like ravens crowding upon the body of a fallen warrior. Under pretence of rescuing the original text from the injuries of age and ignorance, of tearing asunder the veil of mysticism and allegory in which the poet, indulging the taste of his age, had mantled his eternal truths, they plunged the Divine Comedy into an ocean of doubt; they racked, they cramped, they stretched the sense even of its most lucid poetical effusions, to shape it after their own narrow-minded conceits; they made of it a maze of enigma and mystery, a mosaic of quibbles and acrostics, a monster which timid minds cannot approach without awe and superstition.[18]

We recognize the consequences of such an approach in the comments of Voltaire. Yet, in fairness to the "ravens," one might recall the poem's pretensions. To take it at face value entails reckoning with difficult claims (to truth and realism) and scathing judgments (against Church and Empire).

More to the point, Dante promoted the quest to seek out hidden meanings. He once wrote that the poem was "polysemous" and that, like holy scripture, it consisted of a literal or historical sense, along with three allegorical senses.[19] One can well imagine that the heft of the ostensibly allegorical senses easily outweighed the plain sense of the text. This precluded attention to the poem as an aesthetic object.

The shift from allegoresis to philology is one way of characterizing modern *dantismo*. Its origins are probably not singular. Mariotti and Toynbee saw the poet Ugo Foscolo (1778–1827) as an important forerunner of critics who later encouraged readers to disregard the accretions of an unwieldy commentary tradition. At the turn of the twenty-first century, Teodolinda Barolini and Robert Hollander incline toward regarding Erich Auerbach as the decisive voice in reorienting criticism around the poem's literal-historical sense. There is no doubt that Auerbach's approach to the poem is anchored therein, and that it leaves behind the quagmire of theological allegories. Nor is there any doubt that Auerbach was one of the two or three most influential readers of Dante in the twentieth century. His expositions of Dante are indeed a landmark in modern philology.

They did not emerge ex nihilo. As modern rehabilitators of the poem, the German Romantics figure centrally in this history. Admittedly, it can be a challenge to accept such a claim, for the bombast of Romantic rhetoric has a way of coloring Romantic philology. It is sometimes necessary to distinguish the latter from fits of enthusiasm. The Romantics' enthrallment to the mystical can seem an insuperable obstacle. To be clear: they marveled over the allegory of the *Commedia*. Schlegel's first essay discusses Dante's claim of polysemy. It wonders at the mysterious force of the poem's riddles, comparing the *Commedia* to an obscure hieroglyph (AWSW 3:225).[20] Unlike earlier commentators, however, Schlegel blanched at the thought of trying to pry open the poem's mysteries. He believed that to do so would be futile (226). Whatever the source of Dante's poem (dream, vision, or voyage), its execution was poeticized (*hinzugedichtet*) (215). Accordingly, the poem demanded philological exposition, not demystification. When the poem begs for allegoresis, Schlegel does not yield; he expresses frustration (342). His commentary reads like a textbook case in the historical-critical method. His recuperation of the *Commedia* may sometimes have been (dis)colored by quasi-religious veneration, in other words, but it began in the academic seminars of Göttingen where modern philology was born.

It turns out that Auerbach's understanding of the poem is rooted in what Schlegel sees as the cardinal virtue of Dante's allegories: their stake in history. To see that virtue is to see a difference between traditional allegory and Dantean allegory: the former reduces human figures to "marklosen Schatten" (weak shadows), robbing them of dramatic force (226). Dante avoided that pitfall. His Virgil may well be a personification of earthly wisdom, for example, but he retains the texture of his historical profile. This profile is maintained throughout the poem, as in Virgil's embrace by Sordello, another Mantuan poet (*Purg.* 6.75). Dante's characters have not been whittled to pawns in a game of allegory. Independent of their symbolic meaning, they have "Bestandheit" (solidity). The poem's allegory, thus underpinned by history, allows Schlegel to describe the reading experience as one of walking "überall auf festem Boden, umgeben von einer Welt der Wirklichkeit und des individuellen Seins" (everywhere upon solid ground, surrounded by a world of reality and individual being) (AWSW 3:226). Schlegel articulated how Dante's practices of signification avoided the deficiencies that rendered medieval allegory unnatural. In doing so, he raised the prominence of the poem, established parameters for Romantic discussions of allegory and symbolism, and set the course for subsequent readings.

Schlegel's role in the formulation of this view has been forgotten, or almost never acknowledged. His elision is due to the enormous shadow cast by Hegel, who contended that allegorical interpretation had run roughshod over texts since the time of Friedrich Schlegel and C. G. Heyne.[21] The *Commedia*, he believed, suffered especially from this vice (404–405). But Hegel's reading betrays inconsistencies. After all, he singles out the *Commedia* as a text that is indeed rife with allegories, albeit of a special variety: Dante's personifications hover between the universals of "eigentlicher Allegorie" (actual allegory) and the particulars of the lives of the people whom Dante represents (515–516). Beatrice is simultaneously Lady Theology as well as the woman whom a nine-year-old Dante once spied in Florence. The characters of the poem thus have one foot in allegory, the other in history. Hegel's description does no more than repeat what Schlegel had already written. A century later, Auerbach echoed this view by rejecting the apparent opposition of allegory and history—in Dante, they were both present.[22] Auerbach's innovation was to go a step further, to interpret the figural structure typologically. This was the central thesis of his book on the poet, *Dante als Dichter der irdischen Welt*. He credited Hegel (and Schelling) with the initial insight, but Hegel owed his conceptualization to A. W. Schlegel.[23] Modern *dantismo* may trace its origins to Auerbach, but Romantic philology looms in the background.

Well before Auerbach, fundamental tendencies within Romanticism found footing in Schlegel's comments on Dante. His interpretation of Dantean allegory, for example, prefigures the Romantic eschewal of allegory in favor of the symbol. Both rhetorical devices involve a sign that stands in for its referent, but as Jeremy Tamblin has written, allegories seemed to the Romantics artificial and mechanical, whereas symbols looked to be organic.[24] The latter participated in the being of their referents, and thus bore the appearance of necessity, whereas the former were chosen at the discretion of a poet. The distinction holds true for both German and English Romanticism. William Blake, for example, contrasted allegory with vision and pointed to the latter as the product of inspiration, the former of memory.[25] Coleridge asserted that the origins of allegory were to be found in conscious speech, those of symbolism in the unconscious mind.[26] Karl Solger said much the same, writing of allegory and symbolism as forms of art based on conscious and unconscious mysticism.[27] Determinable by the poet, allegory looked to be arbitrary. The hitching of its signs to their referents depended only on the poet's whim. Yet, in the case of the *Commedia*, as Schlegel had begun to show, the symbolic structure operated differently. Its "personifications" were flesh-and-blood personages, often contemporaries of Dante, who lent the poem solidity. Rooted in history, rather than spun from fancy, the figural structures infuse the poem with the character of objectivity. Dante could not have deployed Saint Bernard of Clairvaux, for example, to illustrate carnal sins in quite the same way as he did with historical adulterers like Paolo and Francesca. The signs of the poem were not arbitrary inventions. They developed organically out of and were contingent upon history. The series of symbolic interlocutors whom Dante interviews has its source not in the poet but in a patrimony the poet shares with readers. The objectivity of this system encompasses the whole geography of the afterlife, not just its dramatis personae. Heaven, Hell, and Purgatory may have borne the marks of the poet's imagination, but on a primary level, they were expressions of a common physicotheological structure. There was a science (*Wißenschaft*) that underlay the imaginative poetics (AWSW 9:130). Unlike the flimsy allegories of the past, the edifice of the *Commedia* comprised semiotic elements that had been quarried from a common worldview. These features denoted the poem's stake in myth. By channeling a "christlichen Mythologie" (Christian mythology), Dante had composed a poem whose signs were native to the narrative in which they appeared (AWSW 3:238). A. W. Schlegel had altered the terms by which the *Commedia* was read and, in doing so, made clear that the recuperation of the poem carried implications well beyond academic philology.

FROM PHILOLOGY TO PHILOSOPHY: DANTE AND THE BIRTH OF GERMAN ROMANTICISM

The *Commedia* spoke to fundamental tenets of the emergent Romantic school. Foremost among them was the imperative to link poetry and philosophy. One could do worse than summarize early German Romanticism as an endeavor to do just that—in a word, to give philosophy a beautiful form. In this respect, A. W. Schlegel's engagement with Dante was only a precursor, albeit a vital one, to his brother's and Friedrich Schelling's more inventive and strategic thinking about Dante. To them, the *Commedia* represented a persuasive answer to the fundamental aesthetic question of the age: what would a new mythology look like? To understand why the question was posed, and why it was answered with the *Commedia* entails inquiring after the origins of German Romanticism.

After all, the enthrallment of a German avant-garde to the cynosure of medieval Catholic art is unexpected. One would be excused for surmising, for example, that the recuperation of the *Commedia* belonged not to the radicals of Jena but to the Christians of Heidelberg some two decades later. Or that Schelling's preoccupation with Dante might have arisen during his later years, when he pursued matters of myth and religion. Friedrich Schlegel's engagement with Dante, one might likewise assume, must have overlapped with his 1807 conversion to Roman Catholicism, or with his service to Metternich and the empire. Oddly enough, such suppositions do not reflect the circumstances. Schlegel and Schelling's first and most significant engagement with the *Commedia* occurred in tandem with the highpoint of early Romantic activity, just as the former composed the seminal tract on Romantic poetics, *Gespräch über die Poesie* (*Dialogue on Poetry*, 1800). Schelling's period of intense devotion to Dante ran concurrent with some of his most daring steps in philosophy, namely his break from Fichte and his early collaborations with Goethe and Hegel. The point is not that the innovations of the Romantic school owe in any narrow sense to the engagement with Dante, but rather that the Catholic poem aligned unexpectedly with the aesthetic innovations and philosophical radicality of the Romantic avant-garde.

The enthusiasm for Dante was unexpected, too, on a more mundane level: namely, that of taste. Like Friedrich Schlegel's more general warming to romantic (i.e., postclassical or "modern") poetry, his reception of the *Commedia* represented a departure from his predilection for classicism. He was among those, as noted above, to whom the name of Dante sounded the bells of barbarism. Aversion of this sort was the result of how he had positioned himself in the *querelle des Anciens et des Modernes.* In a word, Friedrich Schlegel was a grecophile. But like the major German grecophiles of his era, he differed from French neoclassicists by sidestepping narrow considerations of form. Instead, he pursued a classicism that was rooted in anthropological, religious, and philosophical phenomena. Like Winckelmann, he was a Platonist who wished to discover the ideality of Greek art. Specifically, he wished to know what made Greek poetry different from modern poetry. Schlegel's *Über das Studium der griechischen Poesie* (*On the Study of Greek Poetry*, 1795–1797) hypothesized that Greek poets privileged the beautiful, modern poets the interesting. The difference helped to shape contrasting cultural landscapes: the Greeks' appeals to objective principles of beauty enabled an artistic culture to flourish. The moderns relied on subjective experience to locate *das Interessante* (the interesting), *das Frappante* (the striking), and *das Piquante* (the delightful). In its headlong race toward novelty, modern poetry prevented the coalescence of a community around shared aesthetic priorities. There was no artistic culture to speak of—only a series of coexisting egos, each one driven by an insatiable quest for the new.

Friedrich Schlegel's Romanticism was not a straightforward reversal of this position, but a reshuffling of its terms. It started when he began to see new affinities between Greek and romantic (i.e., modern) poetry. The advent of new ideas in philosophy and philology helped him along the way. Fichte's *Wissenschaftslehre* (*Science of Knowledge*, 1794) sparked his interest in the philosophical and rhetorical dimensions of subjectivity, above all in the reflexive potential of irony, which carried special attraction for an admirer of Socrates like Schlegel. The preoccupation with irony was an inducement to reconsider modern texts. So, too, was Friedrich August Wolf's 1795 hypothesis that Homer's epics were the work of multiple authors, which suggested to Schlegel the possibilities for artistic co-creation that existed among apparently isolated poets. Modern poetry, therefore, began to take on the character of a grand composite in the making (*im Werden*), the process of which drew poets toward harmony on the vanishing horizon of history. Thus Schlegel's definitional statement on Romantic poetry (*Athenäumsfragment* 116) opens with a series of predicates denoting its propensity for movement toward union.[28] Romantic poetry is a "progressive Universalpoesie" (progressive universal poetry), and it is charged with conjoining disparate elements of life and literature. Among its tasks are "vereinigen" (to unite), "in Berührung setzen" (to place in contact), "mischen" (to mix), and "verschmelzen" (to amalgamate).

"Sie umfaßt alles, was nur poetisch ist" (It encompasses all that is poetic), Schlegel writes. There was no poetry too small or too remote to be caught up in the romantic tempest and absorbed by its growing corpus—thus the proliferation of the fragment and the fragmentary novel; the concept of the *Roman* as a hybrid of forms; and the interpenetration of diverse media in Romantic art. Romantic poetry was a hodgepodge in whose quest for universality there was room even for the eccentric and the monstrous (*Athenäumsfragment* 139). Eclecticism of this sort contrasted with the tidiness of classical genres, which Schlegel came to describe as "lächerlich" (laughable) (*Lyceumsfragment* 60). On the other hand, the incremental movement of poetic fragments toward union in a cosmic-aesthetic mosaic suggests an affinity with classicism after all; the anticipation of a harmonious world bound by poetry was in its fundamentals a translation of eighteenth-century Germany's view of Greek antiquity.

The challenge posed by a poetry *im Werden*, however, is that it is never finished. Even if the promise of universality infused the theorization of romantic poetry with momentum, the poetry was still predicated on the unflagging dynamism of the subject. Its generation would somehow have to be sustained. Until 1800, this burden had fallen on each poet, who had to summon from the ego a new and distinctive poetic vision. It was a solipsistic affair, the creation of new art being directed by "nur jeder allein, jedes Werk wie eine neue Schöpfung von vorn an aus Nichts" (each solitary individual, with each work being like to another new creation ex nihilo) (KFSA 2:312). Given the myriad iterations of this process, the novelty of the new creation could not prevent its generation from looking something like re-creation, like an exhausting reinvention of the wheel. New poetry, to be sure, was new poetry, and that counted for a great deal; but Schlegel saw the poet as a social being who demanded "Gegenliebe" (requited love) and "Mitteilung" (communication) (KFSA 2:285). If the development of poetry proceeded unchanged, splintered along the borders of subjectivity, then poetry ran the risk of falling silent (KFSA 2:311). The diagnosis was straightforward: modern poets lacked a "festen Halt" (firm foothold), a "mütterlichen Boden" (maternal ground), which would assuage the demands of novelty that had been placed upon them. Above all, they lacked a "Mittelpunkt" (midpoint) that could orient them around one another and galvanize their efforts (KFSA 2:311).

THE NEED FOR A NEW MYTHOLOGY

In 1800, it looked to Schlegel as if the midpoint of that yet-to-materialize circle could be supplied by a new mythology. This was the simple assertion that governed his abstruse *Rede über die Mythologie* (*Speech on Mythology*). Schlegel followed a course adumbrated by Heyne and Herder, dispensing with the Enlightenment axiom that myth was no more than a fictional etiology employed to hoodwink the unlearned.[29] He regarded it instead as an intrinsic dimension of language and poetry. For a time, he wrote of it as the unvarnished essence of poetry. "Das Wesen der π [Poesie] besteht allerdings im μυθος." (The essence of poetry exists in *mythos*) (KFSA 16:255). That lofty notion did not, however, liberate myth from associations with the supramundane—angels, gods, and other celestial beings. Schlegel's talk of myth thus spanned a conceptual gamut. It was at once internal to and constitutive of all poetic expression, yet also an overarching system of symbolic elements—"hieroglyphs," as he called them. In the case of the former, Schlegel had been probing myth's raison d'être and mining it for as much theoretical force as he could muster. In the latter case, he had raised a practical question: What would a new symbolic system look like?

If a new mythology were to exist in more than just theory, it required an organized network of referents. A new mythology would have to be a mythology *of* something. To Schlegel, the matter was clear: "Der Kern aller Mythologie ist die Idee der Natur" (The kernel of all mythology is the idea of nature) (KFSA 16:266). Here the Zeitgeist was at work, for the reception of Spinoza in recent decades had added urgency to the consideration of nature as a concern of philosophy. Young idealists like Schelling, with his elaboration of a so-called *Naturphilosophie*, and Franz Baader, too, opened new channels of thought in the wake of the Kantian moment. The philosophical trajectory of Schelling's publications reflected the fact that Fichte's subjective idealism was on the cusp of being turned inside out. The force of these shifts is evident in the conjectures of Ludovico, the speaker in Schlegel's *Rede*, who emphasizes that the source of the new mythology must be sought in the science of nature. The development of *Naturphilosophie* and the revival of Spinoza had signaled to Schlegel the emergence of a new realism out of the spirit of idealism. It was the sign of an incipient harmony between the subjectivity of transcendental idealism and the objectivity of materialism. Myth would be a bridge between subject and object.

This perspective lent the prospect of a new mythology a religious sheen. Its ability to mediate between the realms of the ideal and the real signaled a unique epistemic function—one that seemed to verge on that of revelation. Schlegel's eagerness to proclaim that function was spurred by Spinoza, who ironically had been regarded as the bogeyman of European atheism.[30] Schlegel embraced Spinoza after reading Schleiermacher argue that the essence of religion lay neither in morals nor in metaphysics, but in feeling and intuition (*Anschauung*).[31] That assertion originated in one of the more tantalizing claims in Spinoza's *Ethics*: there exists a form of direct, intuitive knowledge (*scientia intuitiva*), which, when exercised, grants the knowing subject the feeling of blessedness. To a Platonist like Schlegel, the notion resembled the Greek ideal of *theoria* (KFSA 2:270). Spinoza thus became a fixture in Schlegel's pantheon. The doctrine of intuitive knowledge supplied conceptual force to the idea of a new mythology. The new mythology would not be an arbitrary assemblage of hieroglyphs, mythical because of their mysteriousness, but rather a system of hieroglyphs that provided for communion between nature and spirit. When Schlegel revised the *Rede* in his later years, he glossed *Mythologie* as a "symbolische Anschauung" (symbolic intuition) and a "symbolische Naturansicht" (symbolic view of nature) (KFSA 2:311–312). By that point, he had long been an orthodox Catholic, but the Spinozan idea of a revelation of the universe afforded by myth proved inextricable from the speech.

The significance of Schlegel's intervention lay in his effort to fix the position of poetry and aesthetics amid the tumultuous developments in idealist philosophy. In recent decades, Herder had written of myth as a *Symbolsprache* (language of symbols), and Karl Philipp Moritz had conceived of it as an autonomous domain of art. They paved important avenues out of the Enlightenment's reduction of myth to aetiology.[32] Schlegel followed these paths into the sphere of idealism by theorizing the possibility of a new mythology as a mode for the subject to know the object. As he put it in two kinetic metaphors, mythology was a pillar of cosmology as well as a counterweight to ontology: art provided for a knowledge of nature in a way that the philosophy of being could not (KFSA 16:263). It served as a mode for the cognition of the universe. He returned frequently to the notion that nature lay at the center of a new symbolic language.[33] In myth, the subject found a window onto the universe.

Schelling, meanwhile, had weighed similar ideas since his years as a student at the Tübinger Stift.[34] There, either he or one of his friends, Hegel or Hölderlin, drafted the fragment of a manuscript that raised the prospect of forging a new mythology. The anonymous author of the so-called *Älteste Systemprogramm des deutschen Idealismus* (*Oldest Systematic Program of German Idealism*) articulated a series of philosophical imperatives, culminating in the unambiguous assertion: "Wir müssen eine neue Mythologie haben, diese Mythologie aber muß im Dienste der Ideen stehen, sie muß eine Mythologie der *Vernunft* werden" (We need to have a new mythology, but this mythology must stand in service of ideas; it must become a mythology of *reason*).[35] Ideas had to be given aesthetic form before they could attract the interest of anyone other than academicians. Only once reason had been given beautiful shape would the standards have been met to live not just in an age of enlightenment, but as Kant had distinguished, in an enlightened age. Here, as in Schlegel, the new mythology possessed unitive force. In a society plagued by ignorance and anomie, it was intended to foster social coherence around rational ideas. A new mythology was the organic counterpoint to the unnatural machine of the state. It promised to overcome the limits of discursive reason. Whether the product of Schelling or not, the *Systemprogramm* outlined paths of inquiry that the Swabian philosopher pursued assiduously in the years just after 1800, which is also to say, just after his collaboration with the Schlegel brothers in Jena and during his formulation of the tenets of absolute idealism.

Whereas Friedrich Schlegel rhapsodized about the promise of a new mythology, auguring its role in the future of idealism, Schelling spent years carving out a space for art and myth in his multiple iterations of an idealist philosophy. As his system matured, the role of myth accrued weight. His anonymously published *Allgemeine Übersicht der neuesten philosophischen Literatur* (General overview of the most recent philosophical literature, 1797–1798) conceived of Greek mythology as a transformation of a "Schematismus der Natur" (schematism of nature). Schelling affirmed, in fact, that all theory culminates in mythology (SW 1:472). Such reflections gave way to a more programmatic statement on aesthetics and myth at the end of the *System des transcendentalen Idealismus* (*System of Transcendental Idealism*, 1799). There Schelling posits the artwork as the objective revelation of the union of conscious and unconscious activity in the absolute. Generally, such representations of the absolute lie beyond the realm of possibility, he believed, because the objective arises only from the division of the absolute. The artwork, however, presents a unique set of circumstances: it is created consciously by an artist who, despite his consciousness, is compelled to create by an external power (HkA 9/1:317–318). The artwork is a site of mediation, in other words, between the freedom of spirit and the determinacy of nature. The point is not to be underestimated, for it was this tension that propelled the *System* in the first place. Here was an idealist philosophy crowned by its veneration of art.

The significance of the artwork is borne out in Schelling's philosophy inasmuch as it assumes the revelatory status it possesses in Schlegel. Here, however, the object of the revelation is not a conceptually fuzzy notion of nature or the universe; it is a clearly delineated first principle: that of absolute identity. Schelling's "absolute" encompasses the totality of subject and object, each one manifesting as a different potentiation of the otherwise indifferent identity of being. He believed concepts were insufficient in arriving at a cognition of that identity of being (i.e., the so-called *Indifferenzpunkt* [point of indifference]), but in the *System*, he held that an aesthetic intuition could grant knowledge of it: "Was also der Philosoph schon im ersten Act des Bewußtseyns sich trennen läßt, wird, sonst für jede Anschauung unzugänglich, durch das Wunder der Kunst aus ihren Producten zurückgestrahlt" (What the philosopher thus allows to be separated in the first act of consciousness is—though otherwise inaccessible for any intuition—reflected back by the miracle of art and its products) (HkA 9/1:325–326). The observation results in the unavoidable and tantalizingly Romantic conclusion of the *System*: all "currents" of philosophy must return eventually to the "ocean" of poetry, whence they had emerged in the primeval age of humankind. Even the instrument by which this process would happen, according to Schelling, was clear: mythology (HkA 9/1:329).

More difficult was the matter of knowing *how* a new mythology would constitute itself. That lacuna became a central concern for Schelling in the period of his identity philosophy. The effort to think through it, and the prospect of myth's reinvention, governed significant dimensions of his philosophy of art. At the time, his identity system had been predicated on the view that the dualism of nature and spirit was always subsumed in the unity of the absolute. That dualism, Schelling sought to show, was an illusory perception of a monist absolute. But as in the *System*, cognition of the absolute demanded special tools. The artwork stood out for its ability to grant a particular representation of the absolute in its indifference to the particularity of nature and the universality of spirit. This realization found precise formulation in paragraph thirty-nine of Schelling's posthumously published lectures on the philosophy of art: "Darstellung des Absoluten mit absoluter Indifferenz des Allgemeinen und Besonderen im Besonderen ist nur symbolisch möglich" (Representation of the Absolute with absolute indifference of universal and particular in the particular is possible only through symbols) (SW 5:406). Schelling glosses the material of the representation as *Mythologie* and elaborates what he means by proposing mythology as the particular symbolic representation whereby the absolute can be accessed. In short, the capacity of mythology to offer a presentation of the indifference of the absolute hinges on its synthesis of two forms of representation: schematism and allegory. The former denotes acts of signification in which the particular is represented by the general, as for example in the case of language. The latter refers to acts of signification in which the general is represented by the particular. In symbolism, which manifests itself as mythology, neither does the particular represent the general nor does the general represent the particular. Instead, the actors of the mythological artwork—gods—exist with indifference to both. Their meaning (*Bedeutung*) is intrinsic to themselves, and as soon as one assigns them other meanings, "sind sie selbst nichts mehr" (they themselves are no longer anything) (411). The term *Synthesis*, which Schelling uses, is thus something of a misnomer; it suggests that both schematism and allegory are at play in the symbol. But mythology combines these modes of representation in a way that evacuates each one of its representational force, resulting in a net-zero pattern of signification. There is thus no object of allegory, no object of schema. As the representation of the indifference of the absolute in particular form, Schelling's concept of mythology was arguably the most defined example of autonomous aesthetic theory in the age of Goethe.

Notwithstanding the originality of Schelling's position, his doctrine of mythology reflected and refined the impulses, prejudices, and concepts of aestheticians in the age of Goethe. Friedrich Schlegel and Johann Gottfried Herder had written of myth as a *Symbolsprache* before Schelling developed a doctrine of the symbol. Karl Philipp Moritz, now recognized as the theoretician of Goethe's autonomous aesthetics, had characterized the Greek gods as defined by limitation and historicity, all the while arguing that the mythological sphere they inhabited constituted a world unto itself—an absolutized realm of fantasy.[36] He had shed the Enlightenment's preoccupation with myth as a device of etiology and approached it instead as an autonomous poetic sphere. So, too, did A. W. Schlegel, when he reckoned with myth in a course of lectures on aesthetics, not as an instrument of primeval history, but as a creative act of the organ of *Fantasie* (KAV 1:441). Schelling's writings exemplified the culmination of these views. He bristled, for example, at the conjecture that Homer could have been engaged in something as mundane as allegorizing natural phenomena, or creating "Kindermährchen" (children's fairy tales) from such allegories (SW 5:409). To admit that possibility was to give room to the Romantic anxiety that artistic representation could be reduced to a mechanical operation, perhaps even an arbitrary one. A new mythology, as the author of the *Systemprogramm* had written, was an organic counterpoint to the unnatural machine of the state. Schelling described the realm of the gods as a "Totalität, eine Welt" (totality, a world) (399). His careful attempt to vouchsafe the gods' aesthetic autonomy, and to ward off the specter of allegory—particularly in light of Moritz's comments on historicity and fantasy—suggests an affinity to A. W. Schlegel's interpretation of allegory and history in the *Commedia*. In all three cases, there reigns an effort to tame the excesses of allegoresis by affirming the primacy of local meaning.

Friedrich Schlegel and Friedrich Schelling, to put a point on the matter, shared a conviction about the crises that plagued modern society. They and their contemporaries lacked the social cohesion that they believed had unified previous civilizations, foremost among them the Greeks. Divisions ran deep in other ways too, for the advent of Kantian and Fichtean idealism signaled not just the alienation of one human subject from another but, just as insidiously, the alienation of the human subject from the world. To the Romantics who wrestled with these problems, among whom I provisionally count Schelling, art looked to be a restorative instrument, especially when it took the shape of mythology. This perspective did not materialize ex nihilo; Moritz, Herder, and Lessing had supplied momentum to the Romantics' theorization of art, poetry, myth, and religion. That is to say nothing of the influence exercised by Goethe's oeuvre, nor of the legacy of Schiller's tracts on aesthetics. Yet the new mythology was a Romantic project. Friedrich Schlegel and Friedrich Schelling did the heavy lifting.

DANTE AND THE NEW MYTHOLOGY

For all the headiness of its theory, the new mythology turned on an unavoidable practicality: what would it look like? This matter capped the speculative froth unleashed by Ludovico in Schlegel's *Rede über die Mythologie*. Upon concluding, his interlocutors brim with questions: Why has he deployed Spinoza, a philosophical writer of "barbarische[r] Form" (barbaric form), as myth's primary representative? Might not Plato or Jakob Böhme be better representatives? Is Christianity amenable to the plan, such that the gods of old might be dispensed with? On the other hand, are not the gods of antiquity and the mysteries of the Greeks to be venerated? A veritable debate ensues. It reaches its inflection point when Camilla, in the lone question posed by a woman, gets to the crux of the matter. What might Spinoza look like in beautiful form (KFSA 2:327)? After all, the new mythology was an ineluctably aesthetic undertaking. Camilla's question not only gets right to the point, it is tantalizing because it amounts to a request that Ludoviko write the missing pages of the fragmentary *Systemprogramm*. Or at least that he sketch it in abstract. He obliges:

> Wer etwa dergleichen im Sinne hätte, würde es nur auf die Art können und sein wollen wie Dante. Er müßte, wie er, nur Ein Gedicht im Geist und im Herzen haben, und würde oft verzweifeln müssen ob sichs überhaupt darstellen läßt. Gelänge es aber, so hätte er genug getan. (KFSA 2:327)

> (He who had something like this in mind could only do it, and want to do it, like Dante. Like him, he would have to have just *one* poem in his soul and heart; often he would have to despair of whether it could ever be represented. But were it to succeed, he would have done enough.)

The response he elicits warrants further quotation for its anomalous tone. "Sie haben ein würdiges Vorbild aufgestellt!" (You have proposed a worthy model) affirms Andrea: "Gewiß ist Dante der einzige, der unter einigen begünstigenden und unsäglich vielen erschwerenden Umständen durch eigne Riesenkraft, er selbst ganz allein, eine Art von Mythologie . . . erfunden und gebildet hat" (Certainly Dante is the only one—all by himself—who, amid some favorable and countless trying circumstances, has invented and formed a type of mythology through his own enormous strength) (KFSA 2:327). The name of Dante defuses the debate at once. In a strange contrast to the preceding hubbub, in which no agreement could be reached, there is now enthusiastic support for the project's icon. As Andrea says, Dante was the only precursor who had showed the way to create something like a mythology. Dante is unexpectedly unobjectionable. He has unique status in the dialogue.

The consensus around Dante reflects the Romantics' robust agreement on the formal realization of a new mythology. Friedrich Schlegel, after all, was not the only one to regard him as the model of the new mythology. His brother, some ten years after first publishing on Dante, explained to the attendees of a lecture in Berlin that Dante's poem represented the realization of a scientific mythology (KAV 2/1:154). The elder Schlegel began to describe the *Commedia* as a "Darstellung des Universums" (representation of the universe), taking up his younger brother's catchphrase (KAV 2/1:148). Around the same time, Schelling was delivering much the same message, having published on Dante in the *Kritisches Journal der Philosophie* (*Critical Journal of Philosophy*) and lectured on him in his *Vorlesungen über die Kunst* (*Lectures on Art*). Dante was "urbildlich" (archetypal), according to Schelling, for demonstrating how modern poets could create mythological artworks (SW 5:156). In the years around 1800, Schelling and the Schlegel brothers may have quarreled over many affairs, personal and intellectual, but their estimation of Dante was a paradigmatic moment of Romantic *Symphilosophie*. To them all, the *Commedia* represented a pleroma of Romantic poetics, a blueprint for the composition of a new mythology.

The evidence for this claim is persuasive but not immediately apparent. There were few systematic treatments of Dante or the *Commedia* in the heyday of early German Romanticism. The nearest thing to one is Schelling's essay *Über Dante in philosophischer Beziehung* (*On Dante in Relation to Philosophy*). Beyond it, there are a smattering of notebook fragments, comments in lecture cycles, and Friedrich Schlegel's frequent but by no means coherent notations on Dante in the *Gespräch über die Poesie*. The dearth of a systematic exposition of the *Commedia* demands a synthesis of the Jena Romantics' mélange of fragments on Dante's poem. Following here is an outline of those features of the *Commedia* that emerge repeatedly across the writings of the Schlegel brothers and Schelling. It is a heuristic, of course, and for that reason, imperfect: there are repetitions and overlaps. Nevertheless, it helps to cut through and organize what might otherwise seem a morass of Romantic hyperbole. Indeed, that morass may well induce us to view the objects of Romantic study as mere palimpsests onto which the Schlegel brothers inscribed their cultural-poetic agenda. There are times when the rhetoric of Romanticism becomes self-reinforcing, to be sure; but the salient aspects of these figures' reception of the *Commedia* have their roots in the poem.

1. Reflexive Subjectivity

Poetry was not Romantic if it was not reflexive, according to Walter Benjamin.[37] It is not a controversial point. Reflexivity emerges as a guiding principle in Friedrich Schlegel's definitional fragment of Romantic poetry, where he writes that Romantic poetry alone can be a "Spiegel der ganzen umgebenden Welt, ein Bild des Zeitalters" (mirror of the entire surrounding world, an image of the age) (*Athenäumsfragment* 116). Were that the essence of it, the line would suggest that reflexivity amounts to mimesis, albeit on a vast scale. But Schlegel refines his point with three qualifications: (1) Romantic poetry hovers between the artist and his object; (2) it exists in that intermediate zone, "frei von allem realen und idealen Interesse" (free of all real and ideal interest); (3) its reflection multiplies like an "endlose Reihe von Spiegeln" (endless row of mirrors) (*Athenäumsfragment* 116). Together these descriptors designate a position and a potency. Romantic poetry is neither a mere reflection of nature nor a mere expression of an author; it is both. In this sense, the language of the *Spiegel* is not entirely apt, for Schlegel does not have in mind the reproduction of reality. Nor, to take up M. H. Abrams's metaphors, is this the matter of a lamp. Romantic poetry hovers between and reflects both subject and object. It stages the perpetual interpenetration of spirit and nature. Its character of *perpetual* reflection signals the endless potency of that reflection. That is to say nothing, by the way, of its objects of reflection: the entire surrounding world and age. Romantic poetry is nothing if not reflexive.

In mirroring its poet's soul, the *Commedia* manifests more than a modicum of Romantic reflexivity. It manages this, in particular, by compounding the poet's layers of subjectivity. Dante the poet writes of Dante the pilgrim, though if the narrator is Dante the poet, then the historical personage (i.e., Dante Alighieri), is a third Dante. The subjectivity of the author comes unspooled. He begins to resemble the kaleidoscopic images cast by Schlegel's endless row of mirrors, but the result is not the chaos of a funhouse. The poem's reflexivity makes possible unusual gambits. Stretched over time, the valences of Dante's subjectivity account for the efficacy of his numerous prophecies. The pilgrim wanders the afterlife on Easter weekend 1300, but the poet writes in the decades thereafter; he is able thereby to record "prophecies" from the residents of the afterlife, which, owing to the disjunction in time, appear true. Prophecy became an articulation of his compounded subjectivity. The mirrors have provided for the illusion.

Romantics were anomalous in attending to and celebrating the *Commedia* for such devices. To their predecessors, texts of such autobiographical substance were unseemly. It was the reason why Dante launched the *Convivio* with a justification for having written about himself in the *Vita nuova*. To the *lumières* of later centuries, as Luzzi has written, the impersonal duty to society outweighed the individual drive to moral excellence.[38] To the Romantics, however, the poem's reflection of the authorial subject helped sketch what the poeticization of Fichtean idealism might look like. Schlegel twice described the *Commedia*, for example, as "die gesamte Transcendentalpoesie" (the entirety of transcendental poetry) (KFSA 16:143, 157). The formulation appears to have sat well with him, for he published it in the *Athenäumsfragmenten*: "Dantes prophetisches Gedicht ist das einzige System der transzendentalen Poesie, immer noch das höchste seiner Art" (Dante's prophetic poem is the only system of transcendental poetry, still the highest of its kind) (*Athenäumsfragment* 247). The visions and prophecies of the poem were more than mystical window dressing. They were narrative structures that embedded the subjectivity of the poet in the life of the world. This alone did not make the *Commedia* a model for the new mythology, but without it, the poem would have been merely mimetic.

2. Encyclopedic Objectivity

A dazzling display of subjectivity, to be sure, the *Commedia* likewise embodied the other half of Schlegel's dictum on reflection: it was a paradigm for the representation of the world. Mimesis, in other words, constitutes the poem's "universalism"—but only in a propaedeutic way. What made the *Commedia* uniquely universal was the scale of its mimesis. The Schlegels and Schelling were unanimous in characterizing the poem as an encyclopedic representation of Dante's world. This set Dante apart from every other idol in the Romantic pantheon. "*Dante* ist unter allen mod.[ernen] Dichtern *allein, encyklopaed[isches]* Bild des Zeitalters. Sh[akespeare] ist das nicht" (Among all modern poets, *Dante alone* is an *encyclopedic* image of the age. Shakespeare is not) (KFSA 16:161). By composing the vision of a vast world from which the reflection of the poetic subject was inextricable, he had balanced on the wings of reflection. Poetry inclined generally toward one or the other, as Schiller's *Über naive und sentimentalische Dichtung* (*Naïve and Sentimental Poetry*, 1795–1796) had argued. The *Commedia* was unique for having done both. It synthesized the objective and subjective dimensions of poetry, which elsewhere failed to converge (KFSA 16:116). Dante demonstrated how to navigate the bounds of subject and object.

There was another and more basic way the poem was encyclopedic: namely, it resembled an encyclopedia. It gathered, organized, and articulated the science of Dante's age, albeit in poetry. This was by no means some unlikely attribute the Romantics ascribed to it. Encyclopedism—literally, a circle of education (ἐγκύκλιος παιδεία)—was intrinsic to the generic program of the *Commedia*, which one might regard as a medieval Catholic bildungsroman. That is an exaggeration, of course, but not by so great a stretch: the spiritual education of Dante is the central concern of the poem. Unlike in a bildungsroman, however, education tends not to occur via trial, error, and experience, but through dialogic interactions with the dead, across the span of the universe. The result is a veritable encyclopedia of medieval knowledge, a poem whose pretensions are clearly didactic. This did not escape the attention of Romantics, who described Dante as a poet of theological science (KAV 2/1:148). Indeed, Schelling paired Dante with Lucretius as the two authors of didactic poems of nature, and on one occasion, he suggested that poets and natural scientists could learn to depict changes in nature if they studied Dante's depictions of metamorphoses (SW 5:161). In a scientific publication, he went so far as to draw on the *Purgatorio* to show that Johann Friedrich Blumenbach's doctrine of the *Bildungstrieb* was familiar to Dante in the fourteenth century (HkA 8:433). Xavier Tilliette surmised that Schelling's metaphors for the absolute and its cognition relied as much on Dante as on Spinoza.[39] More than just a spiritual autobiography, the poem was a summation of contemporary science—much of it still salvageable.

Its grand sweep of knowledge made the *Commedia* exemplary for the new mythology. The Romantics' undertaking would be to absolute idealism what Dante's had been to medieval scholasticism. That meant, for one thing, that both projects *encompassed* a realm of knowledge; it is also to say that they *communicated* a corpus of knowledge. As the *Systemprogramm* had suggested, a new mythology would advance reason by democratizing science for the *Volk*. That impulse animated the *Commedia*, and was evident not just in its use of the vernacular. More importantly, the poem's symbols (*Symbole*) had united physics and theology in an account that was both legible and pleasant. A. W. Schlegel believed the *Commedia* confirmed the possibility that a scientific mythology could serve as the "Organ des Idealismus" (organ of Idealism) (KAV 2/1:154). He concurred, in other words, with his brother and with Schelling. It was time to resurrect Dante, that "riesenhaften Schatten der Vorwelt" (gigantic shade of the primeval world) (148). The promulgation of idealism depended on it.

3. Classical Modernity

With the advent of Romanticism, Friedrich Schlegel formulated a new historiography of literature. Early on, he had concluded that the distinctiveness of modern (i.e., postclassical) poetry lay in its tendency to abandon the beautiful in favor of titillation. The ascendancy of novelty suggested that modern poetry had relinquished long-standing ideals. Unmoored from such ideals, poetry lost its contours. Genres evaporated. Forms dissolved. Each new work was a unicum, untethered to anything but the mind of its creator. Schlegel could think of no starker contrast to the poetry of antiquity, which he described as "ein organisches Ganzes" (an organic whole); the whole of classical poetry looked to him much like a single long poem (*Ideen* 95). Admittedly, with his esteem for irony and reflexivity, he was enamored with the poetry of extreme subjectivity. But his theory of Romantic poetry was predicated on seeing these unica eventually merge into an organic corpus.

All books should become one book; therein would be revealed "das Evangelium der Menschheit" (the gospel of humankind) (*Ideen* 95). To that end, he and Novalis corresponded about the composition of a new Bible, stylizing themselves as evangelists. Novalis approached his novel, *Heinrich von Ofterdingen*, as a continuous succession of novels. Totality was to be achieved one book at a time. The focus on the fragment, in other words, was balanced by an idealization of the wholeness that would come from the eventual convergence of all fragments. Modern poetry could be classical without surrendering its Romantic features.

The new historiography underscored the paradigmatic stature of the *Commedia* for the ambitions of early German Romanticism. Here was a poem that, for all its modernity, approximated the fading ideals of the classical world. The encyclopedic scope of the poem had adumbrated the task of modern poets; it spoke not the truth of one man, but the "Identität der ganzen Zeit des Dichters" (identity of the entire age of the poet) (SW 5:153). As such it was prototypical for all modern poets, rendering particular experiences such that they appeared universal and necessary (SW 5:154–155). But in the more traditional vein of imitation, too, Dante had channeled the spirit of the ancients. Schlegel believed that, in his rendering of the Florentine vernacular, Dante had sorted and gathered the noblest features of the common tongue, refining them into poetry of "klassischer Würde" (classical dignity) (KFSA 2:297). Despite limited access to the font of classical poetry, Dante had imbibed (what Schlegel imagined to be) its preoccupation with the idea of a single, grand work (KFSA 2:297). He had found a way of granting coherent vision to an age that had lost the coherence of the classical world. In an echo of his *Rede*, Schlegel said that Dante had seized the most diverse elements of his experience and forced them together into "Einen Mittelpunkt . . . in Einem ungeheuren Gedicht" (a midpoint . . . an enormous poem) (KFSA 2:297). Dante had fulfilled the tasks of modern poetry, and as such, became its father.[40]

In his modernity, Dante signaled how the Romantics might attain something for which they all ached: a collective aesthetic culture. The significance of that foretaste ought not be underestimated. At least since Winckelmann's celebration of the Greeks, German artists and intellectuals had felt bereft—not just of art or beauty, but of the sort of society that emerges when art and beauty are common desiderata. What bound Germans to one another apart from the machinery of the state? These concerns underlay Schlegel's prescriptive discussions of modern poetry, as well as Schelling's. They all but obsessed Novalis, whose idealization of the medieval was a way of mourning the disintegration of an erstwhile organic culture. The *Commedia* suggested the path to its recovery. Against the backdrop of splintering European literatures, it had gathered together lost fragments of the culture and pieced them together in a grand vision of a common medieval age. This was the task of modern poetry, and in having executed it, Dante pointed the way to a new mythology.

4. Substantive Form

That execution relied on structures that the Romantics regarded as inchoate examples of their poetic-philosophical suppositions. Take, for example, the matter of the poem's genre. Despite its title, Schelling wrote, the *Commedia* did not belong to the theater, for its range was too vast. The poem bore a didactic mission, to be sure, but its form resembled no other *Lehrgedicht*. The categories of novel and epic bespoke aspects of the poem too, but they were similarly inadequate in encompassing its scope. The *Commedia* had mixed all these genres, and by virtue thereof, was an "absolutes Individuum, nichts Anderem und nur sich selbst vergleichbar" (absolute unicum, comparable to itself and nothing else) (SW 5:153). In its individuality, the poem confirmed the Romantic view of modernity and its tendencies. Schelling's comments on genre amount to a passable definition of the central bit of nomenclature in the Romantic poetics of Friedrich Schlegel: the *Roman*. The latter had pushed the bounds of the genre in drastic ways, writing that the novel was inconceivable unless it comprised multiple genres and forms (KFSA 2:334–335). As Ernst Behler wrote, the *Roman* so drastically eclipsed the customary bounds of genre that it amounted to a synonym of Romantic poetry.[41] The *Commedia* was one representative of the form that transcended genre. Like Schelling, he saw the poem as an amalgamation of genres: novel, drama, prophecy, epic, lyric, and didactic poem. It had united and synthesized all genres (KFSA 9:104). By the logic of his own terms, Schlegel's most apt description was his simplest: "Dantes Komödie ist ein Roman" (Dante's comedy is a *Roman*) (KFSA 16:91).[42]

The poem's division into three parts evoked the organizational structures of Romantic thinking. To Schelling, whose philosophy of identity was predicated on a triadic structure, it was understandably significant. Like the five acts of a drama, which corresponded to discrete progressions in the action, the three canticles of the *Commedia* were not arbitrary (i.e., they were not merely contingent upon the geography of the Christian afterlife). They represented divisions of knowledge. The realms of Hell, Purgatory, and Heaven thus corresponded to nature, history, and art, which Schelling described as the three great objects of knowledge and culture. One could envision the composition of poetry in the future along similarly trichotomous lines (SW 5:158). Friedrich Schlegel interpreted the canticles as different manifestations of the *Roman*: mimetic (*Inferno*), sentimental (*Purgatorio*), and fantastic (*Paradiso*) (KFSA 16:158). Nor was he alone in wishing to identify features intrinsic to each canticle. Schelling associated them with individual arts: the darkness of Hell foregrounded the role of shape, the dawn of Purgatory brought out the colors of the earth, and the light of Heaven left only pure music (SW 5:162). The poem was thus a harmonious intermingling of the arts, which—not incidentally—rendered it quintessentially Romantic (*Athenäumsfragment* 116).

Bejeweled by figurative riches, the *Commedia* lent itself to the popular orientation of the new mythology. After all, the new mythology aimed at sociocultural transformation through the aestheticization of knowledge. The poem's saturation in painterly images appealed for just this reason: it demonstrated how to render ideas *sinnlich* (*sensual*). That was by no means to be taken for granted in an epic-religious poem. Milton and Klopstock had undertaken similar endeavors, but as A. W. Schlegel wrote, their image-starved epics amounted to a "vergebliches Bestreben eine protestantische Mythologie aus nichts zu machen" (futile striving to make a Protestant mythology from nothing) (KAV 1:461). The resources of medieval Catholicism, on the other hand, were vast. Dante's poem was a bottomless source-book of a once popular iconography. Schlegel thus commended the wisdom of John Flaxman for executing contour drawings of the *Commedia* rather than of *Paradise Lost*, which may have seemed the more natural choice to the English artist (AWSW 9:117–118). Ludwig Tieck and Wilhelm Wackenroder's *Herzensergießungen eines kunstliebenden Klosterbruders* (*Outpourings of an Art-Loving Friar*) (1797) had advanced a similar association of the visual arts with Roman Catholicism; they all but canonized Raphael as their patron saint. Now, the Schlegel brothers, philologists by training, situated Dante in this world: he was the Michelangelo *and* Raphael of poetry (AWSW 9:162).[43] Dante was the "Mythologe der katholischen Religion" (mythologist of the Catholic religion), Friedrich Schlegel said, asserting that he could have been pope (KFSA 6:268). Hyperbolic, to be sure, but there is no doubt that Dante's poem gave prominent display to the visual riches of Catholicism.

The religiosity of the poem had a way, in turn, of shaping how a broader spectrum of Romantic writers perceived its formal structures. Its division into three canticles, as noted above, was regarded as a division of eternal significance, with applicability for subsequent mythologies. *Terza rima*, the chainlike sequence of end rhymes with which Dante linked his poem (aba bcb cdc), became an even more identifiable marker of such poetry. Friedrich Schlegel employed *terza rima* in his ode "An die Deutschen" (To the Germans) and mentioned the rhyme scheme repeatedly in his descriptions of plans for a religious epic.[44] In a retelling of Goethe's "Prometheus," A. W. Schlegel opted for *terza rima*. Clemens Brentano's *Romanzen vom Rosenkranz* (Romances of the rosary) and Karl Immermann's *Merlin* did, too. Goethe, who twice used the form, explained that it required "großen, reichen Stoff zur Unterlage" (grand, rich material for a foundation).[45] Banal though the remark is, it shows how *terza rima* had come uncoupled from Dante's triune numerology and nevertheless retained a whiff of grandeur. One of the rare Romantic examples of *terza rima* in which formal and semantic valences of a poem coincide is Shelley's "Ode to the West Wind," with its contemplation of cyclicality, recurrence, and movement. The (meta)physical landscape the English poem sketches, in which nature is preserver and destroyer, evokes the Spinozism for which the German Romantics had identified the *Commedia* as a beautiful model.

5. Personal Origins

If one investigation haunts the discourse of myth, it is that of its origins. Where and how does myth originate? To what end? Unanswerable as they are, these questions perpetuate the discourse, whether in the work of Hans Blumenberg in the twentieth century or in that of the *lumières* in the eighteenth century. Debates around the matter were especially volatile among German scholars of the 1810s and 1820s.[46] Nor were the early Romantics immune to the matter. Yet, in their quixotic endeavor to create a new mythology—indeed, in their privileging of the new over the old—this investigation found different articulation. In an age of radical individuation, the question had become *who* could create a mythology.

Here, the case of Dante was especially compelling. Within the mythology of the *Commedia* was the origin story of the poem. For in addition to his spiritual journey, the poet documents the genesis of the poem that he knows is destined to be read as sacred literature. Quite apart from a grand vision of the afterlife, with its gallery of the dead, he presents from start to finish the inner drama of an election. Like a prophet, he has been chosen; like an apostle, he has witnessed marvels; like an evangelist, he has been inspired to record his vision. The myth is inseparable from its author.

The inextricability of the author from his mythology rendered the veneration of the poet inevitable. In their veneration, the Romantics relied on the autobiographical portrait supplied by Dante's poetry. The two most poeticized elements of his life—his love for Beatrice and his exile—tend thus to play the precise role that the poet designed for them. Exile, as A. W. Schlegel had written, subjected the poet to hardship and seemed thereby to have predisposed him to exacting and rigorous habits of art and intellect. We cannot know what poem Dante would have written in "Ruhe und Wohlstand" (quiet and prosperity), but the one he wrote in exile is "göttlich" (divine) (AWSW 3:222). Thus it was that Dante, whom artists have long depicted as haggard and severe, deemed the difficult *Paradiso* "der liebste und wichtigste Theil" (the dearest and most important part) of his poem (AWSW 3:224). To Romantic critics writing on the heels of the *Geniezeit* (Age of Genius), Dante appeared Promethean in his ability to overcome disaster. From the death of Beatrice, from exile, from a barbaric age, Dante had wrested the poetry of genius.

The matters of genius and authorial stature recall the outset of the present chapter: Dante's ascent of Mount Purgatory and his conviction that he would suffer for his pride. From the perspective of his critical fortunes, the centuries prior to 1800 amounted to a purgatorial period for Dante. Pressing the analogy further, the early German Romantics were akin to the living faithful whose prayers for the dead diminished the duration of their sojourn on the penitential mountain. For in a little more than a decade, A. W. Schlegel's translations, Schelling's lectures, and Friedrich Schlegel's advocacy raised Dante from accusations of barbarism and fixed him in the firmament of the European canon.

The living pray to the dead for intercession, too. The Romantics' embrace of Dante was more than scholarly advocacy: they eyed the *Commedia* as the locus of a poetics from which their new mythology might emerge. It is the role of Dante and the *Commedia* in the execution of those endeavors that forms the remainder of this book. There were other Romantic poets, like Ludwig Tieck and Joseph Eichendorff, who read and borrowed from the *Commedia* in their novels.[47] Dante surfaces as a character in Tieck's comedy, *Prinz Zerbino*. It was not his only appearance in the modern German canon. But these engagements occurred on different terms. They were proximate to, but independent of, the conceptualization of the *Commedia* as a work of mythic consequence. Chapter two, therefore, attends to the Romantic literature that invokes Dante in its quest to make myth.

CHAPTER TWO

Schelling, Novalis, and the Legitimation of a Dantean Mythology

THEORY WAS ONE THING, execution another. Attempts at realizing the new mythology induced deliberation over stubborn practicalities. Who was positioned to draft a new mythology, or to put it another way, who might be a new Dante? In reading the *Commedia*, it is difficult not to fall under the spell of the author and conceive the achievement as that of a particular genius. The poem is a mythologization of the poet as much as it is of anything else; its protagonist, after all, is its author. This was a practicality that had a way of decentering the focus of the new mythology. At the time, Friedrich Schlegel was writing longingly of a confederation of poets, a "Volk von Königen" (people of kings), among whom no single poet reigned supreme (*Ideen* 114). But the long shadow cast by Dante led to discrepancies in theory and practice. Notwithstanding its orientation toward a culture of *Bildung* and art, the new mythology as a Romantic project pivoted on questions of authorship and authority.

Dante's claims to sacred authority resonated among the Romantic heirs of the *Geniezeit*, who saw poetry and religion as intertwined. This entanglement is almost ubiquitous in the *Commedia*, beginning when Virgil reveals that Dante has been elected for a journey through the afterlife (*Inf.* 2). The remainder of the poem balances the narrative of Dante's redemption with his arrogation of poetic authority. Arguably, that arrogation culminates atop Mount Purgatory, in the Earthly Paradise (*Purg.* 27–33), where Dante states matter-of-factly that his knowledge of the afterlife compares to that of the authors of the Bible. His self-comparison to Ezekiel and John (*Purg.* 29.105), noted above, is the most famous such instance. Astounding though the comparison is, it is perhaps more remarkable that the progression between the "ma io?" of the *Inferno* and the "Giovanni è meco" of *Purgatorio* almost reads as foreseeable. The whole poem is reminiscent of the call narratives of the Hebrew prophets, a fact that leads again to comparisons between Dante and the authors of the Bible. But similar comparisons were du jour among Romantics. Friedrich Schlegel and Friedrich von Hardenberg (Novalis) conceived the idea of writing a new Bible and a scientific Bible (Novalis's *Allgemeine Brouillon*), imagining themselves to be evangelists. Inspiration in these endeavors came from Lessing, who had augured the advent of a new gospel, and from Schleiermacher, who argued that the laws of the universe required proper communication by holy mediators, among whom were poets. Propelled by these notions, the Romantic theorists of the new mythology were responsive to Dante's exercises of poetic authority.

This resulted in at least one predictable outcome: they readily identified the Promethean emblem of the age, Goethe, in their quest for an author of a new mythology. In Schelling's opinion, Goethe's *Faust* was the only contemporary equivalent of the sort of mythology embodied by the *Commedia*. It had a "wahrhaft Dantesche Bedeutung" (truly Dantean significance) (SW 5:732). Friedrich Schlegel singled out Goethe as a new Dante. If his contemporaries followed Goethe's example, there would develop a poetry guided by universal "Ideen" (ideas). The fragmentary character of poeticization would give way to a new, eternal blossom of poetry, and Goethe would be the founder of a new school of poetry, as Dante had been for the Middle Ages (KFSA 2:347). Even the more prosaic academician of the group, August Wilhelm Schlegel, was intrigued by the possibility that Goethe's poetry had demonstrated a way to fuse Spinozistic ideas in Dantean forms. In 1798 he rewrote the Prometheus myth in more than three hundred lines of *terza rima*. The cryptic explanation of the poem he sent to Goethe—"hoffentlich ist das Gedicht nicht so stumm, daß es nicht Kenner über alles Nöthige durch sich selbst sollte verständigen können" (hopefully the poem isn't so mute, that it should be unable to make itself intelligible about the essentials to those in the know)—suggests it was a Dantean versification of the Prometheus ode with which Goethe sparked the *Pantheismusstreit* of 1785.[1] In Weimar, the Romantics believed they had found the heir to Dante.

Around 1800, however, the campaign for a new Dante proceeded only out of the Romantic corner in Jena. Indeed, the Romantics' solicitation of Goethe raised eyebrows in Weimar. Schiller was asked, for example, how Goethe coped with the deification he shared with Shakespeare and Dante.[2] The critic Karl Böttiger gossiped to playwright Friedrich Rochlitz that Goethe had allowed the Schlegels to venerate him with smells and bells.

Through their influence, he claimed, Goethe became an imperious poet.[3] Christoph Martin Wieland wanted to know from Goethe how one could allow himself to be praised in such disgusting fashion by the Schlegels.[4] Johann Gottfried Schadow and August von Kotzebue, both of whom mocked the Romantics' veneration of Goethe, sketched caricatures that attest to contemporaries' aversion to such *Schwärmerei* (enthusiasm).[5] Notwithstanding his legendary ego, Goethe admonished A. W. Schlegel: "Was meine jüngern Freunde gutes von mir denken und sagen will ich wenigstens durch unaufhaltsames Fortschreiten verdienen" (As for the good things that my young friends think and say of me, I at least wish to merit them through tireless progress) (FA 2:4, 559). Goethe's grace belies just how distant he was from pursuing anything akin to a Dantean poetics around 1800.

Indeed, the single greatest impediment to the Romantics' hopes for a Dantean Goethe was Goethe himself. In his eyes, Dante was still the barbarian poet of the Catholic Middle Ages. When Goethe traveled to Italy, and wrote of his sojourn, only his silence over Giotto's frescoes in Assisi was more deafening than the little he had to say of Dante. In comments on Italian literature, he described Dante's poetry as "widerwärtig" (abominable) and "abscheulich" (detestable) (FA 17:331). *Terza rima* meant nothing to him when he received Schlegel's "Prometheus." Its effect on him was that of aversion. He complained to Schiller that the rhymes offered no rest (WA 4/13:71–72). When several Dantean poems were published in the *Musenalmanach* of 1802, edited by A. W. Schlegel and Ludwig Tieck, Goethe mocked the poets' infatuation, writing to Schelling that the volume's contributors were "weder auf Erden, noch im Himmel, noch in der Hölle, sondern in einem interessanten Mittelzustand, welcher theils peinlich, theils erfreulich ist" (neither on earth, nor in heaven, nor in hell, but rather in an interesting middle condition, which is partially awkward and partially pleasant) (WA 4/15: 294). The remark was more trenchant than Goethe knew. The theorists of the new mythology found themselves in limbo: they had conceived a project that the holy poet in Weimar would not deign to christen.

For all this, the new mythology was not exactly dead on arrival. Presupposing even the aid of Goethe, its realization was never going to be once and for all. It was not an imminent project, as Ernst Behler wrote, but rather "one of those more fundamental tasks that . . . manifest both the impossibility and the necessity of their realization."[6] Rhetoric inflected by apodictic certainty masked the assertoric character of the plan. They proceeded, one may glean from the insistence of their calls, as if theory could speak mythology into existence—a difficult proposition, to be sure, but in keeping with Friedrich Schlegel's view that an adequate theory of the *Roman* would have to be a *Roman* (KFSA 2:336). Eventually, the theorization of a mythology would yield a mythology. Or so one could hope. There was no shortage of theoretical furor, after all, just a dearth of poets, rendered more glaring by Goethe's lack of interest. The Romantics, however, were nothing if not resourceful. Theory and poetry emerged in tandem.

For despite the perspicacity of Behler's observation, which could suggest the project never gained footing, there were attempts at a new mythology—a Dantean one at that. These efforts emerged in proximity to the formulation of the project. Schelling and Novalis, some of the first poets of Romantic myth, had participated actively and intimately in the *Symphilosophieren* (co-philosophizing) of Jena. For a time, in other words, the project remained an "in-house" affair, despite its ambitions of vast cultural transformation. Ultimately, Goethe engaged with Dante as well. In each of these cases, the poetics of myth was virtually inseparable from the Germans' incessant teetering between the ideality of spirit and the objectivity of nature. The new mythology, as Friedrich Schlegel had augured, emerged from the wellspring of Idealism, that "großen Phänomen des Zeitalters" (grand phenomenon of the age) (KFSA 2:312). In this respect, as he had in many others, Schlegel aligned with the view of his frequent rival, Friedrich Schelling, who ventured the source of the new mythology would be the new German philosophy. In Schelling's case, however, this was quite explicitly to be identified with *Naturphilosophie*: therein was "die erste ferne Anlage jener künftigen Symbolik und derjenigen Mythologie . . . welche nicht ein Einzelner, sondern die ganze Zeit geschaffen haben wird" (the first distant creation of that future symbolism and of that mythology . . . which will not have been created by an individual, but by the entire age) (SW 5:449). Yet the *Einzelner* (individual) retained significance that was disproportionate to the goals of the mythology.

Articulated in the rhetoric of a collective—"*Wir* müssen eine neue Mythologie haben"[7] (*We* must have a new mythology) (*Ältestes Systemprogramm*), "*Wir* haben keine Mythologie"[8] (*We* have no mythology) (*Rede über die Mythologie*)—the new mythology was conceived as an expression of the Zeitgeist. The *Commedia* lent itself to the propagation of that expression. Yet Romantic mythologies were often more inflected by the poeticized life of Dante than by the structures of his poem. Dante's election to divine knowledge, seeming to confirm Schleiermacher's doctrine of mediators, legitimated the Romantics' view that myth is a revelation of the absolute. In each of the mythic endeavors of Schelling, Novalis, and Goethe, there is a single, male subject who is the recipient of a revelation. In two of them, the subject is—as he was in Dante—a poet. In Novalis, and in a loose sense in Goethe, too, the male subject is on a pilgrimage. In all three of them, a romantic, female muse occupies a salvific role. The *Ewig-Weibliche*, as Goethe called it, was rooted in Dante's representation of Beatrice and his fixation on love—"l'amor che move il sole e l'altre stelle" (the Love that moves the sun and the other stars) (*Par.* 33.145). For that matter, Dante's sidereal imagery figures at least peripherally in the mythic poetry of Schelling, Novalis, and Goethe, too. In theory, the structures of the *Commedia* impressed the Romantics as ideally suited to the demands of a modern mythology; in practice, it was the author of the poem and the iconography of his vision that supplied a new lexicon to the mythic poetics of (Romantic) German Idealism. That lexicon is first visible in the poetic musings that emerged from Schelling's scientific collaboration with Goethe.

GOETHE, SCHELLING, AND THE (DANTEAN) POEM OF NATURE

In the spring of 1798, still under the spell of his first encounter with Schelling, Goethe composed what is often considered his greatest naturalistic poem, "Die Metamorphose der Pflanzen" (The metamorphosis of plants). He described it as an attempt to represent the "Anschauen der Natur" (contemplation of nature) (WA 4/13:200). The descriptor echoes the Spinozism of Schleiermacher's speeches on religion, which bound Goethe and the Romantics once their infatuation with Fichte had given way to a new estimation of the reality of nature. Goethe had been ahead of the curve, writing of Spinoza's religious-epistemic praxis years earlier in his correspondence with Jacobi:

> Wenn du sagst man könne an Gott nur *glauben* so sage ich dir ich halte viel aufs *schauen*, und wenn Spinoza von der Scientia intuitiva spricht und sagt: Hoc cognoscendi genus procedit ab adaequata idea essentiae formalis quorundam Dei attributorum ad adaequatam cognitionem essentiae rerum; so geben mir diese wenigen Worte Muth, mein ganzes Leben der Betrachtung der Dinge zu widmen, die ich reichen und von deren essentia formali ich mir eine adäquate Idee zu bilden hoffen kann. (WA 4/7:214)
>
> (When you say that one can have only *belief* in God, I say to you that I stick to *vision*; and when Spinoza speaks of *scientia intuitiva* and says, "This kind of knowledge proceeds from an adequate idea

> of the formal essence of certain attributes of God to an adequate cognition of the essence of things," then these words give me courage to devote my whole life to the contemplation of things from whose formal essence I can hope to form an adequate idea.)

In its contemplation of the life of the plant, the "Metamorphose der Pflanzen" embodied the ideal of *Anschauen der Natur*, but its scope was hardly that which the Romantics had in mind when they heralded the coming of a new mythology.

Between 1798 and 1800, however, Goethe and Schelling imagined writing an epic *Naturgedicht*, a counterpart to Lucretius's *De rerum natura*. The essence of the unrealized poem, explored repeatedly in scholarship (Adler, Kunz, Nisbet, Plath, Whistler), remains nebulous.[9] Its plans can be pieced together only from a handful of diary entries and letters, especially those sent to Karl Ludwig Knebel, who was at work on a translation of Lucretius. Shortly before lectures at the university resumed, in September 1799, Goethe spent several weeks in Jena pursuing the topics that lay at the heart of the project: he discussed *Naturphilosophie* with Schelling, empirical and transcendental philosophy with Schiller, and elegies with A. W. Schlegel. Prompted by the Romantic figures in Jena, he read Schleiermacher's speeches on religion and works of Romantic literature by Friedrich Schlegel and Ludwig Tieck. It was a frenetic period, and Goethe relinquished his stake in the project. Caroline Schlegel explained to Schelling, "Goethe tritt Dir nun auch das Gedicht ab, er überliefert Dir seine Natur. Da er Dich nicht zum Erben einsetzen kann, macht er Dir eine Schenkung unter Lebenden" (Goethe now surrenders the poem to you; he delivers to you his nature. Since he cannot instate you as his heir, he makes you a gift among the living).[10] At the time, Goethe had resumed work on *Faust*. It must have lent the plan for an epic nature poem the semblance of impossibility. Responsibility for the *Naturgedicht* thus landed squarely in Schelling's lap.

Schelling, meanwhile, had already taken the first steps toward poeticizing his *Naturphilosophie*. In 1799, while composing the *System des transcendentalen Idealismus*, he drafted the satirical poem "Epikurisch Glaubensbekenntnis Heinz Widerporstens" (Heinz Widerporst's epicurean confession of faith).[11] As its title suggests, the poem amounts to a natural philosopher's heretical profession of faith. It lampoons the Romantic encomia of Christianity that had recently been written by Schleiermacher and Novalis. The latter found the contents of his speech on medieval religious unity reformulated to comedic effect. Whereas Novalis had spoken reverentially of "schöne glänzende Zeiten" (lovely, splendid times) (*Schriften* 3:507), Schelling wrote of the same age but employed the doggerel of Hans Sachs (87–89). Schleiermacher's redefinition of religion suffered similar mockery, since it had done no better than propose Christianity as the ultimate expression of religion.

The poem's proximity to the planned *Naturgedicht* is clearest in the (meta)physical confessions of its purported author. In fact, Widerporst's derision of transcendent religious doctrines is probably less incendiary than the materialism he touts: "Die Materie sei das einzig Wahre, / Unser aller Schutz und Rather, / Aller Dinge rechter Vater" (Matter is the only truth, / protector and counselor of us all, / righteous father of all things) (68–70). This standpoint leads Widerporst not just to abandon the ethical models of religious systems but also to invert and vulgarize them: "Mein einzig Religion ist die, / Dass ich liebe ein schönes Knie" (My only religion is / that I love a lovely knee) (77–78). Christianity would merit his respect only if nature vouched for its truth: he would worship in a temple where magnetic force suspended church bells, where crystals formed crucifixes, and where time had led to the formation of petrified Capuchins (150–161). Widerporst revels in irreverence, writing that until this day should come, he will persist in his godlessness (165). As Whistler points out, however, Widerporst's godlessness amounts to more than a satire of transcendence; it includes a genealogy of matter's development into consciousness.[12] Indeed, the poem draws to its conclusion with a robust account of the doctrine of the *Weltseele* and nature's process of unfolding self-consciousness. It is a ribald affair, yet all the same a propaedeutic to the *Naturgedicht* Schelling had conceived with Goethe.

The failure of "Widerporst" underlines the centrality to the new mythology of the practicalities already observed. On the one hand, Schelling's poem looks to be a loose imitation of Goethe's voice—specifically, that of his Faust. Schelling composed the poem in *Knittelvers*, after all, whose melody is inseparable from Goethe's necromancer. There are times indeed when Widerporst's turns of phrase evoke those of Faust. He claims that his naturalism has helped him "durch die *Welt*" (through the *world*) and that it "Leib und Seel *zusammenhält*" (*holds together* body and soul) (49). The rhyme echoes that deepest wish of Faust to know "was die *Welt* / im Innersten *zusammenhält*" (what *holds* the *world together* at its core) (FA 8:382–383). But whereas Faust's language seethes with frustration over the limits of knowledge, Widerporst's jiggles with laughter at the ignorance of his contemporaries. Its scorn figured consequentially in its failure, for the poem was too brazen to publish. Although Friedrich Schlegel wished to release it with Novalis's speech in the *Athenäum*—a tête-à-tête of sorts, between the epicurean and the ultramontanist—neither appeared there. Fichte had recently been dismissed from the University of Jena on charges of atheism. Having endured Karl August's ire over the affair, Goethe advised the Schlegels against publication. Schelling eventually published a short excerpt in his *Zeitschrift für spekulative Physik* (*Journal of Speculative Physics*), but he introduced the poem as if it were the work of an unknown poet (HkA 8:428). The poem reached an impasse that reinforced what the *Commedia* had led the Romantics to believe: the new mythology demanded a voice of authority.

In the renewal of his efforts, Schelling leveraged the philological expertise of his Romantic compatriots. Indeed, he received encouragement from his interlocutors in Jena. They put stock in his endeavor, with Friedrich Schlegel remarking that Schelling's turn to poetry would help him to rise out of "der Rohheit" (crudity) and become a "Genosse der Hanse" (associate of the Hansa) (KFSA 24:309). The remark indicates the Romantic circle's esteem for poetry vis-à-vis the systematic philosophy to which Schelling mostly devoted himself. His new intellectual commerce consisted of nightly tutoring sessions in the *Commedia*—under the direction of the Schlegel brothers. The encounter with Dante was decisive: having read him so earnestly as to solicit specific editions and commentaries from friends and family, Schelling dropped *De rerum natura* and regarded the *Commedia* as the new prototype for the poem of nature (SBD 2:217). He planned to relinquish the colloquialism of Goethe's *Knittelvers* for the clarity of Dante's *terza rima*. By Christmas 1799, he had composed its opening. The Schlegels' lessons were bearing fruit.[13]

"Das himmlische Bild" (The Heavenly Image), as Schelling's editors entitled the thirteen stanzas, endorses the naturalism of "Widerporst" but neglects its promulgation in favor of a new program (SW 10:447–451).[14] Schelling now recounts an election to divine gnosis, or in this case, to the knowledge of nature. For here, the reality of nature may be indisputable, but the central dilemma of the poem is the inscrutability of its workings: "Die starre Brust der Erde liegt verschlossen." (The stiff breast of the earth is locked) (1). Opposite the closed breast of nature is the open breast of a chosen one, whose chest has been struck open by a heaven-sent ray and filled with divine gifts (26). The one who is to unlock the secrets of the earth requires the grace of heaven. It is given freely, albeit to a select few, who must in turn undertake a daring journey "zum Abgrund" (to the abyss) (62).

That journey depends on the guiding light supplied by a romantic partner, his "himmlisch[es] Bild" (74). For all its imagery, the quest is naturalistic and not to be confused with forms of Christian (or gnostic) transcendence. Yet the account of the poet's path toward knowledge of nature recycles the governing images of the *Commedia*: a poet-pilgrim depends on the grace of love to lead him through the obstacles of a cosmological drama of salvation. The whole affair amounts to a Dantean volte-face on the heels of "Widerporst." The jester had turned pilgrim.

Above all else, the poem is concerned with legitimating the authority of the adept who unlocks nature's secrets. "Widerporst" is a credo, the stanzas an account of how and to whom the credo is communicated. Nature is now overshadowed by the matter of its revelation to a select few. Like Schleiermacher's mediators, these few lack the everyman quality at hand in the vulgarity of "Widerporst." As if to underscore the insignificance of his person, Widerporst's confession opens with a series of subjectless verbs: "Kann es fürwahr nicht länger ertragen, / Muß wieder einmal um mich schlagen" (Truly can't bear it any longer, / must strike yet again around me). The words *unser einer* (7), a collective folksy slang, appear some fifteen lines before the word *ich* (22). To be sure, Dante is also an everyman: he is in need of saving. But in most respects, the *Commedia* marks him as an exception to the ordinary, grouping him alternately with Aeneas and Saint Paul (*Inf.* 2), with the classical poets of limbo (*Inf.* 4), and with the authors of the Bible (*Purg.* 29). It is that Dante to whom Schelling aspires in the stanzas. The hero of his poem is repeatedly set apart from the *hoi polloi*: he enjoys a happiness granted to "gar Wen'gen" (very few) (10); he is graced with a glory that "Viele nie empfunden" (many never felt) (15); he strives for an object "Wonach vergebens Tausende verlangt" (for which thousands longed in vain) (68). His self-acknowledged unworthiness to undertake this journey of knowledge intends ultimately, as it did in Dante ("Ma io?"), to foreground his humility and thereby reify his status as prophet (48). It seems no accident that Schelling's two translations from the *Commedia*, *Inferno* 3, and *Paradiso* 2, are the two moments in the poem when Dante includes explicit warnings to readers that he is about to take them where few mortals have ever been. More a song of himself than a song of nature, Schelling's poem displays the authorial fixations that accompanied the propagation of a new mythology.

This is not to say that the mission of the new mythology had been forgotten, just that Dante's exemplarity had reoriented Schelling to the question of legitimation: how could he—an academic, yes, but a poet of no significance—purport to educate humankind in poetry? After all, *Bildung* figured among the primary tasks of a new mythology. Dante had arrived at a bold but simple solution to the same problem: he claimed that his poetry had been commissioned by heaven. Beatrice had counseled him, upon his vision of the apocalypse, to write what he has seen (*Purg.* 32.103–105). She was not God, of course, but she was among the blessed, and the love of the Creator caused her to reach out to Dante (*Inf.* 2.72). It was a clever maneuver. Having starred already in the *Vita nuova*, her reputation provided an intelligible link between the familiar art of Dante's poetry and the unfamiliar art of his prophecy. Schelling followed suit, presenting Caroline Schlegel, the romantic partner to whom he dedicated the stanzas, as his poetic muse and mediatrix. The gifts with which he claims to have been endowed, much like those of Dante, were love and poetry. His quest to unlock the secrets of nature—"die ewige Nacht entsiegel[n] (to unseal the eternal night) (56)—and to record them in poetry required the guidance of his beloved. She could point him to eternal truth (66), and in so doing, enable him to transcend his limits. The romance of *romantische Poesie* drives Schelling's pretensions to knowledge.

Whence the wisdom of romance? Love (*Liebe*, *eros*) is underwritten in Schelling (and Dante) by the cosmic signature of the universe. For love is not reducible to romance, but is instead an organizing force of creation. As Schelling describes in the stanzas, the ray that sunders his poet's chest has been sent from on high, "Herab vom Sitz der ungebornen Liebe" (Down from the seat of unborn love) (25), which, to draw on another lexicon, one might gloss as God. Romance is an earthly experience, afforded by its eternal form. It awakens the poet and draws him onward to access the highest peaks and deepest recesses of the universe. The Romantics were influenced here by the dialogue on love in Plato's *Symposium*, but more proximate to the stanzas was the *Commedia*, wherein the object of the poet's earthly desire has become an instrument of the celestial *amore* that governs the sun, the moon, and the other stars. The stanzas' insistence that love will sustain the faltering poet's quest for knowledge echoes the final lines of *Paradiso*. In beholding the Trinity, when the pilgrim's power of vision fails, it is the synchronization of his will and desire with the momentum of *amore* that preserves for the pilgrim his harmony with the divine. Schelling's pilgrim aims for knowledge of Nature; notwithstanding this difference, it is the propulsive force of love that Schelling says will sustain him. Love, the Romantics suggest, has Reason in addition to its reasons. Friedrich Schlegel conceived the new mythology not just as a symbolic articulation of nature, but one in which fantasy and love were transfigured (KFSA 2:318). The Romantic poet as hero is thus more than a romantic hero: romance is the outward sign of his prophetic calling, his revelatory mission to gather, shape, and articulate an encyclopedic poem of the world.

In the quest to poeticize philosophy, Schelling pursued his own convictions, as Whistler has argued; but these were informed by the religious-poetic programs of Dante and the Early German Romantics.[15] The poet of the stanzas was Dantean, for example, and also a species of the mediator in Schleiermacher's *Reden*. Yet the sacralization of the poet was also a corollary of the crowning lesson of Schelling's *System*: experiential knowledge of the absolute was to be had in aesthetic intuition. What Schelling lacked in his poetry was the authority to promulgate the revelation of his *Naturphilosophie*. "Widerporst" had summoned the voices of Goethe and Hans Sachs. The stanzas intimate how the *Commedia* led Schelling to fashion a new poetic voice. His other poetry of the period sheds light on just how thoroughgoing that concern was for him. He opens "Lebenskunst" (The Art of Life), for example, a poem composed of some thirty-three lines of *terza rima*, with an imperative that sounds as if it could have been drawn straight from the stanzas: "Die goldnen Lehren hört aus treuem Munde; / Wie sie ein Gott mir selbst hat eingegeben, / Empfangt von mir des Lebens sichre Kunde. / Zum Leben ward uns selber nur das Leben" (Hear the golden lessons from a true mouth; / Just as a god supplied them to me, / Receive from me firm knowledge of life. / For living we were given only life) (SW 10:439–440). The last of these verses echoes the stanzas' *Naturphilosophie*, but together they foreground—as the stanzas had—the poet's election to secret knowledge.

There were practical grounds for Schelling's fixation on poetic voice. Goethe ceded his stake in the project of a *Naturgedicht* by October 1800. With the Olympian out of the picture, would Schelling's poeticization of *Naturphilosophie* be received seriously? It was not a trivial concern, given the aspirations of the new mythology. The transition from theory to poetry thus raised dilemmas of a variety that until then could escape notice. Schelling opted to pursue Dantean rhetorical strategies, albeit less convincingly than Dante, whose unique assertions of authority were all the more effective for the guise of humility in which they were presented. Yet Schelling was not without admirers. His work inspired confidence in Caroline Schlegel, who called him her prophet and wrote to him that his work would assuredly culminate in a "herrliche[m] Gedicht" (masterful poem).[16] One of Schelling's pupils in Jena,

Henrik Steffens, was so impressed by the poetic quality of Schelling's *System* (though not necessarily by Schelling's poetry), that he hailed him as a philosopher-poet worthy of the laurel wreath:

> Nichts hat mich so begeistert wie Ihre Transcendental-Philosophie. . . . Ich . . . vergrub mich immer tiefer und tiefer in die Hölle der Philosophie hinein, um von dort aus den Himmel zu schauen, weil ich ihn nicht, wie der dichtende Gott, unmittelbar in meinem Busen habe.—Hier sahe ich nach und nach die Sterne hervortreten—bis plötzlich die göttliche Sonne des Genies aufstieg und alles erhellte. . . . Nicht eine Stelle in dem Buch war mir dunkel. Es ist das wichtigste Geschenk, der transcendentale Idealismus.—
> Und hier lege ich—ich darf mitsprechen—den Kranz vor Ihre Füße, den ein künftiges Zeitalter Ihnen sicher reichen wird.[17]
>
> (Nothing has excited me quite so much as your transcendental philosophy. I dug myself ever deeper and deeper into the infernal cave of philosophy in order to glimpse from there the heavens, which—unlike the poeticizing deity—I do not have directly in my breast. Here I saw gradually the stars emerge until, all of a sudden, the godly sun of genius arose and illuminated everything. Not a single passage in the book was obscure to me. It is the most important gift, transcendental idealism. And here, I permit myself to say, I lay at your feet the wreath that a future age will no doubt grant you.)

It is probably no accident that Steffens describes Schelling's philosophy as a revelation of the heavens that drew him out of philosophy's hell. His words allude to the Dantean persona that Schelling had begun to forge. Most importantly, Schelling was convinced of his creation. Inspired by the *Commedia*, he wrote to A. W. Schlegel that he believed he had found the singular mythology he had been seeking (HkA 3/2.1:212).

Schelling's attempt at a Dantean mythology was fleeting. He abandoned the project of the great nature poem and wrote poetry only intermittently in the years thereafter. The influence of Dante remains apparent, as in "Die letzten Worte des Pfarrers zu Drottning auf Seeland" (The Last Words of the Pastor at Drottning on Seeland) (1802), a gothic ballad composed in *terza rima*.[18] Another of his poems in *terza rima*, "An Dante" (To Dante), grants a glimpse of Schelling's idiosyncratic view of the *Commedia* (SW 10:441).[19] It reports that Dante did not travel through "das Thor der göttlichen

Gerichte" (the gate of divine judgments); instead, he went through the "Herz der Erde selbst zum ew'gen Lichte" (heart of the earth itself, on to eternal light) (10–12). The distinction is noteworthy, for it suggests that the geography of the pilgrim's journey is a validation of the tenets of *Naturphilosophie*: the pilgrim does not attain "den höchsten Sieg" (the highest triumph) through transcendence, but through nature. The essence of this triumph is characterized by the activity of "schauen" (seeing), which underscores that Schelling had located the uniqueness of Dante's pilgrim not in his guarantee of salvation but in his penetration of "nie gesehnen Orte" (never before seen places), where he gained the knowledge of experience (2). Dante was an explorer whose journey impressed Schelling for its terrestrial character. The philosophy of nature was the great truth to be communicated by mythology.

PARALLEL LIVES

Schelling tried to craft a Dantean song of *Naturphilosophie*, but it was Novalis, the poet whose religiosity had exasperated him, who came to be seen as a new Dante. The reason lay less in Schelling's failure than it did—and here again looms the magnitude of Dante the man—in the uncanny similarities between the lives of Dante and Novalis. The most significant articulation of this likeness came from the pen of Ludwig Tieck. When he published the first edition of Novalis's works, he included a hagiographic statement that set the tone for the reception of Novalis well into the twentieth century. The force of Tieck's words lay in his praise for *Heinrich von Ofterdingen*, the novel project that Novalis left unfinished at the time of his death in 1801. Tieck was able to enhance the mystique of the project by stylizing its debt to the 1797 death of Novalis's fiancée, Sophie von Kühn. It was by dint of this biographical detail—"daß ein einziger großer Lebens-Moment und Ein tiefer Schmerz und Verlust" (that a single great life-moment and *one* profound pain and loss) had produced "einen unergründlichen mystischen Gesang" (an unfathomable mystical song)—that Tieck boasted that Novalis, alone among modern poets, resembled Dante (*Schriften* 4:559). Yoking Sophie to Beatrice, he suggested that the biographies of Novalis and Dante had resulted in a spiritual affinity between the poets. The rhetoric by which he made this point evokes the language of Friedrich Schlegel's statements on a new mythology. In his string of qualifying adjectives, all of which center on the singularity of Novalis's biography and the singularity of his poetry, Tieck echoes the words Friedrich Schlegel had used to call for a new mythology in the style of Dante. Anyone who would write a new mythology, Schlegel had contended, would require the singular focus of Dante (KFSA 2:326).

Tieck's words suggested that Novalis had begun to fulfill Schlegel's challenge. *Heinrich von Ofterdingen* was the lone work of Romantic mythology worthy of Dante.

Tieck has suffered criticism for the stylization of this biographical sketch, but to be fair, there were unmistakable parallels between Novalis and Dante.[20] The so-called *Sophien-Erlebnis* (Sophie-Experience), after all, did resemble the relationship of Dante and Beatrice: Sophie's death gave shape to Novalis's major literary endeavors, the *Hymnen an die Nacht* (*Hymns to the Night*) and *Heinrich von Ofterdingen*, much like Beatrice's death had stamped Dante's major works of poetry. Indeed, the shapes of the poets' oeuvres mirror one another in uncanny ways. Just as the *Commedia* was preceded by the *Vita nuova*, a prosimetrum in which Dante aestheticized his lost love, so too was Novalis's masterpiece, *Heinrich von Ofterdingen*, preceded by the *Hymnen an die Nacht*, a prosimetrum that voices an erotic and mystical vision of love and death. Just as Dante, in his political tract on monarchy, had written wistfully of a golden age of European unity, so too had Novalis in his essay on *Die Christenheit oder Europa* (*Christendom or Europe*). Just as Dante had synthesized medieval romance and religious pilgrimage in his masterpiece, so too did Novalis in *Heinrich von Ofterdingen*. Tieck's comparison was well founded.

The similarities were sufficiently conspicuous, anyway, to draw the attention of German writers in the early nineteenth century. A. W. Schlegel saw in Novalis's fusion of science, religion, and poetry an endeavor to move toward the encyclopedism that Dante had achieved in the *Commedia* (KAV 2/1:150). Subsequent representatives and critics of German Romanticism found other reasons for drawing the comparison. Karl Immermann, in his own long poem of *terza rima*, grouped Novalis with Dante and Wolfram von Eschenbach in a triumvirate of poets.[21] He marveled over the anachronistic excellence of his compatriot (14). Heinrich Heine, in his retrospective of German Romanticism, described Novalis's novel as a grand allegorical poem like Dante's *Commedia*.[22] Critics agreed that Novalis stood out from his contemporaries—whether because of the supernal vein of his novel, the broad sweep of his knowledge, or the untimeliness of his poetry. It seemed more fitting to place him next to Dante than next to any living poet. Striking though this may be, it is almost astonishing when one considers that in his entire oeuvre, Novalis does not mention the name of Dante a single time.[23]

This is not to say that Dante does not figure in his poetry, only that Novalis has given no such indication. Silvio Vietta has shown, however, that the romantic female figure in *Heinrich von Ofterdingen*, Mathilde, is the intertextual descendant of Dante's Matelda, the woman who resides in the earthly paradise atop Mount Purgatory.[24] He interprets her as an aesthetic-religious mediatrix in the mold of Matelda and presents Novalis's novel as a document in the trajectory of European secularization and Romantic *Kunstreligion*. In addition to supplying substance to all those comparisons drawn by nineteenth-century poets, Vietta has broadened the parameters for approaching the novel. After all, for two centuries scholars have been discussing the relation of Novalis's novel to Goethe's *Wilhelm Meister* and the tradition of *Bildungsromane* and *Künstlerromane*. The novelty of Vietta's discovery is all the more striking considering that, in addition to Dante not appearing in the writings of Novalis, he also makes virtually no appearance in what has grown to be a considerable corpus of Novalis research.

The traces detected by Vietta, however, run deeper than the Mathilde/Matelda connection, for the *Commedia* does more than provide the model of a mediatrix whose adaptation enables the convergence of art and religion. Dante's poem supplies Novalis with the mimetic strategies to achieve the poetics of myth that he, Tieck, and Friedrich Schlegel all ascribe to *Heinrich von Ofterdingen*. The novel represents a vital testimony to Romantic *Kunstreligion*; it is simultaneously an effort to realize the Schlegelian dictum that the new mythology could be realized only in the way that Dante had written his grand poem.

DANTE, NOVALIS, AND THE DREAM POETICS OF ABSOLUTE IDEALISM

Seminal readings of *Ofterdingen*, most notably that of Albert Béguin, have focused with good reason on the novel's preoccupation with dreams.[25] A few pages into the first chapter, Heinrich's father admonishes him in a line that could serve as the motto against which the novel sets up camp: "Träume sind Schäume" (dreams are just fluff) (*Schriften* 1:198). It is a lesson that neither Heinrich nor Novalis heeds. The narrative includes several dream vignettes whose import ought not be underestimated. To wit, the first chapter includes detailed accounts of two dreams, one of Heinrich and one of his father. Each presages subsequent events of the novel. Other dreams emerge in the narrative, too, including one that foreshadows the death of Mathilde. Vignettes like these form part of the novel's fabric, which is interwoven with fairy tales narrated by the novel's characters. The last and longest of these—a fairy tale told by Klingsohr, Mathilde's father—reads almost exactly like a dream. Its action unfolds with few logical transitions and its characters change bodies and roles. Magical transformations of reality, together with an incestuous eroticism, render it the stuff of a dream.[26] That the first part of the novel should end with so perplexing a tale is oddly fitting, for in the fragment that remains of the second part, reality takes on the hue of a dream. Scholars have not failed to comment on these dynamics, but without knowledge of the Dantean background of the novel, there has been no effort to place *Ofterdingen*'s use of dreams in dialogue with the significant role of dreams in the *Commedia*.

Yet the dreams of *Ofterdingen* are inflected structurally and visually by the *Commedia*. Just as Dante's poem begins with its pilgrim on the brink of sleep (*Inf.* 1.11), engendering ambiguity as to whether what follows is dream or reality, so too does *Ofterdingen* open as its protagonist hovers on the borders of consciousness. In the middle of the night he contemplates a distant blue flower and slips into the phantasmagoria of an unsettling dream. Toward morning, calmer repose induces the dream of a distinctive landscape. It looks to Heinrich "als ginge er in einem dunkeln Walde allein. . . . Bald kam er vor eine Felsenschlucht, die bergan stieg" (as if he went alone in a dark forest. . . . Soon he came to a rocky gorge, which climbed upward) (*Schriften* 1:196) The image of a solitary pilgrim traversing a dark wood before reaching the face of a mountain conjures the specter of Dante's famous lines: "Nel mezzo del cammin di nostra vita / mi ritrovai per una selva oscura" (In the middle of the journey of our life, I came to / myself in a dark wood) (*Inf.* 1:1–2). Dante's pilgrim would have scaled the mountain—symbolic of the good and holy life (Psalm 15:1, 23:3)—had his path not been impeded by three beasts. Eventually, he attains the good life via passage over another mountain, Mount Purgatory, upon which he enjoys the delights of the earthly paradise and the presence of the lady Matelda. The pilgrimage in Heinrich's dream unfolds in the same landscape, though it lacks the infernal way-stations through which Dante had to wend his way. Instead, Heinrich ascends the mountain gorges and discovers a cavern in which he disrobes and bathes in an Edenic spring. The baptismal connotations of his submersion call to mind the baptismal ritual to which Dante submitted in the earthly paradise: there Matelda submerged him in the river Lethe, which expunged his memory of wrongdoing and prepared him for Paradise (*Purg.* 31.91–102). Heinrich's pilgrimage does not take him as far as Dante's. He only ever approaches paradise, represented by the blue flower, in an asymptotic trajectory. Indeed, the opening dream sequence ends just as the flower's corolla begins to reveal itself. Utopia lies just beyond the edge of a dream.

Apart from signaling the Dantean valences of *Ofterdingen*, the opening dream outlines in microcosm key patterns that structure Novalis's thinking. Important is the conjunction of elements once Heinrich has entered the cave. Submerged in the waters of the cave, he experiences waves of erotic delight—quite literally, for the waves of the pool seem to nuzzle him like breasts (*Schriften* 1:197). This prepares the way to the dream's tantalizing climax. Heinrich observes the blue flower that had lulled him to sleep. In its center he begins to see a face (Mathilde's), but he cannot admire it for long, because his mother rouses him from sleep. The juxtaposition of his romantic interest and his mother, of which a Freudian might make much, has a Jungian dimension. Its dual vision of femininity—romance and motherhood—bespeaks two wishes innate in human desire: the wish for romantic fulfillment, and the wish for the protection of the womb. The cave of the dream, vaginal in its imagery, accommodates both such longings. In Novalis, the sequence of images operates metaphorically. It corresponds to the guiding conceptual dynamic whereby he understands the unfolding of time. The human subject inhabits always a middle period, teetering between the memory of a past golden age and the expectation of a future paradise. Caught between the maternal and romantic dimensions of his dream (i.e., between the warmth of the past and the pleasure of the future), Heinrich plays out in his dream the guiding tenets of Novalis's philosophy of history.

This triadic form corresponds to notions of history and art that shaped the Romantics' new mythology. In Novalis's view, the *goldenes Zeitalter* would return in an age of fulfillment. As Hans-Joachim Mähl showed, however, the new age ought not be mistaken for a clone of the first golden age.[27] It will not be a return to primal nature. Instead, it will be an age that unites the universe in harmony while preserving the individuation of each being. Whereas Novalis ascribed the original golden age characteristics like instinct and monotony, he envisioned the new golden age as a time marked by art, harmony, and rebirth. In this conception is overlap with documents like the *Systemprogramm* and the *Rede über die Mythologie*. Novalis, along with the authors of these documents, believed the approximation of a utopia would be generated by art. They even shared the same metaphors in envisioning the art of the future: all three referred to the utopian future as an age in which the sea of poetry would return.[28] Only Novalis, however, represented what that age might resemble.

Split into two parts (*Erwartung* and *Erfüllung*) (Anticipation and Fulfillment), the linear structure of *Ofterdingen* gestures always toward paradise.

Its gestures rely on the narrative of Heinrich's pilgrimage. Setting out from Eisenach, he, his mother, and a group of merchants travel to Augsburg. It is a journey whose waystations are laden with meaning. It was in Heinrich's hometown, Eisenach, that Luther later holed up at the height of the Reformation (1521–1522), and it was in Augsburg where religious peace under Emperor Charles V was settled (1555). In Novalis, for whom the schism wrought by Luther was historically devastating (*Schriften* 3:511), the journey between these cities is more than suggestive: it represents a move toward paradise. The episodes of the novel bear this out. The merchants with whom Heinrich travels, for example, indicate that the northern boy will experience in Augsburg the poetic and romantic charms of the south. Indeed, it is the locus of romance where Heinrich meets and falls in love with Mathilde. But the geography of the pilgrimage is doubly significant, for Augsburg is the city where Heinrich's mother was born. It is thus a return to his origins, indeed to the home of his grandfather, where the festive atmosphere approximates a garden of earthly delights. Heinrich's pilgrimage instantiates the kairos of myth.

There is no mistaking the meaning of his grandfather's home: it is a terrestrial paradise, where the dawn of a new golden age is at hand. Poetry reigns supreme, embodied in the form of two characters: Klingsohr, a poet, and his daughter, Mathilde. The former teaches Heinrich the principles and science of poetry, while the latter, as the living spirit of poetry, inspires in him love and the will to create. In these episodes Novalis embeds biblical images that characterize the scene as unequivocally edenic. Life's pleasures were present to Heinrich like a tree weighed down by shiny fruits—thus the narrator—and evil was not to be found. "Es dünkte ihm unmöglich, daß je die menschliche Neigung von diesem Baume zu der gefährlichen Frucht des Erkentnisses . . . sich gewendet haben sollte" (It seemed impossible to him that human inclination ever strayed from this tree to the dangerous fruit of knowledge) (*Schriften* 1:272). As if he can read Heinrich's thoughts, his grandfather sings a tune that encourages mildness of judgment:

Sind wir nicht geplagte Wesen?
Ist nicht unser Los betrübt?
Nur zu Zwang und Not erlesen
In Verstellung nur geübt,
Dürfen selbst nicht unsre Klagen
Sich aus unserm Busen wagen.

Allem was die Eltern sprechen,
Widerspricht das volle Herz.
Die verbotne Frucht zu brechen
Fühlen wir der Sehnsucht Schmerz;
Möchten gern die süßen Knaben
Fest an unserm Herzen haben.

Wäre dies zu denken Sünde?
Zollfrei sind Gedanken doch.
Was bleibt einem armen Kinde
Außer süßen Träumen noch?
Will man sie auch gern verbannen,
Nimmer ziehen sie von dannen. (*Schriften* 1:272–273)

(Are we not troubled creatures? Is our lot not doleful? Destined to constraint and hardship, practiced only in dissimulation, even our cries may not dare escape our breast.

Our full hearts contradict everything our parents tell us. We feel the pain of longing to pick the forbidden fruit. We would so like to hold sweet youths fast to our hearts.

Would it be a sin to consider it? Nay, thinking is subject to no toll. What remains for the poor child, save for sweet dreams? Keenly though one may wish to banish them, they will never go away.)

The lyrics recall the novel's engagement with the *Commedia*. Heinrich's disbelief that humankind should have turned to the fruit of knowledge mirrors the response of Dante to the sin of Eve. Like Heinrich, Dante reproaches the sin of Eve just as he cognizes the pleasures of the *locus amoenus* (*Purg.* 29.27–30). Heinrich's thoughts are less reproachful than Dante's words, but his grandfather's song responds to his disapproval. It is an entrenchment of the intertext, for the ability of the elder poet to read the mind of the younger poet has its precedent in the *Commedia*. Virgil often reads and responds to Dante's thoughts. Like Virgil, the grandfather has a vatic quality, which is confirmed that evening: Heinrich has a powerful dream that mirrors the images from his grandfather's song. The linkage of the song and the dream indicates one way that Dante's poetics figure in the novel: they help navigate the interstices of world and mind.

It is worth lingering a moment over this dream of Heinrich, for it represents the densest concentration of the novel's borrowings from the *Commedia*. Like Heinrich's first dream, this one occurs in the final hours of sleep. Throughout the *Commedia*, Dante alleges that dreams from the hours just before morning are the most prescient (*Inf.* 26.7; *Purg.* 9.13–18; *Purg.* 27.92–95). The content of Heinrich's dream, too, is saturated in Dantean images. A blue river emerges from a space of greenery, Mathilde paddles by on a skiff, and she sings to Heinrich. Bedecked in wreaths, she looks at him wistfully. Suddenly, the skiff begins to swirl and take in water. Heinrich dives into the river and follows her voice, the current carries him away, he loses consciousness, and Mathilde is drawn under. When he regains consciousness, Heinrich believes he is ashore; indeed, Mathilde clutches him in a tight embrace, enacting the words of Schwaning's song: "[Wir Mädchen] Möchten gern die süßen Knaben / Fest an unserm Herzen haben." Heinrich asks where the river is, Mathilde points to its blue waves above them and indicates that they are submerged in the eternal realm of their parents. She kisses him and whispers a secret word that is lost when he is awakened by his grandfather (*Schriften* 1:278–279). The dream is a transformation of the earlier dream: the submersion in water, loss of consciousness, waking to Mathilde's image, and other scenes are a renewal of those primordial pleasures. As in the first dream, the landscape of this one mirrors the *Commedia*. Now, however, there emerges another forest: the *divina foresta* of the terrestrial paradise. When Dante enters that forest, he hears the melodious singing of a woman, Matelda, whom he observes gathering flowers across a stream. He advances toward her and requests that she, too, move nearer that he might understand her singing (*Purg.* 28.46–48). In his final moments in the earthly paradise, Dante faints from compunction and Matelda draws him into Lethe, upon which she walks as lightly as a bark. She embraces him, submerges him, and purges him of the memory of sin (*Purg.* 31.91–105). As Dante wakes and approaches the shore, he hears the psalm *Asperges me*, but in his recollection, he writes, it was so sweet that he "cannot remember, let alone write it" (*Purg.* 31.98–99). It is the root of the secret word that Mathilde whispers to Heinrich. The entire scene atop Mount Purgatory, in fact, prefigures Heinrich's dream. In the most liminal spaces of *Ofterdingen* there resound the clearest echoes of the *Commedia*.

Leaving aside those echoes, it remains to be asked how and why the (Dantean) dream figures in Novalis's novel. Clearly it is a determinative feature. *Ofterdingen* hinges on dreams—on their interpretation and their fulfilment. So, too, does the *Commedia*. Both texts, as noted already, begin with their protagonists on the verge of sleep. Dante flanks his poem with references to sleep and goes so far as to bracket the literal center of his poem, *Purgatorio* 16, with a dream in the preceding and following cantos. Their deployment is not incidental. They help Dante to straddle the gap between fantastical poetry and truth-wielding prophecy. The stakes are similar in *Ofterdingen*, for the dream marks a space defined by its ambiguous relation to truth and fiction. "Träume sind Schäume," Heinrich's father declares at the novel's outset; yet Heinrich's dreams are harbingers of experience. *Träume* are anything but *Schäume*. The dream is a technique of narration from the *Commedia* that helps to realize a poetics of myth.

The proximity of Novalis's unfinished novel project to the Romantics' new mythology has been probed since Friedrich Schlegel's 1803 review in the journal *Europa*, where he characterized it as an "Übergang vom Roman zur Mythologie" (transition from novel to mythology) (KFSA 3:12). Just what constitutes the mythology of the novel has eluded consensus. With its numerous vignettes and its layers of narration, *Ofterdingen* has proven intractable in yielding signs of the principles by which it operates: does the mythical dimension encompass the narrative? Perhaps just the narratives within the narrative? Or maybe the dreams within the narrative? Wilhelm Dilthey regarded the novel as a work of mythology because, in Klingsohr's fairy tale, he detected the poeticization of a worldview that could explain nature.[29] The fairy tale, however, represents just a single and discrete portion of the novel. Rudolf Haym, on the other hand, conceived *Ofterdingen* as a work of autobiography that came wrapped in mythological dressing.[30] It immersed the author's life in a sea of enchantments. Modern efforts to think through the novel's mythological shape have focused on its characters' relation to life, death, and the hereafter. Elisabeth Stopp, for example, located *Ofterdingen*'s mythology in its poeticization of metempsychosis, citing as evidence the reiterations of the novel's female type—Zulima, Mathilde, Cyane.[31] Dennis Mahoney, on the other hand, identified its mythic dynamic in the motif of death and resurrection.[32] Illuminating though the latter interpretations may be, their approach to myth, colored by its proximity to religion, has tended to decenter the role of poetry.

A reading that construes *Ofterdingen* in relation to the new mythology must not lose sight of the context from which the discourse of a new mythology emerged. Friedrich Schlegel described the new mythology as a "symbolische Ansicht der Natur." The phrase implies that any reading of the novel as an expression of mythology must consider not so much the content of the novel as the representational practices from which that content is generated.

In aligning the novel's mythic dimensions with its eschatological events, Stopp and Mahoney veer away from this more basic Romantic notion of myth as symbolism. Dilthey's description of the novel as a "Verkörperung einer die Natur erklärenden Naturansicht" (embodiment of a view of nature that explains nature) comes close to it (344); in fact, it is a disagreement over the nature of symbolism that begets the tension between the seminal readings of Dilthey and Haym. Whereas the former reads the novel as the poeticization of a science of nature, the latter reads it as a narrative of the interior, a symbolic poetic memoir of Heinrich's artistic development that, while featuring elements like the transmigration of souls, has as its true backdrop Heinrich's own soul.[33] The disagreement recapitulates the epistemological debate of the era: how does one assign primacy in the matters of subjectivity and objectivity? It is a matter of how the philosophy of (subjective/objective) Idealism is to be articulated in the realm of the beautiful. The difference between the readings of Dilthey and Haym hinges on determining whether an idealistic or realistic worldview guides the mimetic execution of the novel. Whereas Dilthey's reading would suggest the primacy of the object, Haym inclines in the other direction.[34] The disagreement is reflective of the protean character of Romantic philosophy in the wake of Kant and Fichte.

Novalis was not nearly as binary a thinker as the choices between the ideal and the real would suggest. In his notes from the composition of the novel, he referred to the dilemma thus: "Poësie ist wahrhafter Idealismus—Betrachtung der Welt, wie Betrachtung eines *großen Gemüths*—Selbstbewußtseyn des Universums" (Poetry is veritable idealism—contemplation of the world as contemplation of a *grand mind*—self-consciousness of the universe) (*Schriften* 3:640). While he seems to offer an easy answer, "veritable idealism," his gloss of the term reveals that poetry is not reducible to Fichte's idealism of the ego. Instead it is a mode of observation that acknowledges the reality of the universe while comprehending it as mind or spirit. It is thus much closer to the philosophy of Schelling following the latter's break from Fichte. Contrary to the poeticization of natural science as proposed by Dilthey, as well as to the mythologization of the interior by Haym, Novalis's definition of poetry corresponds to what Frederick Beiser has described as Novalis's philosophy of absolute idealism and what Dalia Nassar has described as an idealism married to empiricism.[35] He believed that being has subjective and objective aspects. The terms *idealism* and *realism* are adequate descriptors of the universe only if they operate in tandem with one another. As Friedrich Schlegel had heralded in his *Rede*, the new mythology would rest on the harmony of the ideal *and* the real (KFSA 2:314). Recorded in Novalis's notes, the doctrine of poetry outlined above announces *in nuce* the philosophical worldview of *Ofterdingen* and seems to be what Paul Kluckhohn alluded to when writing that *Ofterdingen* was neither realistic nor allegorical, but "ein symbolischer Roman, der . . . das Göttliche im Irdischen aufzeigen will" (a symbolic novel that wants to depict the divine in the terrestrial) (*Schriften* 1:56). *Ofterdingen* is a reconciliation of difference.

The development of Novalis's poetics of absolute idealism—legible in his correspondence with Friedrich Schlegel—represents an early theorization of a new mythology, though the decisive term (*Mythologie*) is absent:

> In meiner Philosophie des täglichen Lebens bin ich auf die Idee einer *moralischen* / im Hemsterhuisischen Sinn / Astronomie gekommen und habe die interessante Entdeckung der Religion des sichtbaren Weltalls gemacht. Du glaubst nicht, wie weit das greift. Ich denke hier, Schelling weit zu überfliegen. Was denkst Du, ob das nicht der rechte Weg ist, die Physik im allgemeinsten Sinn, schlechterdings *Symbolisch* zu behandeln? (*Schriften* 4:255)
>
> (In my philosophy of everyday life I have come upon the idea of a *moral* / in the Hemsterhuisian sense / astronomy and I have made the interesting discovery of a religion of the visible universe. You won't believe how far-reaching it is. I believe I have far surpassed Schelling. What do you think? Is it not the right way to treat physics, in the most general sense, utterly *symbolically*?)

Quite apart from Schelling, or perhaps more precisely, in addition to him, these remarks intimate a plan that anticipates the mythological program of the letter's recipient. Novalis articulates a symbolic program that would not merely poeticize the laws of nature, it would stage the convergence of nature and spirit, the objective and subjective aspects of the absolute, in the material revelation of a new symbolism. Enamored by the prospect of a "Galvanismus des Geistes" (galvanism of the spirit), Friedrich Schlegel enjoined Novalis to undertake a publishable correspondence wherein they would unite religion and physics (*Schriften* 4:498). This was Schlegel's new mythology *avant la lettre*.

The question facing Novalis was how to forge the representation of that which is marked by equally subjective and objective aspects. How to write a "Betrachtung der Welt" that was simultaneously the "Betrachtung eines *großen Gemüths*"? If taken in the direction of Dilthey, such a novel would seem to have granted the fantastical aspect the full weight of reality. If it veered toward the reading proposed by Haym, the narrative would have subordinated its fantastical aspect to the imaginative power of Heinrich's interior. The choice between this dualism, however, was as unnecessary as the choice between Fichte and Spinoza, between idealism and realism. Through his deployment of the dreamscape, Novalis rendered *Ofterdingen* a representation of the complementary faces of the absolute. The dream as a literary device allowed for him to dance across the spectrum of subject and object, beginning already with the opening dream sequence of the first chapter. It stages an incrementally deepening penetration into the interior of Heinrich, via dreams within dreams and caverns within caverns, but it turns out to be no mere solipsism. It augurs the events yet to unfold in Heinrich's life, and as such, it constitutes the subjective complement to the objective narrative that unfolds in subsequent chapters. The same is true in the other Dantean dream of the novel. Inasmuch as its sequence is foregrounded by the song of the grandfather, and fulfilled by the death of Mathilde, it is the thread with which Novalis braids the interior of his protagonist with the actuality of life. Heinrich's discussion of dreams with his father suggests that he is aware of the real—albeit often imperceptible—connections between the workings of his mind and those of the universe: every dream is a "bedeutsamer Riß in den geheimnisvollen Vorhang . . . der mit tausend Falten in unser Inneres hereinfällt" (meaningful tear in the mysterious curtain that falls into our interior with a thousand folds) (*Schriften* 1:198). Dreams mediate between the mind of the subject and the stage of the world. The novel's intermingling of mind and matter represents Novalis's effort to render visible the "Selbstbewußtseyn des Universums." The effort was not lost on Schlegel, who, in an echo of Novalis's own words, regarded *Ofterdingen* as a transition from novel to mythology. Then again, the novel does not exactly guard this as a secret. Heinrich and Mathilde's child proclaims that "die Welt wird Traum, der Traum wird Welt" (the world becomes dream, the dream becomes world) (*Schriften* 1:319).

The more mysterious matter is why Novalis's use of the dream to navigate the representation of the two faces of the absolute should have been inflected by the *Commedia*. It is worth repeating that the name of Dante fails to appear in the six-volume critical edition of Novalis's works. Yet Dante faced a challenge that was similar to the one facing Novalis, who could grant his novel neither the character of pure mimesis of nature nor that of pure expression of interiority. Novalis accounted for the dilemma through the interpenetration of dreamscape and reality, a fiction so effective that it has prompted readers to debate whether he was propagating a doctrine of the transmigration of souls. The similar challenge facing Dante is best illustrated by considering one of the debates that has long governed the interpretation of the *Commedia*. Is it to be read, namely, as *viaggio* or *visione*, as voyage or as vision? The question has been in play since at least the time of Boccaccio, who described a group of Veronese women who, when they saw Dante, noted how his beard and skin had been singed by the flames of Inferno.[36] The stakes of the debate are straightforward: if the *Commedia* is to be read as a voyage, then Dante is clearly a poet. If it is to be read as a vision, however, then Dante is a prophet. Scholarship includes prominent voices on both sides, with Bruno Nardi, for example, having asserted that Dante continued the tradition of the Old Testament prophets and medieval visionaries, while Charles Singleton wrote that "the fiction of the *Commedia* is that it is not fiction."[37] The matter centers on where one locates the poem's reality: in the mind of Dante or outside of it. We are dealing again with the matter of idealism.

As with *Ofterdingen*, the prominence of two positions has led to the illusion that there are only two. Teodolinda Barolini, however, as noted in the introduction, has argued convincingly against a false dichotomy.[38] By reassessing the dreams of the poem and arguing that Dante's empiricism (i.e., his poetry of voyage) operates in tandem with his mysticism (i.e., his theology of vision), she has generated a third reading that overcomes the weaknesses of the other two. Her argument relies on the elliptical remarks at the beginning and end of the *Commedia*, both of which allow readers to infer, though not conclude, that the experience of the *Commedia* is underwritten by sleep (*Inf.* 1.11–12; *Par.* 32.139). These remarks belong to Dante's imitation of Paul, she says, who described being raptured to the heavens and encountering God, yet admitting uncertainty as to whether in the body or not (2 Corinthians 12:2).[39] Mimicking Paul's ambiguity, Dante points to the corporeality of his experience all the while that he veils it in the language of sleep. Barolini spells out the consequences for us:

> Dante chooses a precursor who "went" as well as "saw" . . . who left his mode of going notoriously unexplained, so that an exegetical tradition grew up devoted to explaining what the apostle says he does not know and, increasingly, to debating whether or not Paul saw God in his essence. (148)

Dante employs dreams, in other words, not to undermine the reality of his experience but to blur the lines that would otherwise allow for the distinction between voyage and vision. As Barolini explains, he deploys sleep as a device for representing transitions because it is a "liminal condition that participates in both life and death, standing on the thresholds of both worlds and fully committed to neither" (160). For Dante, dreams are never mere fiction; the sleep that he depicts is the waking sleep of John the Evangelist, who goes "sleeping, with a vigilant face." (*Purg*. 29.144). Sleeping and dreaming function within the logic of the *Commedia*, as Barolini argues so persuasively, so as to mediate between the apparently opposed experiences of voyage and vision, participating in the reality of both without privileging either. As a technique that sustains the actuality of experience and the subjectivity of vision, Dante's poetics of waking sleep afforded Novalis the means to blur the apparently insuperable division of idealism and realism.

Ofterdingen may have been an anti-*Meister* novel; it may have been a bildungsroman; it may, too, have been a *Künstlerroman* (artist novel), as scholars have long written; but these characterizations fail to account for the ambition that the Dantean program of the novel reveals. To be sure, its fanciful character has attracted romantic readers and repelled realists, its blue flower becoming a shibboleth for all those of soft heart. But to reduce the novel's reception to an assessment of the enchanted hue of its world, as if one had to choose between the pragmatism of *Wilhelm Meister* and the idealism of *Heinrich von Ofterdingen*, is to miss the stakes of the novel. Its movement back and forth through the realm of reality and the realm of the dream, indebted to the dream poetics of the *Commedia*, shows a thoroughgoing effort to grant poetic form to the dynamism of reality that was inherent in Novalis's conception of the absolute. The stakes here are worth underscoring: the Dantean dimensions of the novel do not limit themselves to Matelda/Mathilde, but extend to the novel's entire deployment of dreams, which stretch from the beginning to the end of the fragment. The novel is arguably the single most significant poetic endeavor to resolve in representational form the dilemmas of post-Kantian Idealism. Like Hölderlin's *Hyperion*, it approaches the genre of the philosophical novel, though even that is an imperfect descriptor. *Ofterdingen* does not primarily lay out a set of ideas in a prosaic imitation of nature; it performs them, attempting to grant readers in its mediation of dreams and reality a glimpse of the interstices of nature and spirit. One may call into question the success with which it does so; the third-person narration of the novel, for example, lacks the power to bend truth that Dante is able to exercise in his poem. But like the *Commedia*, *Ofter-*

dingen is a work of religious proportions: its ambition is a revelation of the totality of the absolute.

NOVALIS AND THE MYTHOLOGIZATION OF THE SELF

The extent of Novalis's engagement with Dante opens new ground on which to consider Novalis and his corpus. *Ofterdingen* no longer looks to be primarily a critique of prosaicism, even if that is part of its mission. It is a fulsome expression of Novalis's so-called physics and a distinctive attempt to realize a mythical poetry. The innermost realm of the subject is one with, and not distinct from, the universe. The interweaving of dream and reality approaches a veritable if imperfect poetry of absolute idealism—one that surpasses the didacticism of Schelling's similarly aspirational poetry. But the intertext tempts further exploration: do other features of the novel represent assimilations of Dante's poetry? The possibilities stack up quickly. Like the *Commedia*, the novel recounts the steps of a journey, a pilgrimage to paradise. Like Dante's pilgrimage, that of Heinrich consists in a sequence of interviews in which interlocutors relate their stories and lessons. Heinrich's father describes the dream of his youth; the merchants narrate fables; Zulima describes the tragedies of the crusades; a miner discusses the holy simplicity of his profession; a contemplative in the mountain explains his way of life; Klingsohr provides a lesson in poetry; Sylvester expounds on the nature of the universe. In each case, the pilgrim's desire for knowledge incites a monologue, as Dante's curiosity does in the *Commedia*. The pilgrim in *Ofterdingen* is not identical with the author of the novel, as in the *Commedia*, but he is close: a young poet from north-central Germany whose fiancée, the embodiment of poetic spirit, dies in the bloom of youth. The dead lover is the most obvious of parallels—between Heinrich and Novalis, and between Novalis and Dante. Such is a cursory enumeration of the overlaps between *Ofterdingen* and the *Commedia*. Together, they suggest that Novalis's engagement with Dante, indebted though it was to his dream poetics, extended beyond it. Indeed, they open another possibility, that Dante gave shape not just to *Heinrich von Ofterdingen* but to other segments of Novalis's oeuvre.

In this light, the various comparisons of Novalis to Dante take on a new hue. His early death may have thwarted the realization of the *Ofterdingen* project and precluded it from attaining the status of the *Commedia*, but it contributed to a mythology that sprang up around his person. Since his death, Novalis has become both a canonical poet of Romanticism and a central representative of the Romantic quest for a new mythology. Henrik Steffens's recollection of Novalis from 1841 exemplifies this legacy: "Das ganze

Dasein löste sich für ihn in eine tiefe Mythe auf. Gestalten waren ihm beweglich wie die Worte, und die sinnliche Wirklichkeit blickte aus der mythischen Welt, in welcher er lebte, bald dunkler, bald klarer hervor" (The entirety of his existence distilled itself into a profound myth. Figures were malleable as words to him; the world of the senses glimpsed out of the mythical world in which he lived—at times clearly, at times obscurely) (*Schriften* 4:638).[40] Novalis's poetry was mythical, that is, because he perceived the world as myth. Steffens's statement betrays what the new mythologists failed to discuss: the new mythology relied as much on the mythologization of its authors as it did on a poetics of myth.

Scholars have tended to see the halo surrounding Novalis as the forgery of posthumous promoters.[41] "Novalis became the mythical, quintessential Romantic through Romantic editing," William Arctander O'Brien has written.[42] The principal movers in the campaign were Ludwig Tieck and Friedrich Schlegel. There is truth to that view, but it overlooks the degree to which the poet of myth forges the myth of his poetry. He relies on an *auctoritas* that is ordained by the heavens. This was overt in the case of Schelling's stanzas, where the young philosopher made no bones about proclaiming his election to divine gnosis. The transparency of the maneuver was counterproductive, however, as it all but destroyed the semblance of authenticity. Dante was cleverer, for he went through elaborate steps to convince readers of his humility. He resembled the prophets of the Hebrew Bible, hesitant and astonished ("ma io?"), and was unusually credible. It is more difficult to locate strategic attempts of Novalis to present himself publicly as a poet of the universe, particularly in light of the conspicuous promotional efforts of Tieck and Schlegel. It is tempting to admit that Novalis's life was lived with one foot in the grave, as if his proximity to death endowed him the status of a visionary.

Yet the Dantean resonances of Novalis's poetry shed light on how he molded his status as a poet of myth. The present reading renders some aspects of this endeavor visible: the numerous allusions to the *Commedia* were probably included in *Ofterdingen* not just for the sake of the novel's dream poetics; they were probably also doffs of the cap to the Romantic circle in Jena and to Friedrich Schlegel's conviction that Dante was the exemplar for Romantic myth.[43] For it was at the time of *Ofterdingen*'s composition that the *Commedia* had become nightly reading for the Romantic circle in Jena. It is difficult to imagine Novalis, their regular correspondent, unaware of the devotion to the poem and not expecting an enthusiastic response to his novel's engagement with it. Furthermore, Novalis's intricate adaptation of

Dante's poetics of the dream had a special connection to A. W. Schlegel. The latter had addressed the matter of dreams in Dante in his 1796 commentary on the *Purgatorio.* He discussed dreams with respect to the earthly paradise, focusing on Dante's dream of Rachael and Leah, which prefigures the arrival of Beatrice and Matelda. Schlegel's use of Neo-Platonic terms to describe Rachael's "himmlische Beschauung" (heavenly contemplation) probably intrigued Novalis, an avid reader of Hemsterhuys and Plotinus. So, too, his observation of Dante's frequent use of early-morning dreams to signal prophetic events (AWSW 3:352). Novalis, after all, described both of Heinrich's prophetic dreams as having occurred in the hours just before waking. The *Commedia* may have informed the composition of *Ofterdingen*, in other words, but its coloring of the novel in the context of the Jena circle ought not be neglected: Novalis was seizing the mantle of the circle's mythic ambitions.

Novalis's attempt at a Dantean mythology occasions a reconsideration of his legacy. The notion that his death rendered him clay in the hands of Tieck and Schlegel insufficiently reflects his agency in the process of that mythologization. For, as with Schelling, the composition of a new mythology also entailed thinking through the authority of myth's source. Dante looks to have figured in Novalis's thoughts on the matter. The early death of Sophie von Kühn was probably sufficient impetus to seek consolation in Dante's poetry of mourning and to identify with him. It was something Dante had done upon Beatrice's death, finding solace in Boethius's *Consolation of Philosophy.* It is thus with good reason that several readers have detected an affinity between the *Vita nuova* and the *Hymnen an die Nacht*, each one a collection of poems in which a man mourns the death of his beloved. Both are autobiographical, prosimetric collections (as was Boethius's *Consolation*): Dante's poems are interspersed with his commentary, whereas Novalis's transition over the collection from prose to verse. The focal point of each is the love of the poet for a woman whose life beyond the grave imbues his love with an aspect of mysticism. Both express the wish to join their beloved in death. The similarities are striking, in other words, but as Judith Ryan writes—echoing other commentators—there is "no evidence that Novalis was in fact inspired by the *Vita nuova*."[44] What might it mean if there were? Together with the Dantean thrust of *Ofterdingen*, it would cast a strange new light on the whole of Novalis's slim corpus.

Could the *Hymnen*, in fact, be a sister text to the *Vita nuova*? Dante's volume, like the *Commedia*, is autobiographical: it depended on his curation of memories, all centered on the experience of love. It is a poeticization of the experience of love, but it is many things besides that too. It is an encomium to and glorification of Beatrice, whom Dante analogizes to Christ. He plays up the significance of her name—the blessed one—and makes a show of manipulating a line from Homer to call her the daughter of a god (VN 72). She is awarded the same numerological connotations as God. Her love is salvific. The book, too, is an account of youth. It gestures almost always toward the past, using a reconstruction of memories to outline how the experience of love led to new life. Finally, the book is a precursor to the *Commedia*. In its conclusion, Dante promises to write more of Beatrice when he is better able and prays that his soul might ascend to behold hers in heaven. Novalis's *Hymnen* are likewise the bitter fruit of a tragic romance. They teeter between the recollection of the past and a future beyond the grave. Novalis draws on the "Fernen der Erinnerung, Wünsche der Jugend, der Kindheit Träume" (distances of memory, wishes of youth, dreams of childhood), analogues to Dante's book of memory (*Schriften* 1:131). Like Dante, who is prepared to die and ascend to Beatrice (VN 90), Novalis versifies his "Sehnsucht nach dem Tod" (longing for death) (*Schriften* 1:153). When he writes that he would go "Hinunter zu der süßen Braut, / Zu Jesus, dem Geliebten" (down to the sweet bride, / to Jesus, the beloved), his conflation of Sophie and Christ recalls Dante's analogization of Beatrice and Christ. The *Hymnen* are significant in their own right, but like the *Vita nuova*, they are important in presaging the arrival of the poet's magnum opus. It is difficult, in short, to regard the texts' linkages as happenstance.

Closer inspection reveals that the Dantean traces of the *Sophien-Erlebnis* emerge from the salient images of Dante's *libello*. Integral to this connection is a dream-poem at the outset of the *Vita*. It is numerologically significant, for it is the first poem of the collection as well as the third appearance of Beatrice.[45] It is unique, Robert Hollander has argued, because it is the only one of Beatrice's nine appearances in the book in which she appears to Dante in his sleep.[46] Her appearance in the dream is preceded by the appearance to Dante of a fiery cloud from which emerges the figure of a frightening man, Amore. He announces: "*Ego dominus tuus*" (I am your master) (VN 74). Dante indeed becomes the captive of love, a point the book reiterates (72, 90, 121, 130). Its first poem—"To Every Captive Soul and Gentle Heart"—underscores this enslavement (VN 75–76). The allegorized master, Amore, holds in his arms the figure of Beatrice, draped in crimson. He feeds her Dante's burning heart, and breaking from joy into tears of sorrow, he whisks her off to the heavens. The terror of the encounter wakes Dante from his dream. The poem and its prose commentary are a memorable introduction to the theme of the book: love and the sacrifices to it that Dante will make.

With the images of the dream, the *Vita* supplies the *Hymnen* a lexicon with which to represent Sophie's death. Novalis may well have understood himself as the sort of captive whom Dante addressed, his book an embrace and re-enactment of Dante's grief. He repeatedly depicts himself in the *Hymnen* as a captive. The master whose dictates cause him to suffer is not *Amore* (love), but rather *das Licht* (light), another allegorized figure. *Das Licht* has servants (133); it has chains that bind from birth (135); in the realm of *Licht*, nature is bound by the iron chains of time and measurement (145). *Das Licht* is the source of division, the force that precludes the eternal union of all things. Thus is it a dream that must end the captivity of light and vouchsafe union with God (157). The pain of the daylight must be banished by the release provided by the night. With the erasure of all difference, the poet and his beloved will be one. This is Novalis's wish, repeated in the poems: he would mix himself with her ashes that they might be one for eternity (131). To that end, he gives voice to a prayer inflected by Dante's image of Beatrice consuming his fiery heart: "zarte Geliebte . . . zehre mit Geisterglut meinen Leib, daß ich luftig mit dir inniger mich mische und dann ewig die Brautnacht währt" (delicate beloved . . . consume my body with passion of the soul, that I might airily mingle myself more inwardly with you and then the bridal night might last forever) (133). As with the chains of captivity, it is not an exact replica of Dante's imagery; but it recycles Dante's images in the reinterpretation of a nearly identical experience.

The textual approximation of Dante is at its most intimate in the central poem in the *Hymnen*, "Einst da ich bittre Tränen vergoß" (When I once shed bitter tears). It is the central poem, as Heinz Ritter wrote, because it was the *Urhymne* of the collection.[47] Written in autumn 1797, within months of Sophie's death, it is the oldest and most primal poetic act of the *Sophien-Erlebnis*. It is the foundational myth in what came to define the Novalis phenomenon, the record of his graveside mourning. It depicts the original experience of *Nachtbegeisterung* (nocturnal enthusiasm) and marks the liberation of the poetic subject from his captivity to the light. Overcome by the "Schlummer des Himmels" (slumber of heaven), he witnesses a transfiguration of Sophie:

> die Gegend hob sich sacht empor; über der Gegend schwebte mein entbundner, neugeborner Geist. Zur Staubwolke wurde der Hügel—durch die Wolke sah ich die verklärten Züge der Geliebten. . . . Jahrtausende zogen abwärts in die Ferne, wie Ungewitter. An Ihrem Halse weint ich dem neuen Leben entzückende

> Tränen.—Es war der erste, einzige Traum—und erst seitdem fühl ich ewigen, unwandelbaren Glauben an den Himmel der Nacht und sein Licht, die Geliebte. (*Schriften* 1:135)

> (the region raised itself gently up; above the region hovered my unchained, newborn spirit. The mound became a cloud of dust—through the cloud I saw the transfigured features of my beloved. . . . Millennia stretched by into the distance, like storms. Upon her neck I cried delightful tears for the new life.—It was the first, only dream—and since just that moment have I felt an eternal, unchanging belief in the Heaven of the Night and its light, my beloved.)

Novalis here sketches the contours of the origin myth that came to define his literary oeuvre: the death of the beloved, the salve of the night, the ecstasy of the dream. With the transfiguration of the beloved there emerges a new subjectivity: bitter tears are transformed to delight. The poet has a "neugeborenen Geist," a "neues Leben," a *vita nuova*. In the heart of Novalis's personal mythology, Dante's voice rings clear. The *Hymnen an die Nacht* are, ultimately, a re-creation of the *Vita nuova*.

The degree to which Dante shaped the guiding gestures of Novalis's poetry warrants reiteration of a question: What else does the slim corpus of Novalis owe to the poet whose name he never recorded? That his two major literary works owe so much to Dante makes plausible propositions that might otherwise seem preposterous. Does Novalis's political essay on the unity of Christian Europe represent a reformulation of Dante's political essay on world monarchy? Was his *Sehnsucht* for the unity represented by the Roman pope a transformation of Dante's wish to experience the unity provided for by the Roman emperor? And what about Novalis's self-stylization as a "clearer of new lands," as his adaptation of a medieval family name suggests: Did he adopt as his model in this venture another clearer of new paths? Could Dante, the poet of the vernacular and the voice of the *dolce stil novo*, reside at the heart of the myth that Friedrich von Hardenberg designed? The questions are not as farfetched as they sound.

They return us to a course whose traces have begun to materialize: the disconnect between the Romantics' theorization of a new mythology and their efforts at realizing it. The formal and theoretical appeals to the *Commedia*, delineated in the main by the Schlegel brothers and Schelling, found themselves largely subordinated to the mystery of the person of Dante. It is true that *Heinrich von Ofterdingen*, with its poetic program of dreaming, leveraged the nimble way that Dante had balanced the lines of fantasy and reality and aimed at a mythological expression of idealism. The seminal images of the *Hymnen*, too, lay in Dante's representation of dreams. But Novalis's imitations, like those of Schelling, betray a fixation on the mythology of Dante's life. It is arresting that the poetic record of the defining event of his life repurposes Dante's images of grief. The absence of Dante's name from Novalis's corpus renders the fixation all the more conspicuous: given the multiple intertexts, it reads like a concealment. To let slip the name of Dante would have been to reveal the man behind the curtain. The omission reveals the double bind of Romantic mythology—how to communicate the (Dantean) authority of the project, without disclosing it as historically contingent.

CHAPTER THREE

Goethe's Dantean Mythologies of the Self and of the World

INCIPIENT PREOCCUPATIONS with authority and life altered the horizons of the new mythology. Its focus no longer stretched to the distance; it turned inward. Whereas Friedrich Schlegel had speculated that a new mythology would organize the disparate talents of the age, the cases of Schelling and Novalis highlighted a challenging new priority: a mythic poetics demanded first of all a reconceptualization of the self, a reimagining of the poet's relation to God and world. The ground upon which each of them made his attempt—the sacrosanct space of divine election—was consequential for the fledgling project. Its utopian force was deferred, its outward-facing trajectory subsumed by more immediate needs. More urgent than an imitation of the organizing principles of the *Commedia* was the appropriation of Dante's voice, the re-creation and inhabiting of his life. The ineluctable question of myth's origins had eclipsed its conceptualization as aesthetic form.

Inseparable though it was from the *Commedia*, the symbolic record of Dante's life materialized first in the *Vita nuova*. It had situated him in a tradition of Western writers of the self. Conceived as a text of retrospection, it alternates between two voices: an editor in the present and a poet in the past. Its alteration between past and present renders it similar to Boethius's *Consolation of Philosophy*. Its attention to spiritual development and conversion, on the other hand, approximates Augustine's *Confessions*, and with it, the origins of Western autobiography. As an account of development, the collection pivots on a specific *canzone*—"Donne ch'avete intelletto d'amore" (Women who have understanding of love). The editorial voice represents the song as a personal breakthrough; indeed, it is an early articulation of the so-called *dolce stil novo*, in which eros leads to beatitude. Conversion, by this account, turns on the artist's passage beyond the stagnant waters of convention. Through Dante's practice of self-editorialization, the song became a touchstone of the new style: in the *Commedia*, a Tuscan poet remarks upon it as such (*Purg*. 24.49–63). Like the final lines of the *Vita nuova*, which augur the *Commedia*, it is an example of how Dante's texts cohere in ways that allow him to build a mythology of the self. He orchestrates a polyphony of voices across texts, each suffusing the other with meaning.

The persistent rewriting of the self reveals the perspicacity of the early Romantics' alignment of Goethe with Dante. Their idol in Weimar was perhaps the only poet to have aestheticized his life as elaborately as Dante. There is no grand poem of Goethe's life, as the *Commedia* is for Dante, but there is a vast corpus—some 133 volumes in the *Sophien-Ausgabe*—that is a memorial in its own right. As Nicholas Boyle has written, Goethe was the "supreme product" of the age of paper.[1] A register of his texts of the self would need to include multiple fragments of autobiography, volume upon volume of journals and correspondence, and the testimony of his lyrical poetry. Notwithstanding the heterogeneity of this corpus, the comparisons of Dante and Goethe usually begin and end with a consideration of the *Commedia* and *Faust*. That maneuver—performed with varying degrees of success[2]—elides their most significant bond: a propensity to mythologize the self. Goethe, it is to be noted from the outset, was not invested in the Romantics' mythological undertaking; yet the propensity toward self-mythologization, as well as the Romantics' efforts to adopt him, render his role in the historiography of the new mythology indispensable. His proclivity for automythology is a natural departure point for the inquiry at hand.

AUTOMYTHOLOGY

If it is a platitude to note the fictions of autobiography, what authorizes a concept of automythology? Consider two source texts of the autobiographical genre, Augustine's *Confessions* (397) and Rousseau's *Confessions* (1769). They reveal myriad overlaps in the lives of their authors. Each moved from the periphery to the center of a world-historical power; each undertook significant travel and held diplomatic posts; each was a convert to Roman Catholicism; each perceived his libido to be the source of considerable personal trouble; each struggled to cope with having fathered offspring out of wedlock. Most saliently for us, each of them relied on acts of retrospection to write autodiegetic narratives. Yet there is a marked difference in their narration: whereas the events of Rousseau's life appear scattershot, his development all but aimless, just the opposite is true of Augustine. The smallest events of his life are shot through with meaning. The ostensibly trivial details of his youth often presage the momentous events of his maturity. His life is organized by a typological hermeneutic. Consider two examples: Augustine's emergence as an adolescent from a Roman bath—which signaled to his father the arrival of his manhood—foreshadows his baptism.[3] His theft of pears in a garden (29), an adaptation of events of Eden, is another typological mytheme. Its fulfillment occurs with Augustine's conversion in a garden of Milan (146). Rousseau, by way of comparison, depicts a similar moment of horticultural transgression. He and a friend reroute an irrigation system from an important tree to a sapling they wish to tend. It is an episode charged with interpretive prospects, but the narration neglects to exploit them. It is a bit of one-off mischief, any meaning of which is circumscribed by the parameters of the episode. The contrast helps define the peculiarity of Augustine's inscription of the self. Whereas Rousseau's life amounts to a lottery, his *Confessions* the record of its gains and losses, Augustine's life has the hermeneutic density of a poem, his *Confessions* the exposition of its meaning. As Nietzsche once wrote, the holy man knows to write his life such that it signifies something.[4]

Automythology relies on mythic and religious patterns of representation to generate a surplus of hermeneutic value: it saturates a life with meaning. To use Blumenberg's term, it infuses a life with *Bedeutsamkeit* (significance).[5] The presence of fiction is taken for granted, as the title of Goethe's autobiography, *Dichtung und Wahrheit* (*Poetry and Truth*), admits. More vital than its facticity is its formal design. Augustine's *Confessions* is neither history nor autobiography, but a superimposition of "Genesis patterns" on the events of its author's life.[6] Mythology is not singular in its ability to produce meaning via form, but it possesses something that other discourses lack: an "established repertory of procedures," which provide for the inscription of experience in an objectively accessible foundation.[7] In addition to Blumenberg's observation that myth possesses a repertory of procedures, one might speak of its repertory of symbols, which broadens the lanes of access to that foundation. The procedures and symbols of myth, as Augustine demonstrates, are transferable. They enable the mythological inscription of the self.

The automythological use of such symbols and structures (e.g., Dante's [purported] use of the *quadruplex sensus*), has a pluripotent effect. It militates against what Paul de Man identified as an aporia of autobiography—the "defacement" of the autobiographical subject through the privative nature of language.[8] De Man pointed to the tension between the formal impulse of diegesis and the actuality of a life. Each motivates the other, but language cannot help but signal the absence of the life. In the shift from autodiegesis to automythology, however, there occurs a transformation: automythology gathers the caprices of a fate like that which governs Rousseau's *Confessions* and organizes them into a legible unity. It is Goethe's *life*, for example, and not just his autobiography, that is regularly conceived as an artwork, as one finds in the title of Rüdiger Safranski's recent biography, *Goethe: Kunstwerk des Lebens* (*Goethe: Life as a Work of Art*).[9] As a consequence of this reifying effect, automythologies often result in the de facto canonization of their authors, whose lives appear unusually whole. The lives of Augustine, Dante, and Goethe are exemplary in this respect. More to the point, in adopting established modes of hermeneutic signification (typology, scriptural allegory, etc.), automythology inscribes the life of the author in a hermeneutic tautology: subjectivity loses whimsicality and takes on the appearance of necessity. Subject (author) and object (universe) are inextricably integrated. The meaning of one does not exist without the other.

Structures and symbols of myth permeate Goethe's texts of the self. They encompass his traditionally aesthetic forms, like the lyric, as well as his mundane forms, like the letter. Nor are they bound by period. They shape his mature as well as his youthful self-presentation. Already in 1765, for example, he corresponded with his sister in terms that anticipated the more complex automythological devices of his later autobiographies. Consider the example of a letter he writes to Cornelia from a spa in Wiesbaden. Its garden was overrun by snakes, reported Goethe, who boasted of having slaughtered one of them. His subsequent description of other obstacles in the primeval landscape merits attention:

> Neulich verwirrten wir uns in dem Walde, und mußten Stundenlang in selbigem, durch Hecken und Büsche durchkriechen. Bald stellte sich uns ein umschatteter Fels dar, bald ein düstres Gesträuch und nirgends war ein Ausgang zu finden. Gewiß wir wären biß in die Nacht gelaufen; wenn nicht eine wohlthätige Fee hier und da . . . den rechten Weeg uns zu zeigen gebunden hätte. Da wir denn glücklich aus dem Walde kamen. (WA 4/1:7)[10]

> (Recently we got lost in the forest and had to creep through its hedges and bushes for two hours. Soon there appeared to us a cliff wrapped in shadow, then a gloomy thicket; there was no way out in sight. We would certainly have been running into the night, were it not for a kindly fairy . . . who bound herself to show us the way, for which reason we came happily out of the forest.)

The letter is hardly coy in its evocation of mythical topoi. The serpent's connections to Genesis are obvious enough. To Cornelia, a student of Italian, so, too, must have been the allusions to the gambit of *Inferno*. The intertexts make an everyman of Goethe, who, at the age of fifteen, was a bit presumptuous, or at least zealous, in comparing himself to these seminal examples of fallen man. Yet he was prescient, too, if for no other reason than that it was not the last time he suggested he had lost the right path in the forest, and certainly not the last time that mythological topoi structured the shape of his self-representation.

His mature autobiographies, *Dichtung und Wahrheit* and the *Italienische Reise* (*The Italian Journey*), coalesce around narratives that intertwine complex mythemes. The former juxtaposes mutually reflective scenes in which Goethe represents his maturation and genius as Promethean.[11] His identification with the Titan, apart from engaging the discourses of the *Geniezeit*, figures in the construal of his subjectivity as necessary and quintessential. The absolute character of his existence all but flanks the body of the text. At the outset of book one, he describes the favorable astrological sign under which he was born, as if his life had been sanctioned by the universe. The final book of the autobiography, meanwhile, outlines the conflict between Goethe's Promethean nature and a concept he calls *das Dämonische* (the demonic). Efforts to define the concept have bedeviled scholars, as Kirk Wetters has explained, but even our amorphous image of it reveals why it concerns an automythological narrative.[12] For as Goethe describes it, the demonic is akin to chance or contingency, which is to say, it poses an existential threat to the notion of subjectivity as necessary and absolute. Goethe's response to the demonic—he claims always to have fled from it "hinter ein Bild" (behind an image) (MA 16:820)—confirms as much. From start to finish, *Dichtung und Wahrheit* is a text of the self that draws on the representational structures of myth.

The *Italienische Reise*, meanwhile, leverages biblical episodes as frames for isolating and underscoring the events of Goethe's life. Appropriations from the New Testament, linked carefully to the Christian calendar, as Vittorio Hösle has shown, saturate the text.[13] Goethe's many identifications with Christ merit special attention; their frequent iterations reveal the traces of a program. The episode Goethe describes on March 25, 1787 (i.e., on the Feast of the Annunciation), is exemplary in this respect. Goethe and a companion, Christoph Heinrich Kniep, sit on a terrace and enjoy a view of the Gulf of Naples. The romantic partner of the latter, angelic in appearance, ascends to the terrace. She reminds Goethe of the angels depicted in representations of the Annunciation. In the wake of the encounter, there arrives a flash of insight: Goethe comes closer to conceiving of the *Urpflanze* (MA 15:276–277). The adaptation of the biblical episode, which depicts Goethe's botanical work as divinely inspired, presages a set of similar appropriations of events from the life of Christ. As Goethe sails from Naples to Sicily (April 2), he sequesters himself in his cabin and works on the unfinished drama, *Torquato Tasso*, consuming nothing but the eucharistic meal of bread and wine. After three days "im Wahlfischbauch" (i.e., like Jonah, a Hebrew type of Christ), he emerges from his cabin in good spirits: he has nearly finished the work on his drama (MA 15:283). The return journey to Naples, too, takes its shape from other episodes in the life of Christ.[14] The mythography of the Judeo-Christian tradition yielded strategies for the signification of the self. What did its transmission signify?

The culminating scenes of the *Italienische Reise* suggest that Christ's meaning to Goethe's autobiography inheres in his status as a figure of renewal and new life. The proposition hinges on two encounters—one aesthetic, the other romantic—that occur when Goethe has returned from the south to Rome. He meets a young woman from Milan. The two form a quick bond, sealed by Goethe's instruction to her in the English language. The affair founders as quickly as it had begun: Goethe learns that the woman is engaged to be married. But the engagement is broken off, and she falls deathly ill. Goethe visits her devotedly, sometimes twice a day, and eventually learns that she credits his visits with her recovery. Goethe reports much of this in his essayistic account of the events of December 1787, composed over four decades later in 1829. The disjunction in time reveals how much of the episode must be the work of retrospective composition. Indeed, it is striking for its arrangement: the narration of the affair flanks Goethe's study of Raphael, as if the events were interdependent. Goethe's discussion of Raphael's *Transfiguration* reads in fact as an oblique commentary on the unfulfilled romance. That discussion centers on a disagreement of interpretation:

does the painting, whose upper half depicts Christ's transfiguration and whose lower half depicts the healing of a sick child, constitute a unity, or not?

> Wie will man nun das Obere und Untere trennen? beides ist eins: unten das Leidende, Bedürftige, oben das Wirksame, Hülfreiche, beides auf einander sich beziehend, ineinander einwirkend. Läßt sich denn, um den Sinn auf eine andere Weise auszusprechen, ein ideeller Bezug aufs Wirkliche von diesem lostrennen? (Dezember. Bericht). (MA 15:540)

> (How can one wish to separate the upper and lower parts? Both are one: below is suffering and neediness, above is potency and aid, both of which relate to and interact with one another. To put the matter another way, can an ideal relation to the real be separated from the image?)

Goethe's assessment lacks evidentiary force. After all, the painting does have two distinct halves (figure 3.1). Whence, then, the adamance of his conviction? By a logic of substitution, it appears, the painting has come to represent Goethe's role in the encounter with the Milanese. Like the sick child who is healed by Christ, she has been restored to life by a figure of genius who is experiencing his own transformation. Her convalescence and his potency are fatefully linked, as Goethe reiterates in the final pages of the *Italienische Reise*, confessing her perpetual place in his soul (April. Bericht) (MA 15:650).

The centrality to Goethe of the affair, particularly his choice of its emblem, illuminates the stakes of the Christocentric mythology in the *Italienische Reise*. To interpret his life in Italy under the sign of Christ is to mark it as *transfigured*, to mark it *renewed*. The sense is not religious, but automythological: the symbolic valences of Christ lend an aged Goethe the images to communicate the meaning of his years in Italy. It was a period of glorious transformation. These identifications with Christ, tantamount to a program, form the mythological sinews of the autobiography. But the transfiguration of Christ is not the only mytheme through which Goethe announces the dawn of new life. The resurrection, as one might well expect, figures here as well. On April 8, 1787—marked *Ostersonntag* (Easter Sunday) in the diary—Goethe describes a scene of Christian anagnorisis: a man from Malta, who recognizes Goethe as a German, asks for news from Thuringia,

fig. 3.1. Raphael (Raffaello Sanzio), *The Transfiguration*, 1520. Oil on wood. 410×279 cm. Pinacoteca, Vatican Museums. Scala / Art Resource, NY.

ultimately asking after the trendsetting author of *Werther*, whose name he has forgotten. Goethe records his response:

> Nach einer kleinen Pause, als wenn ich mich bedächte, erwiderte ich: die Person, nach der ihr euch gefällig erkundigt, bin ich selbst!—Mit dem sichtbarsten Zeichen des Erstaunens fuhr er zurück und rief aus: da muß sich viel verändert haben!—O ja! versetzte ich, zwischen Weimar und Palermo hab' ich manche Veränderung gehabt. (MA 15:301)
>
> (After a short pause, as if I were pondering the matter, I replied: "The person after whom you so attentively inquire is none other than I—myself!"—With the most visible sign of astonishment he drew back and called out: "Much must have changed!" "Oh yes," I replied, "between Weimar and Palermo I have changed a great deal.")

The Christological mythos at work in the *Italienische Reise* serves Goethe in the segmentation of his artistic life. The identification with Christ authenticates Italy as a caesura in the biography. Christ marks Italy as the advent of Goethe's new life.

NEW LIFE

Edward Said wrote that the rhetoric of transfiguration is common to the late style of writers and artists.[15] If true, it must apply doubly to Goethe, whose long life made him a de facto late stylist for nearly half of it. Thus does the notion of new life, an archetype unto itself, accrue significance across the decades of Goethe's long career. In 1775, as a promising young writer engaged to Lili Schönemann, its prospect was unsettling: "Welch ein fremdes, neues Leben!" (What a strange, new life!) he exclaims, going on to pray that love let him loose (MA 1/1:264). Things had changed by the time of his old age. Invocations of new life, by then synonymous with rejuvenation, litter the lyrics of Goethe's final fifteen years.[16] The late poems, which often memorialize personal relationships, evince an eagerness to see the glimmer of new beginnings. Beset by the (demonic) forces of life, the automythologist aimed to shore up the foundations of his existence. *Neues Leben* (new life) was a useful figure in that venture.

Yet where to source it? In the effort to absolutize his life, Goethe relied on the coordination of his person with canonical semiotic referents. In their universal recognizability, Prometheus and Christ vouchsafed the communicability of an aestheticized existence. They plucked the poet from the Duchy of Weimar and made of his life an emblem that would be comprehensible across centuries and continents. Their symbolic currency, however, did not stretch far enough to encompass Goethe's automythological impulses. The rhetoric of *neues Leben*, linked though it is to Christ, points to Dante. It was his *Vita nuova*, after all, that consecrated new life a topos of European rhetoric. Dante's life supplied an iconography to mark the decisive junctures in Goethe's inscription of his life.

Goethe's exploitation of Dante's life, playful in the early letter to Cornelia, became earnest by middle age. For in the early 1780s, he faced circumstances that resembled the spiritual quagmire in which Dante once found himself. At nearly thirty-five years old, struggling with the move to Weimar, he had reached the crisis of middle age, the "mezzo del cammin di nostra vita." He had traded the imperial city of Frankfurt for the backwater of Weimar, where the brilliance of youth seemed to have lost its luster. It may not have been equivalent to Dante's exile from Florence, but it felt like a similar crisis.[17] Thus does the 1783 poem "Ilmenau"—a meditation on Goethe's relation to Weimar and its duke—teem with the Dantean images that had emerged inchoate in the letter to Cornelia.[18] It is a ballad in which Goethe recounts his journey as a pilgrim into an "Anmutig[es] Tal" (pleasant valley), where a waterfall rushes melodically down the face of a mountain cliff (26). He prays that this *locus amoenus* might be a "neues Eden" (new Eden), a pre-lapsarian garden where he can forget about the toils of the earth. The scene approximates the *divina foresta* of *Purgatorio*, until nightfall, when its affinity to a dark forest becomes clear: "Im finstern Wald, beim Liebesblick der Sterne, / Wo ist mein Pfad, den sorglos ich verlor?" (In the dark forest, under the stars' gaze of love, / Where is my path, which I carelessly lost?) (29–30). Here is the unmistakable voice of Dante's pilgrim in his crisis at the outset of the *Commedia*. (*Inf.* 1.1–3). "Ilmenau" translates the topography of Dante's life to Goethe's Thuringia.

Its Dantean orientation is soon confirmed: the pilgrim's abandonment of the right path yields a visionary experience. No sooner is he off the path than he is in a "Zaubermärchen-Land" (fairytale land) (35), observing a campfire that is presided over by four figures. One of them, a phantom of himself, laments a crisis of self-alienation: "Wer kennt sich selbst? Wer weiß, was er vermag?" (Who knows himself? Who knows what he wants?) (100). The lament is intertwined with the decision to uproot to Weimar: "Ich bin dir nicht imstande, selbst zu sagen, / Woher ich sei, wer mich hierher gesandt" (I am not in a position even to say, / From where I come, or who sent me here) (96–97). Goethe's phantom compares himself to Prometheus, but in this case, it is not the galvanizing image of a hero who defies the gods (as it was in Goethe's ode). It is the image of a man who has once done something heroic, but now sees only limits. It is the portrait of a defeated poet, a man who would seek new life some three years later in Italy. Now, however, he coaxes himself into believing he has found it. For with the end of the phantom's speech, the poet shuns the dream. It dissolves, the sun re-emerges, and the poet claims to have discovered himself: "Es lebt mir eine schönre Welt; . . . / Ein neues Leben ist's, es ist schon lang begonnen" (There lives in me a more beautiful world; . . . It is a new life, already long begun) (163–165). The sign under which he describes the resolution of his crisis—*neues Leben*—echoes Dante's *vita nuova*. Three times in the poem he gives voice to it as a formula: twice as a prayer, and finally as an acknowledgment of his rediscovery of himself in Weimar.[19] It reads as more wishful and illusive than convicing. Only later was it infused with the realism of old(er) age.

In fact, "Ilmenau" yields a repertory of images and topoi that recur across Goethe's lyrical record of the self. They surface a quarter century later in "Mächtiges Überraschen" (Mighty surprise), the first poem in a cycle of sonnets. Goethe reflects on the disappointment that threatens to follow from the interruption of a life's course. The poem operates as an extended metaphor—its subject, a river. Unleashed from the mountains, it rushes toward a valley where it will unite its waters with those of Father Ocean. Suddenly, it is interrupted—Oreads have dammed its course—and it sprays in a crash of waves. No less anthropomorphized than the nymphs, the river must learn to cope with unexpected circumstances: "Sie [die Welle] schwankt und ruht, zum See zurueckgedeichet; / Gestirne, spiegelnd sich, beschau'n das Blinken / Des Wellenschlags am Fels, ein neues Leben" (WA 1/2:3) (It [the wave] sways and rests, diked back into a lake; / Stars, mirroring one other, behold the flashing / Of the surf upon the rocks, a new life).

This is not the *locus amoenus* of "Ilmenau," but the features of that landscape render this one familiar: the mountain forest, the valley at the foot of the mountain, the rush of falling water, the ocular connection to the stars (cf. "Ilmenau": "beim Liebesblick der Sterne"). The repetition is not accidental; the crisis that once had to be resolved in that landscape has again reared its head: a youth marked by brilliance has found its path blocked. How, after the promises of youth, to reckon with the disappointment of the present? The invocation of *neues Leben* no longer marks the end of a dream. Instead, in an act of reconciliation, it lays claim to and reinterprets the bitterness of unfulfilled promise. In the refrain of new life, and in the store of images that culminates in it, the Dantean tropology of Goethe's automythology is discernible.[20]

Concentrated though it is in these poems, that record emerges from incipient forms that populate the early autobiographical lyrics. In 1775, already, they are visible in "Auf dem See" (On the lake). The poet is a boater on the sea of the world (a guiding metaphor in the *Commedia*). Here again, there looms a crisis of subjectivity, albeit from the other side of middle age, which is to say, from the perspective of youth. Instead of the disappointment of middle age, there looms the anxiety at the prospect of that disappointment. The young poet is concerned that his path will be derailed by the temptation of dreams:

> Aug, mein Aug, was sinkst du nieder?
> Goldne Träume, kommt ihr wieder?
> Weg, du Traum! so gold du bist;
> Hier auch Lieb und Leben ist. (WA 1/1:78)
>
> (Eye, my eye, why do you sink down?
> Golden dreams, will you return?
> Away, dream! Gold though you are;
> Here, too, is love and life.)

In the mirage of golden dreams hovers the enticement of a golden age, a vital notion for Romantics like Novalis, but a fantasy shunned by Goethe. The words with which he banishes it anticipate those with which he banishes the dream-vision in "Ilmenau" ("Verschwinde, Traum!" [Vanish, dream!]). The injunctions mirror one another, as, too, does nearly every image of nature across the three poems we have been following. And although there is no explicit resolution of the crisis of the dream in new life, this is for the simple reason that, to the young poet, the life to which he returns his gaze is still new. Indeed, the poem's first line is an expression of delight on that very note: "Und frische Nahrung, neues Blut / Saug ich aus freier Welt" (And fresh nourishment, new blood / I suck from the whole world). Admittedly, the biographical circumstances of its composition call that expression into question: written on the heels of the break from Lili Schönemann, its affirmation of the freshness of the present reveals the fragility of that new life. The poem demonstrates Goethe's early mastery of the images that came to bear the weight of the engagement with Dante.

The lexicon of images in this trio of lyrics is of special significance because it emerges out of Goethe's seminal reflections on myth in the early hymn, "Mahomets Gesang" (Mohammed's song) (1772). The topography of the hymn displays obvious affinities to the later lyrics. Its subject, as in the sonnet, is a river that hurtles down mountain cliffs, through clouds, and into a valley, whence it rushes off to join Father Ocean. It is, as commentators agree, a meditation on the Islamic prophet as the locus of a new religion.[21] Conceived as a powerful river whose course will not be stopped, he hears the cry of his suppliant brothers, tributaries who wish to be borne to the eternal father. They bemoan myriad travails: desert sands have consumed them; the sun has sucked them dry; "Ein Hügel / Hemmet uns zum Teiche" (A hill / hems us into a pond), they say, in a figure that anticipates "Mächtiges Überraschen." The river-prophet gathers the entire race (*Geschlechte*) and leads it to its ocean-paradise. The poem, to be sure, is a meditation on the origins of myth. More specifically, though, it is a representation of the socioreligious force of mythic genius, an exposition of the rallying power of a new mythologist. Together with its poetic descendants—those poems of the self we have been tracing—the hymn illuminates the mythical terroir from which Goethe's lyrical record of the self emerges.

These lyrics, of course, do not amount to Goethe's only record of the self; nevertheless, they are significant for their range and primacy. Their vast arc stretches some five decades into the final stages of the *Faust* project. Their origins, moreover, may be more primal than is at first evident—in particular, the metaphorical transformations of water. Wellbery identifies images of liquidity as intrinsic to the discourse on genius; already this renders them distinctively Goethean.[22] But an insight of Blumenberg raises the prospect of something altogether more fundamental. In a reflection on Goethe's experience of the 1755 earthquake in Lisbon, he observes that Goethe's traumatization developed into two fixations: one on the security of the cornerstone of the family house in Frankfurt, another on the stability of the ground itself. Blumenberg argues on this basis that Goethe's poetry, from a very early age, entered into dialogue with the vulcanistic-neptunistic debate that drove much of his natural-scientific investigation.[23] If figurations of the cornerstone represent one dimension of that debate, it stands to reason that the riparian and oceanic figures represent the other. The development of such an argument lies beyond our scope, but its prospect focalizes the matter at hand: the lyrical record whose traces we are tracking exhibits primal images and networks of images in Goethe's inscription of the self.

Specific though they are to their author, such patterns of representation possess symbolic and discursive resonance. "Mahomets Gesang," as Wellbery explains, is more than a meditation on the development of myth/religion; it is a localization of its origins in the figure of the genius, who creates rather than imitates.[24] It speaks, as such, from the purview of the *Geniezeit*, participating in a discourse of which the hymn's author is only one interlocutor. His contribution to the discourse, however, proved fecund. The central dyad of the hymn, for example, figured in the Romantics' theory of myth.[25] Friedrich Schlegel, writing to Novalis, had singled out Mohammed as a vital model in their conjectures around a new religion (*Schriften* 4:508). Furthermore, they and Schelling relied on oceanic figures to conceptualize the flow of poetic history and its eventual return to the sea of myth.[26] The theorization of the new mythology, in other words, engaged with figures that Goethe had formulated a generation earlier. He was the rare prophet who is heeded in his own land.

The Dantean poems that emerge from the hymn, however, do not proclaim Goethe's genius; instead they register the impediments to its fulfillment. In "Ilmenau" and "Mächtiges Überraschen," his talent is thwarted from attaining its apparent destiny. In these records of unfulfilled ambition is an idiosyncratic approach to Dante. Unlike Schelling and Novalis, Goethe does not summon Dante in an act of imitation. He exploits Dantean tropes in order to wrest aesthetic form from the tedium and disappointment of his maturity. Whereas Dante's notion of new life is virtually synonymous with youth, and the romance of youth, Goethe adapts the concept to the circumstances that materialize precisely when youth is gone, hope is dashed, and promise is spent. *Neues Leben*, in contrast to *vita nuova*, comes to presuppose maturity. It is a salve for the wounds one acquires in the *selva oscura* (dark forest), as "Ilmenau" shows. If one accepts it as such, it can be grace in a moment of crisis. *Neues Leben* is not the paradise of youth, but it tempers the bitterness of that most Goethean of dispositions, the *Entsagung* (renunciation) of maturity. What would new life be if this were its final note?

Late in Goethe, there is a shift in the symbolic constellation whose points we have charted: the Dantean tropology of the lyrics spills over the bounds of the autobiographical. Indeed it reaches most forceful expression in the opening scene of *Faust II*, "Anmutige Gegend" (Pleasant place), whose title echoes the "anmuthiges Tal" of "Ilmenau." Like that poem, the scene is a translation of Dante's earthly paradise. It is an instantiation of the *divina foresta* as *locus amoenus*. Having abandoned Gretchen to die, Faust is purged of the memory by the waters of Lethe (4629).[27] In this, he resembles Dante, whose sojourn in the forest entailed purgation in the same river (*Purg*. 31.94). The cleansing act generates the sensation of new life. "Des Lebens Pulse schlagen frisch lebendig" (the pulses of life beat lively anew), Faust declares, in the first line of a monologue that is wound together in a chain of *terza rima* (4679).[28] It is headed to the summative insight of the drama: the dazzling light of Apollo's chariot will force Faust to turn from the sun and behold the light's reflection in the spray of a waterfall. Its lesson: the perpetually mediated character of knowledge. Already it is clear that the scene renews the Dantean topography of the earlier lyrics; but in this moment of insight, it clutches the subtext all the more firmly. For in the earthly paradise, Dante, too, is granted a vision of existential import. He witnesses a chariot like Apollo's, drawn by a griffin. The griffin is an allegory of Christ, whose image Dante glimpses in the reflection of Beatrice's eyes (*Purg*. 31.118–126).[29] The experience and its representation prefigure that of Faust. In each case, a protagonist relies on mediation for the acquisition of knowledge. In the one, it is the celestial woman who mediates the light of truth; in the other, it is nature.

In all its rudiments, "Anmutige Gegend" is another iteration in Goethe's adaptation of Dantean topoi; it signals, nevertheless, a new stance. It is worth reviewing the course that leads here. Early in Goethe's poetry, a semiotic lexicon of myth and genius materializes around the figure of Mohammed. No sooner had the lexicon emerged than its terms imbued Goethe's mythicizing lyrics of the self. Yet these lyrics are not facile mythologizations of the self as genius. They center on the obstacles to the realization of genius in the course of a life. "Auf dem See" betrays anxiety over its slippage into the realm of the dream. Like a self-fulfilling prophecy, the bête noire comes to life. The collapse of genius haunts the dream forests of "Ilmenau." Goethe banishes it as if it were a chimera, the refrain of *neues Leben* a promise to keep it at bay. But the refrain, it turns out in "Mächtiges Überraschen," had been illusive. The current is hemmed in, after all, its mythic course dammed. Bereft of its force, *neues Leben* is reduced to an act of interpretation: a word to sweeten the bitterness of resignation. Yet, in "Anmutige Gegend," the course has shifted. The scene retains the basic elements of the Dantean topography, but it moves now in a wholly different direction: it dispels the actual horrors of Faust's life, and in so doing, it renders his new life actual. The governing images in the lyrical automythology have migrated to Goethe's mythology of the world.[30]

DAS ALLERLIEBSTE FRAUENBILD
(THE DEAREST IMAGE OF WOMAN)

The spur for the Dantean strains in *Faust II* may well have been a minor German translator, Karl Adolph Streckfuß. In 1824, he sent Goethe his translation of the *Inferno* for review. The communication was fruitful for both parties. Streckfuß received a mildly positive blurb from Goethe. Meanwhile, Goethe tried his hand at translating the *Inferno* and wrote a comment on the structure of Dante's hell (MA 13/1:425–428). The encounter with Dante, which lay in the last decade of his work on *Faust*, foregrounded ethical and epistemic questions of concern to Goethe. That view seems to be borne out by the poem that Goethe dedicated to Streckfuß:

> Von Gott dem Vater stammt Natur,
> Das allerliebste Frauenbild,
> Des Menschen Geist, ihr auf der Spur,
> Ein treuer Werber, fand sie mild.
> Sie liebten sich nicht unfruchtbar,
> Ein Kind entsprang von hohem Sinn;
> So ist uns allen offenbar:
> Naturphilosophie sei Gottes Enkelin. (MA 13/1:186)
>
> (From God the Father stems Nature,
> That dearest image of Woman.
> The Spirit of Man, a faithful suitor on her trail,
> Found her mild.
> They loved each other not unfruitfully:
> A child of lofty reason was their issue.
> Thus is it revealed to us all:
> Naturphilosophie is God's granddaughter.)

The poem alludes to a discussion of usury (*Inf.* 11.94–111), in the course of which Virgil explains that according to the design of creation, human art imitates God's generative act. In this scheme, art descends from nature alone, whereas, according to Goethe, *Naturphilosophie* comes from nature inseminated by a masculine "spirit." It is a curious reading, to be sure, and its context—an obscure occasional poem—makes it prone to neglect. But it was significant enough that, one year later, Goethe reiterated the point in a review of Fritz Jacobi's correspondence. He scolded the polemicist for having undervalued nature and nature philosophy, writing, "Da lobe ich mir unsern

Dante, der uns doch erlaubt, um Gottes Enkelin zu werben" (Here I praise our Dante, who allows us to court God's granddaughter) (FA 1:22, 815). The comparison corroborates the earnestness of the lines to Streckfuß and does something more besides: it repeats the dedicatory poem's gendered and romantic dynamics. This marks another innovation upon Dante, for whereas he traces a genealogy that appears thus:

God the Father
|
Nature
|
Human Art

Goethe's genealogy reveals a modification:

God the Father
|
Nature (female)—Spirit (male)
|
Nature philosophy

The grandchild is different, as noted, but so, too, are her parents. Art has only one progenitor in Dante's model, which is looser in its effort to analogize human ingenuity and divine creation. Goethe's analogy is biologically determined. He accentuates the gendered roles of nature and spirit by incorporating the language of courtship and union. It is not merely a justification of nature philosophy, it is a genealogy that appraises the fruitfulness of a particular parentage.

The issues are clarified by Goethe's essay of the same year, "Naturphilosophie" (1826), which compares the pursuit of knowledge to the pursuit of representation. Their affinity helps explain the poem's substitution of *Naturphilosophie* for Dante's *arte*. But the essay, which proposes that scientific and artistic methods come down to the "Grundwahre" (foundationally true) (MA 13/2:336), resembles the poem in figurative respects too. Proposing that the test of truth lies in praxis rather than speculation, the essay dons the gendered figures of the poem:

> Wenn der Mann, überzeugt von dem Gehalt seiner Vorsätze, sich nach außen wendet und von der Welt verlangt, nicht etwa nur daß sie

> mit seinen Vorstellungen übereinkommen solle, sondern daß sie sich nach ihm bequemen, ihnen gehorchen, sie realisieren müsse . . . (MA 13/2:336)
>
> (If the man, convinced by the contents of his resolutions, turns outward and demands of the world not just that it matches his ideas, but rather that it accommodate them, obey them, realize them . . .)

The *man* of science theorizes, engages the world, and desires, while the world (*die* Welt) bends to his presuppositions. Evident therein are biblical resonances of gender concepts that had long shaped the language of science: the male scientist as active, female nature as his passive object. Unlike the most vociferous instances of such language, however, as charted by Pierre Hadot (2008), the essay does not advocate the domination of nature and discovery of its secrets. Its use of gendered figures subjects scientific method itself to scrutiny. For as Goethe explains, he wishes to distinguish between truthful and illusive pursuits. The latter remain "tot und fruchtlos, ja sogar wie eine Nekrose anzusehen" (dead and fruitless, indeed even like a necrosis) (MA 13/2:336), whereas the former—to take up again the language of the poem—"lieben sich nicht unfruchtbar" (love each other not unfruitfully). The truth of nature is fecund.

It can be difficult to posit that Goethe witnessed something of this truth in Dante. His 1826 assessment of the *Commedia*, after all, was equivocal. On the one hand, Dante seemed to be a poetic *Augenmensch* (eye-man) like Goethe: he represented objects with such fixity of observation that they are visualizable (MA 13/1:425). On the other hand, if the *Grundwahre* is the criterion by which to judge the artistic enterprise, then Goethe is correct that there is something "sinnesverwirrend" (puzzling to the senses) about the geography of Hell, and for that matter, of the afterlife in general (426). As Goethe writes, with a nod to Voltaire, the whole thing has something "Mikromegisches" (tiny yet towering) about it (426). Yet none of this entails that Goethe did not find the *Grundwahre* in the *Commedia*. The fundamental truth of the poem, judging by the lines to Streckfuß, lies in its alignment of art and science (*Naturphilosophie*). This has at least one important consequence for Goethe: in representing these pursuits as divinely ordained, Dante seems to authorize Faustian striving.

It sounds Thomistic, not Goethean, that human activity should be ordained and sanctioned by heaven. Such is the case in Dante, where natural law obtains. Usury, after all, is an act of violence against nature. Yet, in

Goethe's comment on Jacobi, where he uses the verb *erlauben* (allow), he lets slip that we *are* dealing with matters of ethics. How does the natural law of the *Commedia*, evinced by the lines to Streckfuß, harmonize with Goethe's decidedly non-Christian worldview? His adoption of new nomenclature suggests a process of translation: he has transformed Dante's talk of human endeavor (*arte*) to the pursuit of natural knowledge (*Naturphilosophie*). That maneuver, paired with Goethe's metaphysical tenets, enables a more robust translation. The vocabulary of his metaphysics is no secret—it is Spinozan. We can begin by rendering the Christian deity the *natura naturans* (nature naturing), his creation *natura naturata* (nature natured). These translations detheologize (i.e., depersonify) the structures whereby natural law obtains. By the same logic, the providential force of the deity assumes new shape: the purposiveness of God becomes the determinism of nature. Goethe entertained such a notion (cf., "Urworte. Orphisch" [Primal words. Orphic]). In short: these concepts depart from Dante, but they retain a semblance of his universe. Goethe has detheologized the force of the *Commedia*'s ethical vision, all the while that he lauds Dante for that selfsame vision.

Thus it happens that *Faust II*, in its discernment of *das Grundwahre*, reveals important linkages to the *Commedia*. They surface in the text's hyperattentive focus on acts of illusion, which, in central threads of the dramatic narrative, constitute violations of nature. Because of how they leverage the alchemical origins of the Faust material, two such acts stand out as significant: Mephistopheles's scheme to save the Empire from ruin through the creation of paper money and Faust's plan to build dikes and reclaim land from the sea. Each scheme, a manipulation of the elements of earth and water, aims at the generation of value through the inversion of a natural order.[31] Mephistopheles would rescue the Empire by assigning value through fiat to an empty placeholder; meanwhile, Faust plans the creation of a personal empire through radical alteration (and destruction) of the natural landscape. It requires little imagination to locate the affinities between Dante's statements on usury and Goethe's criticism of the capitalist state. Both poets strike at the unnatural means by which capital expands and corrupts.

Dante and Goethe may appear to be strange bedfellows in their criticism of capital, but the conjunction has surprising support. To be sure, it is anachronistic to speak of Dante in such terms, as if he were a proto-Marxist who found his calling five centuries too soon. But as William Clare Roberts has demonstrated, the *Inferno* serves as the organizing model for Marx's *Kapital*. That does not make Dante a Marxist, but it points, as Roberts shows, to a vocabulary of Christian moral discourse that underpins much early socialist thinking. Capitalism generates a "social Hell" whose terrain Marx charted by employing Dante as his guide.[32] No stranger to this moral vocabulary, Goethe was proximate to the circumstances about which Marx wrote. *Faust* not only shudders at the destructive tendency of capitalism, as Hans Binswanger wrote, it relies on medieval allegory to do so, as Heinz Schlaffer observed.[33] For just as the commodity is prized for its abstraction as an exchange value, so too the allegory for its abstraction as a universal form. Schlaffer's argument, which rests on a reading of the *Mummenschanz* (carnival masque)—where allegorical figures use eroticism to hawk their wares—recalls, yet again, the *Commedia*. For while commentators like Albrecht Schöne point to the scene's origins in Renaissance *trionfi* (triumphs),[34] the *trionfi* originate in the allegorical procession that Dante records atop Mount Purgatory (*Pur.* 29). Given the adaptations from that procession in the same act of *Faust II* (see above), as well as his reception of Dante's critique of usury, it is difficult to avoid the conclusion that Goethe's critique of capital operates in tandem with the natural law he had celebrated in (and translated from) Dante.

Intrinsic to the drama's alchemical origins, the criticism of capital figures only as part of a broader concern that resides at the intersection of nature and ethics. Goethe extolled Dante, as noted already, for his insight that human striving is a function of—and therefore subordinate to—nature. Liberating though the insight seems, the proviso is significant. Nature authorizes striving but also determines its limits. The Dantean moments of *Faust II*, in particular, illuminate how the subordination of nature to human striving constitutes acts of transgression. These acts, rooted in Faust's endeavor to achieve mastery over nature, culminate in the Dantean sequence of his death and salvation. He dies amid a massive project of land reclamation. The feat of engineering, in which dikes are employed to ward off the sea, represents the effort of the ego to overcome nature:

> Dort wollt' ich, weit umherzuschauen,
> Von Ast zu Ast Gerüste bauen,
> Dem Blick eröffnen weite Bahn,
> Zu sehn, was alles ich getan,
> Zu überschaun mit einem Blick
> Des Menschengeistes Meisterstück. (11,243–11,248)
>
> (There, in order to look far and wide, I wished
> To build scaffolding from branch to branch,
> To grant my glance a wide path,

To see all that I had done,
To look over in a single glimpse
The masterpiece of the Spirit of Man.)

These lines of overweening ambition point clearly to their source: the *Menschengeist*. In his lyrical adaptation from *Inferno*, Goethe had designated the *Menschengeist* the bridegroom of nature. Here, however, rather than work in harmony with her, it beats her back in a monumentalization of the ego. Faust's network of dikes, modeled on the geo-engineering of Flanders, is not intrinsically hubristic; but coupled with his solipsistic desires, as well as their ramifications (e.g., the murder of Philemon and Baucis), it is a form of violence against nature. This symbol is not without precedent. In the ring of Hell, where Dante narrates his encounter with "sodomites," he describes the embankments that circle their ring as akin to the dikes of the Flemings and Paduans (*Inf.* 15.4–12). There, too, manipulations of the natural landscape reflect the ethical transgression of its inhabitants: for in Dante's system of Hell, sodomites are violators of nature. Faust is in similar territory—quite literally.[35]

His residence on that bulwark against nature is due to the winsome devil, Mephistopheles. Benevolent though he may seem, Mephistopheles's evil inheres in his radical resistance to an ethics that is circumscribed by nature. His paper-money scheme inverts nature, Dante would have said, by obviating the place of human *arte*. That Mephistopheles would favor such an inversion is evident in his self-definition, "der Geist der stets verneint" (the spirit who always denies) (1338), in the utterance of his innermost desire, "alles was entsteht, / ist wert, dass es zugrunde geht") (all that arises / merits only to be unmade) (1339–1340), and most importantly, in the bargain he strikes with Faust: the quest to grant the latter a beautiful moment would strip Faust of his innate will to strive. It would make of him a Belacqua, the man whose listlessness thwarts him from summiting Mount Purgatory (*Purg.* 4). The endeavor to content Faust is an effort to rob him of his will. It is to turn him against nature.[36]

It is small surprise, then, that the *Commedia* looms large when Mephistopheles is robbed of Faust's soul. He regards it as his booty but is thwarted by a chorus of angels. As cherubs descend and ascend, they strew roses that turn to fire and burn Mephistopheles and his devils. This image, like those of the next scene, "Bergschluchten" (Mountain gorges), resembles Dante's Empyrean, where angels pollinate the grand rose of Paradise by descending from above and distributing petals of love (*Par.* 31.1–18). The difference in "Grablegung" (Entombment) is that the roses turn to fire and burn the devils, who find themselves bewitched by the angels' buttocks (11,767–11,800). The Dantean intertext clarifies the sense of the scene: just as the sodomites' landscape had served as a symbol for Faust's violations of nature, so, too, does their punishment. In the seventh circle of Hell, in an allusion to the biblical Sodom, Dante's sodomites suffer to be rained upon by tongues of flame. That Mephistopheles and his demons suffer the same fate has little to do with Goethe's views of sex. That is clear from the work of Robert Tobin and W. Daniel Wilson.[37] It functions rather as a symbol that casts into relief the essence of Mephistopheles's evil, his aversion to nature and being. To be clear, to highlight the Dantean intertext is not to claim that Goethe is concerned with personal acts of sexual morality; *Faust II*, after all, is ultimately a reckoning with the grand forces of Western modernity. It is to claim, instead, that Goethe draws on the imagistic archive of the *Commedia* to grant evil symbolic form as a violation of nature.

Where, then, is nature in the contest? It appears nowhere as such in *Faust*. Yet, in the allegorized drama, it is virtually omnipresent in other figurations. If the eponymous striver represents the impulses of an overweening *Menschengeist*, then the drama's instantiations of woman represent the bride whom he shuns, *Natur*. Throughout the drama, as Harold Jantz argued, the figures of woman point to and denote the processes of birth and rebirth: Margareta, Helena, Galatea, the Mater Dolorosa, to name a few.[38] All these women, as is clear, too, from the epithet of their ideal form, *die Mütter* (the mothers), represent a force of creation, of nature, of *natura naturans*. Thus is it the essence of salvation, as at the end of the drama, to sit in contemplation of the Mater Gloriosa. Nature appears as woman, or as the Chorus Mysticus sings, the *Ewig-Weibliche* (eternal feminine). This strategy of representation establishes a duality in the drama's final contest. Whereas Mephistopheles represents a force of annihilation, the drama's female figures are his antithesis. They are the beating pulse of nature, the generative energy of creation. The action of the drama attests as much, but the idea was anticipated in Goethe's statements on Dante. His judgment of Jacobi, the poem to Streckfuß, its adaptation in the essay "Naturphilosophie"—together these statements designate nature a salvific force, fit to be granted symbolic form in the image of woman. Their conjunction inheres in the Dantean vision of Faust: Beatrice communicates to Dante the light of truth, which the latter glimpses in the spray of water.

Nature as woman, its negation—the devil. Opposed though they are, the poles of this antipode have one thing in common: symbolic origins in the *Commedia*. For just as Goethe manipulates Dante's circle of sodomites, so too does he draw on Dante as he conceives the eternal feminine as a force of salvation. He almost certainly relies on a pair of complementary death scenes where, as in "Grablegung," there occur cosmic battles for the souls of the deceased.[39] The details are significant. In this pair of passages, Dante records the death narratives of Guido da Montefeltro and his son, Bonconte da Montefeltro. The father, a sinful mercenary, converted and became a friar. But in an ill-conceived pact with the pope, he agreed to provide political guidance in exchange for the guarantee of his salvation. Upon his death, Saint Francis came to claim his soul, but a devilish cherub snatched it away. The case of his son is a study in contrast. The younger Montefeltro died in battle with the name of Mary on his lips. For this, his soul was fetched by an angel, and Satan was left to bemoan his deprivation. The contrast in episodes fixes the symbolic terms for the battle over Faust's soul. The elder's pact with the pope is an antecedent to Faust. He ought to be had by the devil. But it is the case of the younger Montefeltro, with his dying prayer to the Virgin, that presages the actual fate of Faust. He is saved by the eternal feminine.

Our course brought us to *Faust* via the Dantean lyrics of Goethe: their patterns of signification had spilled over the bounds of the self. They moved from the automythological to the mythological, concentrated in the edenic scene that opens the drama's second part. They span the five acts of the drama, culminating in its celebration of Mother Nature.

From texts of the self to a text of the world, the migration of Dante in Goethe's ouevre signals a struggle in orientation that has been evident elsewhere in Romanticism. A new mythology must navigate the bounds of subject and object, mind and world. *Heinrich von Ofterdingen* maneuvered these complications via a poetics of the dream. Situated in the broader context of its author's legacy, however, the novel pointed to a tension that surfaces here, as well: Romantic authors undertook a Dantean poetics that could not escape the shadow cast by Dante's mythology of the self. Goethe's lyrics, as the near silence of scholarship on their Dantean traces attests, kept Dante at arm's length. The automythological impulse avails itself of a Dantean lexicon faintly, carefully, reserverdly. With the transition to *Faust*, and the suspension of the automythological project, the pull of that tension slackens. The presence of Dante announces itself, in *terza rima* even.

Yet *Faust*, this text of the world, clings to residues of the automythological. For all its world-historical pretension, the drama reads as a resolution to the failures that haunt the automythological narratives and lyrics. The latter evinced anxieties over the dessication of genius. The former, too, were plagued by crises: both the *Italienische Reise* and *Dichtung und Wahrheit* culminate in painful breaks. The former ends with Goethe's separation from the Milanese, the latter with his flight from Lili Schönemann. It is not mere chance that Faust, upon fleeing Gretchen, finds himself in an edenic alpine meadow. Goethe had fled to the Swiss Alps upon the break with Lili. The observation is not merely to affirm the autobiographical texture of *Faust*, it is to underscore that the aporias of the automythological narratives demand resolution. Goethe, as he said of his confrontation with the demonic, flees behind an image. *Faust II*, with its Dantean topos of new life, marks the displacement of the automythological project. The *Ewig-Weibliche*, which saves Faust, is not so impersonal or abstract as the *natura naturans*. It is Goethe's personal savior, sourced from the *Commedia*'s sanctioning of nature. As he had underwritten the automythological lyrics, so, too, does Dante underwrite the mythology of *Faust*.

Scholars are often reluctant to countenance the prospect of a meaningful engagement of Goethe with Dante—as compared, for example, with his engagement with Shakespeare. Goethe usually appears indifferent to, or even hostile toward, Dante. Some of that hostility has been noted already. By the mid-1820s, however, the distance Goethe maintained had given way to new approximations. He began to reckon with Dante as a figure of consequence. Johann Peter Eckermann, his secretary, recounts a winter evening in 1824 when he found Goethe in contemplation of a colossal bust of Dante in the light of two candles. "'Nun?' sagte Goethe . . . 'wer ist das?'" Eckermann: "'Ein Poet, und zwar ein Italiener scheint es zu sein.'" ("'So?' said Goethe . . . 'Who is that?' 'A poet, and it looks to be an Italian.'") "'Es ist *Dante*,' sagte Goethe" ("'It is *Dante*,' said Goethe.")[40] Eckermann is surprised to report that Goethe spoke of Dante "mit aller Ehrfurcht, wobei es mir merkwürdig war, daß ihm das Wort *Talent* nicht genügte, sondern daß er ihn eine *Natur* nannte, als womit er ein Umfassenderes, Ahndungsvolleres, tiefer und weiter um sich Blickendes ausdrücken zu wollen schien" (with tremendous reverence, which stood out to me, because the word *talent* did not suffice for Goethe to describe Dante; instead, he called him a *nature*, as if he wished to express thereby something more comprehensive, profound, and visionary) (174). Some two decades after the height of Dante furor in Jena, his aversion dissipated. The poet who once bemoaned the restlessness of *terza rima* now recommended it for grand purposes.[41] He lacked the fervor of a convert, perhaps, but not by so vast a measure.

Goethe's engagement with Dante, like that of Novalis, maintains a curious silence. Its traces in the lyrics, rarely though they get noted (e.g.,

Steiner), elicit refutation (e.g., Hirdt).[42] The hope of this chapter is to have argued more persuasively for the signs of that engagement, and in doing so, to have advanced our view of Dantean myth as a persistent phenomenon of German Romanticism. The present survey of Goethe's engagement, which spans lyrics of the self and a drama of the world, demonstrates the range of the Italian icon to accommodate mythical ventures. It is noteworthy, for example, that he underwrites two of the most significant European critiques of modernity in the nineteenth century: Goethe's *Faust* and Marx's *Kapital*. Yet this reading turned up, too, the tendency we saw in Schelling and Novalis: the poet rarely exploits the mere forms and structures of the *Commedia*. More often, he channels Dante's myth of the self. Thus *Faust*, all the while that it adopts an ethics of nature from the *Commedia* and applies it to a social vision, is never not also participating in the automythological enterprise. The iconic Dantean brackets of the drama, "Anmutige Gegend" and "Bergschluchten," signal resolutions to the crises of the lyrical automythology: genius, drawn on by the feminine, now triumphs in new life. It is equivalent neither to Schelling's slavish imitation of Dante nor to Novalis's personal identification with him; and still, in addition to the poetry, it is a significant reckoning with the myth of the poet. As such it complicates that avalanche of philology that, while struggling to locate or even rejecting the signs of such an engagement, would nevertheless insist upon the spiritual bond of a generic greatness.[43] Further, it dispels the notion that Goethe only ever disdained or feared Dante. Friedrich Gundolf wrote, for example, that Goethe intuited the depths of Dante's soul but shrank (*zurückschrak*) from peering into it, fearing that he could not plumb the abyss.[44] It points hyperbolically to the threat that is suggested by Novalis's silence: the instrumentalization of a Dantean poetics will fail if it is identifiably imitative. To retain its import for the age, mythology must be generative, not imitative. Its model, the *Commedia*, is thus a blessing and a curse. It blazes a trail that threatens to burn those who would follow it too closely. Goethe maintained that distance, but in our final chapters, we witness a series of conflagrations.

Part II

Neo-Romanticism

CHAPTER FOUR

Trespassing the Sign

The Mad Flight of Gerhart Hauptmann

IF ROMANTICISM WAS AN ILLNESS, as Goethe once said to Eckermann, then we might deem it a disease of the ear.[1] Its spread in the German realm was a result of the lecture, as Sean Franzel has written.[2] From Berlin to Cologne to Vienna, the Schlegel brothers propagated Romanticism in university lecture halls. Schelling's preoccupation with Romantic aesthetics and myth spread similarly. Attendees of the German Romantic lecture circuit included the likes of Coleridge and Wordsworth, whose further transmission of the illness owed, again, to a tickle of the ear: the lyrical ballad. It would be an oversight to write off visual symptoms of Romanticism, but it is difficult to countenance that any of them had significance proportionate to the crescendo found in Beethoven, Brahms, Liszt, Schubert, and Wagner. Romanticism lodged itself in the ear.

The observation obtains when we recall the seminal articulations of the *neue Mythologie*. The *Systemprogramm* formulates its argument along the contours of speech. We *hear* so often of a religion of the senses, its author states, that it is time to *speak* of a new idea: "wir müssen eine neue Mythologie haben" (we need to have a new mythology).[3] A similar exhortation appeared a few years later, when Friedrich Schlegel wrote that the time had come to generate a new mythology. More to the point, his exhortation appeared in a *Rede* (talk) on mythology. The intellectual debts of that *Rede* are traceable to Schleiermacher's *Reden* on religion. It is no accident, then, to write of the *calls* for a new mythology, or to conceive of the Romantics as its *heralds*. The new mythology was born of oratory.[4]

With the dissipation of Romanticism proper, the Dantean strain of its mythology went silent. Goethe's (auto)mythicizing texts, it is true, revealed a compelling interpretation of the *Commedia*. Its accommodation of the poem to the tenets of *Naturphilosophie* rendered the *dantismo* of *Faust* affine in spirit to the poetry of Schelling. Yet Goethe's position vis-à-vis the *neue Mythologie* was avuncular: he had been adopted, if not annexed, by the younger generation. By the time he published the second part of *Faust*, their project had long since dissolved. The new drama may have anticipated the world to come, but in this respect it was belated. These circumstances did not spell the demise of Dantean mythologies; with the end of the *Kunstperiode* (Age of Art), however, Dante's poetry became the territory of academic philology. His respite there was fleeting, for Romanticism returned with a vengeance.

Neo-Romantics, mostly between 1890 and 1945, entertained the siren song of myth. Its notes echo, as they did once before, in these writers' flights of oratory. Striking efforts to renew German Romanticism thus surface in the post–World War I lectures of three writers: Gerhart Hauptmann (1862–1946), Hugo von Hofmannsthal (1874–1929), and Rudolf Borchardt (1877–1945). But in their addresses to the public, we do not hear the tones of Romantic fantasy; instead, we find the distress signals that spurred figures like Schlegel, Novalis, and Schelling to propose a new mythology in the first place.

The central source of distress, for the Romantics and their heirs, was the perception of an epochal crisis. A crisis—literally, the point at which a disease turns for better or worse (κρίσις)—indicates the decisive juncture before which the Romantics and Neo-Romantics believed themselves to be standing. In the case of the former, the French Revolution had exacerbated conditions of anomie: the events across the Rhine demanded a collective reckoning. The splintering of social factions, particularly the division between the *Philosophen* and the *Volk*, required mending. Art was the recipe du jour, but even in this respect, as Friedrich Schlegel indicated, there was no "mütterlichen Boden" (maternal ground) from which a common art could emerge. There were only solitary poets, each one isolated from the next. Conceived as a remedy to these circumstances, the new mythology was given wings.

Equally profound was the crisis of the World War and its aftermath. In an echo of the past, German intellectuals developed programs of the *Geist* in the face of their fragmented culture. In 1927, at the University of Munich, Hofmannsthal spoke of "unsere vielzerklüftete Kultur" (our much-divided culture).[5] So great was the cleft between the educated and the uneducated that he identified *Schrifttum* (writing), rather than *Literatur* (literature), as the space where a conservative revolution was unfolding (23). At its vanguard were Nietzschean seekers—poets, prophets, scholars—who longed to represent wholeness in a world riven by division. Their instruments were the drama as a mythos of the self, the novel as a retainer of cosmic secrets, and the fairy tale (32). Above all, these seekers wished for *Bindungen* (connections) (38–39). The echoes of the new mythology are unmistakable: a mythic impulse in literary forms was tasked with generating social cohesion. Hofmannsthal's speech lacks the optimism that colors Schlegel's *Rede über die Mythologie*, or the *Systemprogramm*, and he distinguishes between the Romantics and his seekers.[6] But the need to do so betrays what listeners have already guessed: a new Romanticism is at hand, and as the solitary geniuses of the nation forge new bonds, the culture once promised by the new mythology will materialize.

On the other hand, some figures openly encouraged the linkage to Romanticism. Two months after his idol, Hofmannsthal, had spoken in the same auditorium, Borchardt—poet, translator, orator—delivered a searing jeremiad on similar topics.[7] His speech, "Schöpferische Restauration" (Generative restoration), diagnosed a degenerate culture in crisis. Evidence thereof lay in the changes wrought by capitalist expansion: the replacement of the theater by the cinema, the newspaper by the tabloid, the specialty shop by the department store (*Reden* 242).[8] The urbanization of German society and the growth of capitalism had resulted in catastrophic changes in the *Volk*, now reduced to "eine Abfallsmenschheit und ein Menschheitsabfall" (a humanity of waste and a waste of humanity) (247). Similar challenges had been confronted once before by the German Romantics. Their magical grasp of language had disabled the mechanistic and dehumanizing tendencies of the eighteenth century. But that poetic talent vanished. There prevailed now only linguistic poverty (248). For this reason, Borchardt prescribed that Germans "setzen das Werk der Romantik schöpferisch fort" (creatively resume the work of Romanticism) (250). He attempted to graft his program of cultural restoration onto the healthy trunk of German Romanticism. He conceived of himself as a new *Wortführer* (spokesperson), an ambassador akin to A. W. Schlegel, whose lectures had popularized the German spirit throughout Europe. The renewal of the German language would open a space for a national revival of Romanticism.

It did not take the War to elicit such remarks from Gerhart Hauptmann. By the time he received the Nobel Prize in 1912, he was well on his way toward such a revival. For like the Romantic theorists of *Kunstreligion* (religion of art), Hauptmann proclaimed poetry to be the source of authentic religion (CA 6:693). Like Friedrich Schlegel, who longed for the aesthetic unity that classical mythology represented, Hauptmann asserted that poets only ever sought the accomplishment of an all-encompassing totality: "Eigentlich sucht der Dichter ja immer nicht Werke, sondern das Werk" (The poet is never actually searching for works, but for the work) (699). It was the totalizing language that lay behind the mythological impulse.

The catastrophe of war made such a project all the more urgent, as did the birth of the fledgling Republic. In 1921, Hauptmann voiced concern over national disunity: "Deutschland ist uneins, Deutschland ist zerklüftet und zerrissen" (Germany is at odds with itself, Germany is divided and broken) (CA 6:717). The Germans had been through Dante's Hell, he said; like Dante, they must now climb the purgatorial mountain (728). That was no endorsement of the terms of Versailles. It was an acknowledgment that, with the loss of their throne, there was the need for a new national ideal (730). Hauptmann looked to the past to find it. He speaks thus of the most precious treasure of the German heart—love (730). It is a Romantic vision of the national ideal, but not just for its fantastical quality. It is a hearkening back to the utopianism that animated German Romantic statecraft. It is the love of Novalis's *Glaube und Liebe* (*Faith and Love*) (1798), which—with a dedication to the king of Prussia—had envisioned a kingdom inflected by republicanism.[9] Hauptmann, again, turns to Romantic remedies.

Did these diagnoses of crisis signify a resumption of the *neue Mythologie*? The question presupposes the reality of the initial project. Romantic poets had made genuine efforts toward its realization, but its culmination had always been a dream, articulated in the apodictic language of certainty. To resume the project was to adopt the telos, to be sure, but the rhetoric as well. It is thus the case that, in the language of these figures, there resound the echoes of those old calls for myth. Hofmannsthal speaks of a "Prozess, in dem wir mitten inne stehen" (process whose middle we occupy), and Borchardt heralds a program that will proceed from "Mittelpunkten" (midpoints) (250).[10] Schlegel's *Rede* reverberates in this language. He had claimed that a mythology was the missing "Mittelpunkt" of contemporary poets, but that they were "nahe daran eine zu erhalten" (close to obtaining one). Consider the resonance that ties together the statements of Hauptmann, Schelling, and Schlegel:

> Ich würde nicht hier stehen, wäre ich ein Schwarzseher. Dabei *verhehle ich mir* die dunklen Wolkenbildungen *nicht*, wovon ein großer Teil unseres Horizontes noch umlagert ist. *Aber ich setze* ihnen die Kraft der neuen Tage, die Kraft der kommenden Sonnen *entgegen*. (CA 6:721)

> (I would not stand here if I were a pessimist. Nor, however, do I make a secret of the dark clouds that beset a great part of our horizon. Yet I oppose to them the force of new days, the force of coming suns.)

> Ich *verhehle* meine Uberzeugung *nicht*, daß in der Naturphilosophie, wie sie sich aus dem idealistischen Prinzip gebildet hat, die erste ferne Anlage jener künftigen Symbolik und derjenigen Mythologie gemacht ist, welche nicht ein Einzelner sondern die ganze Zeit geschaffen haben wird. (SW 5:449)

> (I make no secret of my conviction that, with the philosophy of nature, as it has emerged from the idealist principle, we find the first, far-off draft of that future symbolism, that mythology, which not an individual, but rather the whole age will have created.)

> Wir haben keine Mythologie. *Aber setze ich hinzu*, wir sind nahe daran eine zu erhalten, oder vielmehr es wird Zeit, daß wir ernsthaft dazu mitwirken sollen, eine hervorzubringen. (KFSA 2:311)

> (We have no mythology. But I posit we are close to obtaining one, or rather it is becoming time that we should collaborate earnestly toward bringing one forth.)

The point is not to claim an intertextual influence, but to underscore the rhetorical structures that cohere in and across these proclamations of cultural transformation. The Romantic wrests the promise of a new dawn from the age of need. That promise resounds in the rhetoric of the Neo-Romantic.

There is, of course, a significant difference between moments. The revivals of Romanticism are inextricable from the achievement of national unity. Whereas the sole German marker of the Romantics' calls for a *neue Mythologie* was their language, the calls for a revival of Romanticism are intertwined with the fate of the German state. For all the distinctions Hofmannsthal draws between the Romantics and his seekers, the sharpest distinction is that the latter contribute to the spirit of the *nation*, as the title of his talk indicates: "Das Schrifttum als geistiger Raum der Nation" (Writing as the spiritual space of the nation). For Borchardt, the rehabilitation of the Romantic is a national project, for the dissipation of Romanticism occurred, in the first place, because of its migration abroad—to

England, France, and elsewhere on the Continent. For Hauptmann, too, the new dawn was a promise to the nation. It is thus that he augurs not just a "kommende Kirche" (coming church) but a "neue[s] Reich" (new kingdom) (CA 6:721). Likeminded poets, including Stefan George and the circle around him, pursued similar aims: a *geistiges Reich* (spiritual kingdom), a *neues Reich* (new kingdom), and a *geheimes Deutschland* (secret Germany). The totalizing gesture of Romantic myth was adopted not just in a moment of crisis but in a moment of national crisis. The new mythology had once promised an ill-defined unity. By the First World War, it had taken on national contours.

The remainder of this book traces the contours of these endeavors, each of which, like its Romantic predecessors, envisions a new mythology according to a Dantean model. In the rhetoric of Hauptmann, there emerge voices from the depths of *Inferno*.

FIERY TONGUES

Rhetoric is much like fire, Dante believed: wielded improperly, it burns. That is a lesson of *Inferno* 26, where he and Virgil interview an oratorical master who suffers eternity while trapped in a tongue of flame. The encounter with that master, Ulysses, is overdetermined by linguistic forms. Take, for example, Virgil's counsel that Dante should fall silent while he interviews Ulysses: he explains that the Greek man might disdain Dante's language (*Inf.* 26.73–75). It is a strange request from a Latin poet, but an indicator of Ulysses's linguistic pride and savvy. His affinity for tricks of the tongue is confirmed when, a moment later, he appears standing within a giant tongue of flame. It is as if he were indeed nothing but a great, flapping tongue (*Inf.* 26.89). That tongue delivers one of the most memorable speeches of the *Commedia*, the only one in *Inferno* that is delivered by a figure from classical antiquity apart from Virgil. Ulysses recounts the rousing speech with which he (in Dante's manipulation) convinced his shipmates to sail beyond the known limits of the world:

> "O frati," dissi, "che per cento milia
> perigli siete giunti a l'occidente,
> a questa tanto picciola vigilia
> d'i nostri sensi ch'è del rimanente
> non vogliate negar l'esperïenza,
> di retro al sol, del mondo sanza gente.
> Considerate la vostra semenza:
> fatti non foste a viver come bruti,

ma per seguir virtute e canoscenza."
    Li miei compagni fec' io sì aguti
con questa orazion picciola al cammino,
che a pena poscia li avrei ritenuti;
    e volta nostra poppa nel mattino,
de' remi facemmo ali al folle volo,
sempre acquistando dal lato mancino. (*Inf.* 26.112–126)

    ("O brothers," I said, "who through a hundred
thousand perils have reached the west, to this so
brief vigil
    of our senses that remains, do not deny the
experience, following the sun, of the world without
people.
    Consider your sowing: you were not made to live
like brutes, but to follow virtue and knowledge."
    My companions I made so sharp for the voyage,
with this little oration, that after it I could hardly
have held them back;
    and, turning our stern toward the morning, of our
oars we made wings for the mad flight, always
gaining on the left side.)

Two transgressions emerge in this account. One is the Adamic sin of transgression: Ulysses trespasses the boundaries of humankind. As for the other—he persuades his shipmates to do the same. The sin of fraudulent counsel is what has landed him in Hell (*Inf.* 27.116). But the former sin, which the poem describes as a "trespass of the sign" (*segno*) (*Par.* 26.117), is related to that misuse of language. Consider, for example, that the third man whom the poem identifies as having trespassed the sign is Nimrod, the builder of the tower of Babel. It is an intricate network of intratextual references that amounts to something fundamental: language runs the risk of transgression. It demands an ethics.

Dante is the exemplar of such an ethics, the poem implies. He is a corrected Ulysses, a typological fulfillment of the Greek warrior and orator. As Glenn Most has written, Ulysses is Dante's "dark twin."[11] He compares their curiosity, but there are other points to consider, too. Both embark on journeys to the end of the world, and in important senses, it is speech that governs the terms of their journeys. Ulysses travels by ship, and to describe his poem, Dante favors the metaphor of the ship (*legno*, *barca*). These navigators share an uncommon destination—Mount Purgatory (*Inf.* 26.133–135), the one foundering on its shores, the other scaling its peak. Each construes his voyage as one of virtue and knowledge, marked to some extent, too, by solitude (*Inf.* 26.16, 100).[12] So keen are the similarities that Dante, upon seeing Ulysses, leans with desire toward the tongue of flame, perhaps as if to kiss him (*Inf.* 26.69). But no kiss, indeed no word escapes Dante's lips. He shows self-restraint. As he begins the exposition of the encounter, he announces that he will restrain his wit and be guided by virtue (*Inf.* 26.21–22). Here the difference between men is pronounced. For, whereas Ulysses subjects virtue to wit, Dante—to take him at his word—does just the opposite. The contrast is not merely that between a loquacious Ulysses and a silent Dante. After all, the latter opens the canto with a damning prophecy of Florence's destruction (*Inf.* 26.7–12). The contrast, then, is between a fraudulent explorer and a prophetic pilgrim. Ulysses employs speech and leads men to their deaths. Dante, a prophet of men's deaths, submits in silence to a guide who will lead him to life.

It is worth tarrying over the matter of rhetoric because, for the rehabilitators of a Dantean Romanticism, the matters of rhetoric—argument, elocution, style—proved essential. Borchardt and George advanced their programs of cultural transformation via ornately stylized receptions of Dante. The former regarded his medievalizing translation of the *Commedia* as the space wherein he could renew the German language. The latter undertook a similarly stylized interpretation, albeit in a process that encompassed his person as well as his poetry. Hauptmann, the orator, leveraged Dante's journey in a metaphor that envisioned the process of Germany's spiritual rebirth. In his poetry and prose, he did much more besides. The revival of the Romantic proceeded via rhetorically charged adaptations of Dante.

But what of the ethical demands of language, inherent in the *Commedia*'s negative judgment of fraudulent rhetoric? Is it too much to think that rhetoricians like Borchardt and Hauptmann, avid readers of the poem, might have assimilated, or even just cognized facets of Dante's philosophy of language? It is not as if Dante's ideas were irredeemably obscure. He was always known as a theoretician of language and style—a founder and proponent, for example, of the *dolce stil novo*. His attention to the instruments of style, and to the use of language, are outlined in the treatise *De vulgari eloquentia*. His use of the vernacular, along with his criticisms of papal authority, rendered him an analogue to Martin Luther among Reformation-era Germans. The Ulysses episode, moreover, has long been one of the most celebrated cantos of the entire poem, surpassed only by the encounters with Paolo and Francesca and Ugolino. To return, then, to the rhetorical obsessions of the Neo-Romantic rehabilitators of Dante: What happens to the ethical constraints Dante places upon the use of language, when the *Commedia* becomes a crucible of Neo-Romantic poetics?

Apart from asking after a philological reception, the question inquires after the terms of these figures' rehabilitation of Romanticism. For if the renewal of Romanticism depended on and aimed for the forms and reformations of language, then it is reasonable—if not vital—to ask after the ethical and teleological criteria that gave shape to language in such programs of renewal.[13] The same question, to be sure, can and should be posed of the Romantics' formulations of a new mythology. These calls, too, were determined by rhetorical contexts; they were born of oratory, as I have claimed. Yet they were not devoid of ethical deliberation. It is not without significance, for example, that the *Systemprogramm* fragment opens with the laconic notation, "—eine Ethik." The manuscript's discussion of aesthetics, and its call for a new mythology, is entirely purposive: it rests on the view that truth and goodness are wed in beauty. A vestige of the Romantics' heritage of Enlightenment, that notion all but disappeared from the efforts to revive Romanticism.

By the time of such revivals, beauty as an ethical good had been supplanted by language. There is no pithier summation thereof than that voiced by Hauptmann—"Sprache ist Seele" (language is soul) (CA 6:888). At first glance, the formulation resembles the old notion that language is a mark of rationality, a quality that separates humans from beasts. But in Hauptmann's copulative, language is no instrument of rationality. It is its equal, or rather, its substitute. The shift absolutizes language in a way that evacuates it of responsibility to a normative good. To employ another lexicon: it represents the triumph of rhetoric over dialectic, the anxiety that Plato had expressed in the *Gorgias*. The hegemony achieved thereby packs force, for language figures henceforth in the imperative mood. Beyond a mere mode of communication, language dictates to its speakers. In language, Hofmannsthal explains, there are forces that "wirken auf uns ein und werden unmittelbar gewaltig" (exert an impact upon us and become immediately potent).[14] Hofmannsthal's notion extends, again, to his Neo-Romantic brethren. Hauptmann speaks of the need to serve language ("dienen," CA 6:888). Borchardt, in a similar vein, discusses the obligations of the *Volk* to its poetry. The latter establishes demands (Forderung) of the former. It is the rare instance in which the etymology of the *Dichter* (poet) and his *Dichtung* (poetry) display their relation to the *Diktator* (dictator). In the veneration of the *Romantik*, the forms of language reign supreme.

In such a worldview, the Ulysses of *Inferno* comes to represent a fiendish patron of the Neo-Romantic enterprise. Again, Glenn Most's reading of Ulysses proves insightful: the Greek orator represents what Dante could be, were it not for the ethical constraints of his Christian faith.[15] Not that figures like Hauptmann, Hofmannsthal, or Borchardt conceived of Ulysses as such. Yet, in the exhortations they render to their compatriots, we detect the rhetorical maneuvers by which Ulysses led his shipmates to their deaths. Consider, to that end, the rousing *peroratio* of Hauptmann's 1937 radio address, "An die deutschen in Übersee" (To the Germans overseas):

> Ihr Männer und Frauen deutscher Zunge, die ich nicht sehe, nicht höre, obgleich ich mit ihnen verbunden bin—ihr seid selber eines, vielleicht das wichtigste Kapitel des deutschen Schicksals und Deutschen Buches! Ich ersehne den Geschichtsschreiber, ersehne den Dichter, der dieses nicht an Grenzen gebundene Deutschland darzustellen und zu glorifizieren berufen ist. Es dürfte kein zimperlicher Moralist oder etwas dergleichen sein—so wenig es die Pioniere gewesen sind, die in leichten Barken den Ozean überschritten haben, todesmutig und muskelhart. Sie waren getrieben von etwas—von was? Nein: die Goldgier allein war es nicht, ebensowenig nur die Flucht vor der Not, ebensowenig die Illusion allein wie bei Kolumbus, der das Paradies und seine Ströme finden wollte. Nein, da war überall zugleich ein beinahe unbewußter kategorischer Imperativ. Es wurde nach einem Befehl gehandelt, dessen Ursprung im Irdischen nicht zu finden ist. Schwestern und Brüder in aller Welt! Ich sage euch in doppeltem Sinne: Lebt wohl! Das ist mein immer lebendiger Wunsch an alle meine Mitmenschen und soll hier zugleich ein Abschied sein. Ich bin heut fünfundsiebzig Jahre, und wir werden uns kaum noch wieder sprechen. Lebt wohl! (CA 6:890)

> (You men and women of German tongue, whom I do not see, do not hear, even though I am bound to you—you yourselves are one of, if not the most important chapter of German fate and of the German book! I long for the historian, long for the poet, who is called to represent and glorify this Germany that is bound to no borders. Under no circumstance may it be some sniveling moralist—no more so than the pioneers were, who in light barks crossed the ocean with courage and muscle. They were driven by something—what was it? No, it was not just lust for mammon, nor was it flight

> from hardship, just as it wasn't an illusion, except for Columbus, who wished to find Paradise and its currents. No, there was everywhere at the same time an almost unconscious categorical imperative. There was a command whose origins lay in no earthly source. Sisters and brothers in all the world! I say to you in two senses: Farewell! That is my ever-living wish for all humanity and here it tokens our parting. Today I am seventy-five years old and we will hardly ever speak again. Farewell!)

Summoning the force of pathos, Hauptmann exhorts his compatriots—one might say with Dante—to "trespass the sign." For in these final lines, he is unmistakable in the desire to surpass limits, to realize a German nation that is bound not by a border, but by a tongue. That prospect of nation-qua-tongue, to be rendered glorious in the texts of the poet and historian, represents the further unfolding of Hofmannsthal's conservative revolution: the nation as an intellectual-spiritual space, the German language its sovereign.

Hauptmann advances the idea by transmogrifying the Romantics' new mythology in a furor of Ulyssean rhetoric. The *deutsches Buch* of which he speaks amounts, after all, to a nationalization of Romantic concepts of mythology (cf. Schlegel, *Ideen*, 95). It is the nakedness of that nationalism that leads him, stifling the sensation of shame, to stipulate the sole criterion of those who would mythologize the German nation: whatever else they might be, they may not be moralists. Language must suffice without an ethics. And like the Greek captain's companions, blandished into following their "higher sowing," the national poets of Hauptmann are prodded by the allusion to unconscious and inexorable forces. It matters not that Ulysses appeals to origins, Hauptmann to imperatives. In neither case is it the rhetorician's goal to locate a truth, but instead, to remove a qualm. To sweeten the deal, he promises no less than the world: in the one case, a world beyond the West; in the other, a boundless Germany, stretched to the furthest corners of the earth by a colonialism of the soul. Once formulated as a project that would serve reason, the new mythology, in Hauptmann's hands, has become a Ulyssean mad flight (*folle volo*).

HAUPTMANN'S DANTEAN MYTHOLOGIES

From *Promethidenlos* (1885) to the Atreus tetralogy (1940–1944), Hauptmann plunged frequently into the currents of utopian and mythical thinking. Such ventures often situated themselves in one Romantic context or another. His novel of a shipwreck, *Atlantis* (1912)—its name an allusion to a Platonic myth—depicts in its second half a new community of Romantic artists in New York City. It is as if the Nazarenes of Rome, a late bloom of the *Romantik*, had been reimagined in the global center of commerce. *Die Insel der großen Mutter* (*The Island of the Great Mother*) (1924), another novel of shipwreck, approaches the emergence of a new mythology as a social experiment: what happens when a group of Western women, shipwrecked on an island in the South Sea, establishes its own social order? A marker of his interest in J. J. Bachofen and the science of myth, the novel reflects how Hauptmann, like later Romantics, turned to the past as well as to the east in the quest to examine the development of myth. Representative of these turns, too, are Hauptmann's polishings of old myths, as well as his syncretistic combinations of Western and Eastern mythologies. Romantic conceptions of myth were rarely distant from his thinking.

Is it a surprise to find, then, that in what Hauptmann deemed to be his crowning efforts at such a mythology, he settled on the example of Dante? From the First World War until his death, he labored on two long, mythical narratives. One of them, *Der große Traum* (The great dream) (1942), he finished. He deemed this epic in *terza rima* to be his *Faust*.[16] Dante appears in the poem and accompanies Hauptmann through a shadowy and unsettling dreamscape. The other decades-long affair on which Hauptmann worked, *Der neue Christophorus* (The new Christopher) (1917–1946), is an unfinished mythological novel. Its protagonist, Bergpater Christoph, shares characteristics of Dante and Hauptmann. On the one hand, his life's dates coincide with Hauptmann's, and like him, the Bergpater wears a Franciscan habit and cincture. Like Hauptmann, the Bergpater is not actually a Franciscan. He is a sage whose brown tunic betokens his distance from the world. The novel describes him, on the other hand, as a twin of Dante (CA 10:738), though the resemblance has less to do with appearance than with the men's affinity for utopianism. The hybridity of the Bergpater suggests that Hauptmann understood himself as an heir not just of Goethe, to whom he was frequently compared, but of Dante as well. In his personal mythologies, Hauptmann channeled the Romantics' quintessential model.

The meaning of Hauptmann's endeavor vis-à-vis the Romantics' *neue Mythologie* is ambiguous. On the one hand, his recapitulation of Romantic symbols and rhetoric creates an assonance with the earlier project. The name of Dante rings the bell of Romantic myth, as does the Bergpater's particular esteem for him. He cites at length from the *De Monarchia* because Dante's wish to renew the *pax romana* prefigured his utopianism. Similarly utopian notions—a golden age vouchsafed by a central monarch—underlay the *neue*

Mythologie, as in Novalis's *Christenheit* speech.[17] But this is not the only affinity. The Bergpater describes Dante as the possessor of special "Organe" (organs) that perceive the coming of a "neues Weltalter" (new age of the world) (CA 10:741). The metaphor of the organ, as Leif Weatherby has observed, figured centrally in the Romantics' theorization of myth.[18] The proclamation of a coming new age, furthermore, alludes to Lessing's *Die Erziehung des Menschengeschlechts* (*The Education of the Human Race*) (1777), a source text of the Romantics' formulation of a new mythology. Finally, like Lessing and his Romantic admirers, the Bergpater understands his mission to be in the service of all humankind (773). Hauptmann thus grafts the protagonist of the novel onto the Romantic discourse of myth. If there were any doubt, it vanishes upon reading how an interlocutor responds to the Bergpater's statements: "Der neue Mythos! Der neue Mythos!" (The new myth! The new myth!) (746).

In significant respects, however, the Bergpater's conceptualization of myth diverges from that sketched by the early Romantics. His disagreements with a Protestant pastor cast such distinctions into relief. The latter regards the Bergpater's preoccupation with myth as suspect, for in his view, the truth of scripture suffices to confirm the salvific reality of Christ (CA 10:768). The Bergpater affirms that reality, but he finds its confirmation not in the "nackte Tatsachenbericht" (naked record of facts) of scripture; instead, he locates its source in the living and ever developing work of mythos. His rationale becomes clearer in light of another circumstance: the Bergpater is the caretaker of a boy, Erdmann, who represents a reincarnation of Christ. Scripture that would exclude him, or other incarnations of the divine, is by its nature deficient. In this respect, Hauptmann still resembles early Romantics like Schleiermacher or Hölderlin—the one with his doctrine of mediators, the other with his openness to Christian and Greek deities. But Hauptmann flies beyond the Romantic in the Bergpater's reflections on the relation of myth, truth, and reason. His belittling characterization of scripture applies not so much to the factual record of scripture as it does more broadly to facts, truth, and reason:

> Vernunft ist etwas, wodurch uns, wie dem Taucher in der Taucherglocke am Grunde des Meers, ein Leben ermöglicht wird, in dem wir uns zu bewegen und zu erhalten vermögen, ohne zu ersticken und zu ertrinken. (CA 10:808–809)
>
> (Reason is something that, like the diving bell does for the diver at the bottom of the sea, makes possible a life in which we can move and sustain ourselves, without suffocating and drowning.)

Reason may be necessary, but its necessity is overshadowed by its insufficiency. It grants just barely the means to survive the ocean of myth, much less traverse it. "Wahrheit" (truth) verifies this inasmuch as it draws us from the "Gärtlein der Vernunft" (little garden of reason)—note the condescension of the diminutive—and presents the sort of infinity known only to one lost at sea (CA 10:794). Unlike in the early Romantic context, myth no longer serves reason—it looms above, behind, and around it.

The metaphor of the ocean is not incidental. One form of it or another surfaced in Goethe, Schlegel, Schelling, and Novalis. Hauptmann is leveraging that topos of Romanticism, as he had in *Atlantis* and *Die Insel der großen Mutter.* It was disaster at sea, after all, that led to their respective episodes of myth formation. But whereas the Romantics' figuration of the sea signaled the primordial truth of myth, Hauptmann's use of the metaphor betokens its menacing profundity. *Der neue Christophorus* renews and hypostasizes that metaphor, which its eponymous character indicates. He derives his name from Saint Christopher, the man who saved *Christ* from drowning by *bearing* him across a river. In Hauptmann, the navigation of myth demands a captain. It demands a Ulysses.

What had become of myth, that it should require such a figure? Conceived by the Romantics as an instrument of knowledge, and wielded for the purpose of social cohesion, the new mythology began as a collective effort. In the actualization of a Dantean mythology, its scope narrowed. Romantic poets struggled with matters of legitimation. Who was fit to create myth? Who might claim to stand at its origins? How could this authority be vouchsafed in poetry? In Hauptmann, these questions have both crystallized and given way to a new concern. No longer is there a question of who is authorized to create myth; instead there is an injunction to follow the one who can navigate its waters. This is the function of the Bergpater, as well as a central concern in *Der große Traum*. The shift is indicative of a transformation in the conception of myth from the Romantics to Hauptmann. No longer is myth a totalized realm of the aesthetic, wherein one intuits the absolute. No longer is myth a sphere that has been forged under the manipulation of the artist or the poet. No longer is it a "realm" that is separate from reality, into which one can "enter" and receive communications of truth. In Hauptmann, myth is reality, and reality is myth. Existence is an ocean of mystery. Everyone is "in den großen Mythos des Daseins hineingestellt" (thrown into the great myth of existence), the Bergpater asserts, in a formulation that recalls Heidegger's *Geworfenheit* (thrownness) (CA 10:745).[19] This is myth on a new order and grand scale.

If myth is omnipresent—a vast and profound ocean—then the pressing question is not how to reinstantiate it, but how to traverse it. Myth shifts from a matter at the nexus of aesthetics and epistemology to the terrain of metaphysics and existential deliberation. Consider the Bergpater's remarks near the end of the novel:

> Der menschlichen Sprachen sind Legion. In ihrem Ein-und-Alles sind sie ein Meer ohne alle Ufer: sie sind ein einziges Meer, ein einziger, weltumfassender geistiger Ozean der Unendlichkeit. (CA 10:881)

> (Human languages are legion. In their totality they are a sea without a shore: they are a single sea, a single, world-encompassing ocean of infinity.)

Without getting lost in the distinction between *Sprache* and *Mythos* (*mythos* = utterance, speech), we find that Hauptmann postulates a metaphysics that is rooted in language and myth. *Sprache*, which he had once defined as *Seele*, has moved a step further. It is now the *Weltseele* (worldsoul), as the allusion to Goethe's "Eins und Alles" suggests. *Sprache / Mythos* is the substrate of all existence. Such a metaphysics poses a formidable dilemma: how to navigate the infinite babble, the endless mystery of life. When myth envelops all in obscurity, the collective enterprise of the Romantics loses its sense. Shall the blind lead the blind? Hauptmann's transformation of myth reassigns agency from the collective to the individual, to the Ulyssean pilot at whose command language bends, twists, and moves.

In Hauptmann's late texts, where events of mythical significance confound understanding, the demand for such a figure looms. *Der neue Christophorus* and *Der große Traum* center on hermeneutically charged episodes of mythic import: dreams and visions; cycles of death and rebirth; battles of cosmic significance. Their syncretistic worlds balance on a simultaneity of mythic systems—Christian, Buddhist, Gnostic, Catharist, and Islamic, among others.[20] The result is a morass by design. Little wonder, then, that in the intervals between mythic episodes, *Christophorus* amounts to a series of discourses between the Bergpater and his disciples. The latter require the guidance of the former. The urgency of a guide is all the more explicit in the semiautobiographical verse epic, where Hauptmann, like Dante, requires a guide to navigate a supernatural dreamscape. He can hardly stand his immersion in the realm of myth: "Wer hat in diese Tiefe mich gezogen? / . . . im toten Bildermeere ohne Wogen" (Who drew me into these depths? / . . . in the dead sea of images without waves) (CA 4:997). It is less a question than an existential sigh. In the depths of a world from which there is no escape, he must be led.

The indispensability of leadership underpins *Der große Traum*, which, apart from a last testament of sorts, is a translation of the *Führerprinzip* from the national-political to the intellectual-spiritual domain. It is no secret, after all, that rhetorical prowess was more than a peripheral concern of Hitler. *Mein Kampf* had proclaimed the political utility of rhetoric: the "Zauberkraft" (magical force) of the spoken word was the basis for history's grand revolutions, he had written; no power worked more forcefully upon the masses than the "Gewalt der Rede" (power of language).[21] Hauptmann's language cast a spell too, albeit among a select audience. The secretary of his later years, C.F.W. Behl (1948), wrote that *Der große Traum* had rendered language a musical instrument that augured "bisher ungeahnte Möglichkeiten" (as yet unimagined possibilities). Its force derived from a "Magie des Elementaren" (magic of the elemental).[22] With his stylized habitus, Hauptmann encouraged such impressions. But he was less interested in the role of political *Führer*—there had been discussion of him as a presidential candidate[23]—than he was in one of an intellectual-spiritual profile.

Hauptmann's *Großer Traum* gives shape to that profile in its relativization of traditional repositories of authority, beginning with the Christian deity. According to his Gnostic mythology, the poem's Virgil-figure, Satanael, is an elder brother to Jesus Christ and a Promethean rival to God the Father. More significant than the provenance of this theology, which Guthke traced, is its effect: Satanael is a god-man whose benevolence and nobility contrast favorably with the Christian Trinity.[24] Apart from thereby constituting a critique of Christianity, Satanael usurps a portion of the authority that is intrinsic to the persons of the Trinity. In doing so, he demonstrates the legitimacy of the *Führerschaft* (leadership) that he exercises throughout the dream.

To complement its diminution of the Christian deity, the poem lodges a blistering critique of the Catholic Church and its prelates. Dante serves the opportunity for that critique on a silver platter. Standing with Hauptmann in a German cathedral, he identifies the Church as the source of universal holiness. His discussion relies on the metaphor of the Church as the Barque of St. Peter (CA 4:1003), which assimilates the matter to Hauptmann's oceanic metaphors of myth and nautical metaphors of *Führerschaft*. Indeed the image of the pontiff (Peter) as helmsman—note, again, the Ulyssean dynamics at play—is a conspicuous representation of that constellation of metaphors. But in a double inversion, Hauptmann reveals the *auctoritas* of the Church and of Dante to be a sham. First, he exchanges roles with Dante. Despite the latter's journey through Hell, Hauptmann takes him by the hand into the infernal depths beneath the German cathedral. Dante expresses skepticism: "Du wirst mir schwerlich etwas Neues zeigen" (You'll be hard-pressed to show me something new) (1004); yet that is precisely what Hauptmann does. Thus, in a second inversion, he reveals the underbelly of the Church to be something akin to a scene from Hieronymous Bosch: monks, nuns, and beasts sacrifice and feast on the innocent. In a single canto, Hauptmann excoriates the Roman Church and purports to supersede the visionary status of Dante.[25]

The rivalry with Dante marks a noteworthy, yet generally unremarked milestone in the context of the Romantics' new mythology. Commentators tend to focus on Dante's role as a Virgilian presence in the poem (i.e., a guide).[26] To be sure, he is an ostensible *Führer* in Satanael's absence, but Dante's role as guide is less remarkable than the gradual erosion of his authority as such. For it is not just the case that Hauptmann leads Dante into a subterranean pit and shows him something new. He goes so far as to have Dante acknowledge his *Führerschaft*—"Nun hast du mich geleitet" (Now you have led me) (CA 4:1015)—and to commission him as a sacred poet:

Du bist wie ich der höchsten Wahrheit Diener,
so zeuge nun, wie ich, nach heil'ger Pflicht
für sie, ein freigeborner Theatiner.

Mein Feuergriffel schrieb das Weltgericht.
Mein Auftrag ist, dir Eigenstes zu weisen
und anzuzünden dir dein eignes Licht.

So schreib auch du! Wohlan, folg meinen Gleisen!
Ich lebe mehr in dir als du in mir,
allein, wie Ich und Du sich unterweisen,

so sind in einem Geiste einig wir. (CA 4:1017–1018)

(Like me, you are a servant of highest truth,
So testify for it now according to sacred duty,
Like me, a freeborn Theatine.

My pen of fire wrote the judgment of the world.
My task is to show you the most secret things
And to kindle your own light.

So write! Onward, follow my tracks!
I live more in you than you in me,
But as we instruct one another,

We are united in spirit.)

With the symbolic passing of the torch—an Olympic tradition begun by Hitler in 1936—Dante bestows on Hauptmann the authority to poeticize the truth, while marking him a spiritual *Führer* in the imagery of European fascism. But the gesture is ambivalent. On the one hand, it would seem an honor to be crowned by so venerable a figure. On the other hand, as Satanael insinuates, Dante is a fraud who has not truly been to Hell (1064). The incongruity discloses Hauptmann's peculiar strategem to claim authority. Unlike Schelling and Novalis, who did their best to imitate Dante, Hauptmann attempts to delegitimize him—all the while that he accepts from him a commission and records his vision in *terza rima*!

Assuming the truth of Hauptmann's fiction, the illusive *Commedia* pales in comparison to the final five cantos of *Der große Traum*. For there, in a summary of his engagement with the new mythology, Hauptmann records the experience of his journey to the underworld, as if readers would now encounter the "real thing." The conclusion summarizes Hauptmann's poetics of myth inasmuch as it (1) evokes the Romantic context, (2) renews and instantiates the oceanic-nautical metaphorics of myth, (3) situates rhetoric as the pre-eminent instrument of its navigation, and (4) culminates in a depiction of Hauptmann as a new *Führer.* The equation of a primordial sea with the sphere of mythos suffices to recall the early Romantic treatments of myth. But in a more concrete allusion to the Romantic background, it is an ancient miner—much like an iconic figure in Novalis's *Heinrich von Ofterdingen*—who leads Hauptmann and Satanael into the belly of the earth (1065). Their journey renews the metaphors of myth from *Christophorus*. Into the "Rätselmeer" (sea of riddles) they sail (1067). Shot through with images of the sea of myth, the canto attends to the navigation of those waters.[27] It focuses attention on *Führer* who, like the Bergpater, transport their charges across the mysterious waters; for even though "beredte Münder" (eloquent mouths) fall silent in the realm of mythos, it is the task of those who travel this realm, "unaussprechlich wie es ist, / in Zeichen und Symbolen zu berichten" (unspeakable as it is, / to report in signs and symbols) (1073). By the end of the poem, that challenge appears to have met its match, for Hauptmann spies not just a shore, which would signal an end to the sea of mythos, he sees on the shore the figure of a man who has presumably disembarked upon the conclusion of his journey. It is a projection of himself (1085). In this poem that obsesses over leaders, one of the summative visions is that of Hauptmann as *Führer. Der große Traum* is not just a text that teems with mythical images, it is a text in which the profundity of myth justifies an audacious seizure of poetic authority.

The embrace of the *Führerprinzip* emerges from Hauptmann's erasure of the difference between mythos and logos. It is true that such a distinction has not always been maintained. It was disputed, for instance, by Heidegger, but his endorsement is not exactly exculpatory.[28] On the other hand, the early Romantics conceived of mythos in the service of logos. The project of a new mythology had emerged in dialogue, after all, with the aesthetic philosophy of the German Enlightenment (Heyne, Lessing, Herder). It was audacious, but not irrational. As Beiser argues, early Romanticism was hyperrational.[29] Indeed, its goals looked much like those of philosophers of the Enlightenment. For if, as Kant had written, the eighteenth century was not an enlightened age, but an age of enlightenment, then the Romantic project aimed for no less than the fulfillment of the former proposition. Myth could unite lay folk and philosophers, and by forging new bonds among artists, it could do this with no end in sight. Such prospects could flourish because Romantic philosophy did not render nature irrational or unintelligible. In Hauptmann, however, where mythos signifies insuperable mystery, logos qua rationality goes missing. In the daunting confrontation with an omnipresent and foreboding mythos, such a conception of logos has become nugatory. Instead of the two complementing one another, or compensating for each other, mythos all but swallows logos. Hauptmann thus construes the latter as the instrument of the former—as language, "was der Grieche den Logos nennt" (that which the Greek calls logos) (CA 10:881). With the replacement of reason by language, the realization of utopia no longer depends on the diffusion of art and knowledge. It becomes a project of rhetorical puissance, of the *Dichter* as *Diktator.* Language shapes a new reality.

There is no denying the unsettling character of this transformation. It testifies not just to the dialectic of which Horkheimer and Adorno wrote, but to the consequences they deduced from it.[30] Indeed, the most explicitly troubling implication in Hauptmann's adaptation of Romantic myth is its proximity to Hitlerian fascism. During the years of the Republic, one could write of the longing for a *Führer* without imagining it to be Hitler. Many writers did.[31] Yet in Hauptmann we are dealing with texts whose composition stretches well into the 1940s. Even as he spiritualizes the role of the *Führer*, he cannot help but conjure the specter of Hitler. His preoccupation with a *Führerschaft* grounded in rhetorical force is difficult to conceive independently therefrom.

The intertwinement of those two is all the more apparent because of a peculiar feature in the ethereal setting of Hauptmann's texts: the still central position of the nation. It is not as if, with the sacralization of the *Führerprinzip*, the texts lost sight of national borders. On the contrary, the events of these poetic meditations occur at the interstices of the celestial and the national. The birth of the messianic figure, Erdmann, for example, is accompanied by canonical Germanic symbols: the reawakening of Luther, of Faust, and of the German cathedrals. The eschatological disruption in the arc of time is concentrated in one geographic space. Similar phenomena unfold in *Der große Traum*, which not only alludes to the old national symbols but takes them up in the old disputes of German nationalism, as when Satanael attacks the Roman Church for its plundering of the Germans. In both texts, the dawning of a new age is heralded from Germany.

And yet it is the wrinkles in the texts' national-historical texture that, if they do not mitigate his embrace of a *Führer*, nevertheless generate ambiguity. We thus find that the Bergpater sees the sources of a German world monarchy in the ideological opponents of Nazism. Marx, Engels, Liebknecht, and Bebel, he says, represent the founding fathers of Germany's prospective global empire (CA 10:877). Whatever the contradictions inherent in such a vision, it is an affront to the filiations of Nazism. It is not the only one. A more incisive interrogation of Nazism comes in the form of a suggestive dream. The Bergpater finds himself in a vast compound, some combination of hotel, barracks, and train station. Throngs of people, all of whose faces bear "hoffnungslosen Wahnsinn" (hopeless madness), are pushed and prodded. Meanwhile, elegantly dressed men sit at game tables, looking on idiotically, hatefully, proudly (839–840). The context of a camp is clear. Though it does not fundamentally alter the novel, the dream elicits critical self-reflection from the Bergpater. He prays to be released from his nightmare, to go where "die Wohltat des Logos mich . . . umgibt" (the beneficence of the logos surrounds me) (840). His mind jumps to Luther, wishing to know whether he regrets having sullied reason with words (Vernunft mit Worten besudeln) (840). Is this an accusation, or an inquiry?

In either case, it applies in equal force to the novel and its contents. Yet there is no resolution to the matter. The dream betrays the novel's uncertainty with the stakes of its philosophical-existential program, but the Bergpater goes no further in resolving the ambivalence. It is one more similarity that he shares with Hauptmann.

Ambivalence characterizes the relation of Hauptmann's project to the Romantics' new mythology. Both spring from a discontent with the present, harbor a utopian gesture, and conceive the work toward its realization according to Dantean forms—aesthetic, poetic, and political.[32] In his equation of rhetoric and reason, Hauptmann contrasts unfavorably with his Romantic predecessors. His summative texts on myth, a flirtation with unreason, proffer a naked defense of fascism's claims to authority. In distinguishing between the original project and Hauptmann's rehabilitation, however, the aim is not to exculpate Romanticism so much as to uncover the problematic influence of its resurrection of Dante. The embrace of Dante, intended to model a mythology, resulted in the de facto emergence of that perennial question: whence myth? To situate one's poetic voice in that originary position demanded an *auctoritas*, the search for which overshadowed all else. It was less the case that Schelling, Novalis, and Goethe imitated the *Commedia* than that they conjured Dante. By the time of Hauptmann, the rehabilitation of myth may have retained elements of the original project, but its guiding imperative had become the overweening effort to match, if not topple him. Critics of Romantic myth may well see this as a case in point of Faustian striving. But the fixation on Dante provides another point of reference. When Hauptmann's Bergpater describes himself as a "sprechende Flamme" (speaking flame) (745), he recalls the image of Dante's Ulysses. In the quest to reinstantiate Romantic myth, Hauptmann trespassed the sign.

CHAPTER FIVE

Abolishing History

New Dantean Germanies in Rudolf Borchardt and Stefan George

MYTH IS NEVER OF THE PRESENT. It occupies its own time—perceptible only in a glint of the past or an intuition of the future. This truth stands awkwardly in the way of efforts to generate it. They labor inexorably to restore a past that is inaccessible, to realize a future that is unattainable. The generation of myth aims to break the plane of history.

That aim is evident in the structure of religious calendars, in the organization of liturgical years, and above all, in the celebration of the new year. It was in this respect that Mircea Eliade wrote of the new year as a celebration of the "abolition of history": the inbreaking of mythic time.[1] Religious celebrations of the new year, he explained, are accompanied by rituals of cleansing, purgation, and exorcism because they are an attempt "to restore—if only momentarily—mythical and primordial time, 'pure' time, the time of the 'instant' of the Creation" (54). One need think only of the covenant struck with Noah: the deluge wiped clean the face of the earth, and from the ark there emerged new life. In the revocation of historical time, myth would realize a new creation.

Drawn from the global anthropology of religion, these observations highlight the temporal dynamic that was integral to the Romantic project of myth. We saw it, above all, in the project's metaphorics: in nearly every writer whom we have investigated, the figure of primordial water is fundamental. Invariably, myth involves a return to its depths. This is attested by Schelling's *System* (HkA 9/1:329); Friedrich Schlegel's *Gespräch über die Poesie* (KFSA 2:284); Novalis's *Lehrlinge zu Sais* (*Novices of Sais*) (*Schriften* 1:104); and Goethe's "Mahomets Gesang" and "Mächtiges Überraschen." It is salient in Hauptmann, as well, with the key difference that one remains immersed in it, struggling to stay afloat. Water is native to the geography of prehistory, we know from creation narratives; it is also, as Eliade points out, an instrument of purgation that expunges the residues of history from the present (58–59). Dante was submerged in the waters of Lethe before leaving behind the terrestrial realm. Novalis and Goethe adopted and adapted that very act to their mythic protagonists. In its poetics of myth, Romanticism would abolish history.

Between 1800 and 1900 (i.e., between the Romantic and Neo-Romantic moments), the prospect of such an abolition gained traction. The gulf between present time and mythic time, it seemed, had shrunk. Romantics once conceived of their striving as "unendliche Annäherung" (infinite approximation); it followed an asymptotic trajectory that, without ever attaining its goal, could nevertheless approximate it. Soon, though, the distance to the goal had contracted—by a wide margin. As we have registered in the lectures of Borchardt, Hauptmann, and Hofmannsthal, the age of myth no longer lay in prehistory. It occupied a space in recent memory. In an improbable irony, the likes of which Friedrich Schlegel might have appreciated, the Romantic strivers after a golden age had come to look like the denizens of a golden age. Romanticism had become a myth unto itself, its restoration a (new) new mythology.

The ironic hypostatization of Romanticism manifests itself in the endeavors of two almost murderously opposed translators of Dante, Rudolf Borchardt and Stefan George. Each of these men rendered a landmark germanification of Dante; in each case, the act of translation only begins to account for what was at stake. In their receptions of Dante, Borchardt and George imagined they had broken the plane of history and instituted a new age. The present chapter alternates between the two men, tracing the threads of a history in which their repurposing of Dante would reconfigure time and instantiate a domain of myth.

A NATION OF *DANTISTEN*

Born in Königsberg to a family of Jewish tea merchants, Rudolf Borchardt nurtured a lifelong obsession with the regeneration of a golden age. Tied always to the history of the *Volk*, to whom he struggled to belong, his obsession pivoted upon two historical fulcra: the German Middle Ages and the German Romantic age, the latter representing a recuperation of the former. In a Faustian bargain, Borchardt believed, Germany had surrendered the fruits of medievalizing Romanticism in exchange for political and economic might. Industrialization in the nineteenth century was thus accompanied by a spiritual degeneration of the *Volk*, evident in Germany's many new urban centers. Like Hofmannsthal, Borchardt bemoaned especially the dearth of a national literary culture: "Kein Volk, keine Literatur, keine Philosophie steht an der Stelle, an der die Literatur von Weimar, die Philosophie und die Geschichte von Königsberg und Berlin, die Philologie von Bonn und Göttingen gestanden ist. . . . Wir leben im Interregnum" (No people, no literature, no philosophy occupies the place that was occupied by the literature of Weimar, the philosophy and history of Königsberg and Berlin, the philology of Bonn and Göttingen. . . . We are living in an interregnum) (GW, *Reden* 110). The latter portion of the lamentation was not to suggest that Borchardt was expecting a return of the Kaiser, as various others did. Like Hauptmann, Borchardt believed that poetry, more than politics, set the course of the nation. Indeed, the notion of an interregnum was important to him prior even to the Kaiser's abdication, for it presupposed something more decisive than a political regime: it was predicated on a return to the *illud tempus* of Romanticism.

For a time, the restoration of that stolen birthright of Germans appeared tantalizingly close. Its proximity was due to the hope Borchardt pinned on two Catholic poets, one from Vienna and the other from the Rhineland. Hugo von Hofmannsthal, born to a family of Jewish converts, had made waves as a seventeen-year-old when he published poems that belied his age. In 1891, when he met Stefan George, six years his senior, the latter had already published two volumes of poetry—*Hymnen* (*Odes*) and *Pilgerfahrten* (*Pilgrimages*). He was about to embark on the publication of a new journal, *Die Blätter für die Kunst* (Pages on art), whose twenty-seven-year run formed the mainstay of a new school of German writers and academics. Orchestrated by the elder poet, the 1891 rendezvous in Vienna did not achieve the partnership George had in mind. Hofmannsthal was likely wary of George's romantic designs; for the duration of his career, he maintained a cautious distance from George, contributing only occasionally and early on to *Blätter für die Kunst*. In a statement that registers both his disappointment at this outcome and his hopes for what might have been, George wrote to Hofmannsthal in 1902: "Ich war des festen glaubens dass wir · Sie und ich · durch jahre in unsrem schrifttum eine sehr heilsame diktatur hätten üben können · dass es dazu nicht kam dafür mach ich Sie allein verantwortlich" (I believed firmly that we · you and I · could have exerted for years a very salutary dictatorship in our writing · that it did not come to that, I hold you alone accountable).[2] There resounds an affinity to Hauptmann: the *Dichter* as *Führer.*[3] George was not the only one convinced of their capacity for leadership.

In 1902, Borchardt identified George and Hofmannsthal as the two living poets in whom Germany could place its hope for a spiritual revival. He depicted Hofmannsthal, however, as the brighter star. George was brilliant, but so dogmatic that he diminished the quality of his and his circle's poetry (GW, *Reden* 62–63). He countered modernity with an iron will, whereas Hofmannsthal transcended it. Borchardt's assessment of Hofmannsthal's merits deserves special attention: he demonstrated how to univeralize an age degraded by capitalism; his work betrayed the range and depth of encyclopedism; each of his lyrics was a genre unto itself; each of them follows a trajectory that culminates in a revelation of the coherence of the world (73, 76, 91). His descriptors echo the Romantic paeans to Dante, each of them voiced a century earlier, as Romantics identified him as the model of their mythology. It is fitting to hear these echoes, for "im süßen neuen Stile Hofmannsthals" (in the sweet new style of Hofmannsthal), Borchardt identifies an analogue to Dante's *dolce stil novo* (93). This was more than high praise from Borchardt, an obsessive stylist. It was an expression of hope.

Borchardt's optimism was rooted in the perception of Dante's unique meaning for European literature. When August Wilhelm Schlegel discovered Dante, Borchardt believed, it was a prize of incomparable value. Soon, however, the profits of that discovery flowed in the wrong direction. With the abandonment of his *Commedia* translation, Schlegel put a premature end to the early *Romantik*. Germans lost sight of Dante and were left with the "bastards" of Romanticism. Meanwhile, the English and French acquired its true children—foremost among them, Dante (GW, *Prosa II*, 355–356). The traces of these transfers were writ large across the nineteenth century. German literature devolved into journalistic realism. But in the exquisite verse of the French Parnasse, he perceived the emulation and reinterpretation of Dante's style; in the major poetic cycles of Victor Hugo, he felt the heat of *Inferno*; and in the influence of Dante on Dante Gabriel Rossetti, Borchardt witnessed the rapprochement of medieval and modern literature. "Dante ist es, der mittelbar oder unmittelbar all diesen Zauber wirkt" (It is Dante who, directly or indirectly, effects all this magic) (357). By the dawn of the new century, it was time that the treasure be repaid:

> Ist nicht der Weg der deutschen Romantik, die zu einer europäischen Bewegung wurde, ein Umweg, der sie mit allem, was Jena und Heidelberg ihr gaben, und also auch mit Dante, wieder zu uns zurückführen muß? Zurückführen von denen, die sie uns entliehen und die das geliehene Kulturgut erstatten müssen, wie wir

> selber Shakespeare erstattet haben, wie große Völker erstatten, mit Zins und Zinseszins? (364–365)
>
> (Is not the path of German Romanticism, which became a European movement, a detour, which—with all that Jena and Heidelberg gave it, including Dante—must now return to us? Return from those who borrowed it from us and who must now pay for those cultural assets—as we paid for Shakespeare, as great peoples pay—with interest and compound interest?)

Romanticism was Germanic in origin but had sown its harvest abroad. To seize their birthright, German poets would have to re-enter the stream of Romantic literature by arranging the intersection of Germanic and Latin "Formenwelten" (worlds of forms). They would have to adopt Dante's forms (364–365).[4]

In the emulation of Dante's forms, Hofmannsthal and George signaled just such a repatriation of Romanticism. In one of Hofmannsthal's ballads, composed in *terza rima*, Borchardt intuited a "wundervoll danteske Vision" (marvelously Dantean vision) (365–366). There were other examples he might have cited. Hofmannsthal had written a lyrical cycle, "Terzinen über Vergänglichkeit" (Tercets on ephemerality), in the same rhyme scheme. His fragment of a novel, *Andreas*, drew heavily on Dante, as noted by David Miles.[5] George, too, figured in the repatriation of Romanticism via Dantean forms. But owing to his tutelage under Mallarmé in Paris, Borchardt depicted him as the unwitting vessel of French theories that "im letzten Grunde rein aus Fritz Schlegel und Novalis stammen" (derived ultimately from Fritz Schlegel and Novalis) (GW, *Prosa II*, 365). Above all, the Romantic ideals that George inherited in France were those that had been intertwined with the fate of Dante. Now, he was bearing the "ganze Beute in die Heimat zurück" (whole booty back home) (365). In Borchardt's estimation, Romanticism had never attained an organic end. By appropriating Dante's verse, Hofmannsthal and George breathed new life into a dormant German spirit.

George, in particular, drove the preoccupation with Dantean form to new heights. This was on public display in his translation of thirty-three episodes from the *Commedia*, released in 1909. Although various translations of the *Commedia* had appeared in the nineteenth century (e.g., Streckfuß, Philalethes, Witte, Gildemeister), none was hailed as the formal achievement of George's *Göttliche Komödie*. It was heralded as the first, authentically poetic Dante to exist in German. The preeminent German Dantist of the time, Karl Vossler, saw in its "Impressionismus und geistigen Sensualismus" (impressionism and intellectual sensuality) a superlative attack on the academic translations of the German tradition—albeit a dizzying one.[6] Erich Auerbach judged it similarly, writing that "das Dichterische . . . und dieses allein, war der Trieb und die Absicht dieser Übersetzung, und sie ist die erste, der es gelungen ist" (the poetic . . . and this alone was the motivation and purpose of this translation; and it is the first to succeed as such). He suggested that George's translation ought to be read at least as widely as his poetry.[7] A backhanded compliment, perhaps, but it pointed to a basic truth about George's poetry: it had become increasingly intertwined with that of Dante.

By George's accounting, it was not primarily Dante's worldview that appealed, but the structures and resonance of his poetry. His affinity for Dante emerged from a fixation on matters of form and *elocutio*. This much is evident in the foreword he affixed to the publication of his collected *Commedia* translations. He did not intend to render "einen vollständigen umguss" (a complete recast)—note the shapely metaphor—of the poem. The goal was never that of philological excavation. He was not driven by the desire to uncover the poem in its totality, as if the scope of its vision were what made it unique. The object of George's aspiration lay elsewhere: "das dichterische · ton bewegung gestalt: alles wodurch Dante für jedes in betracht kommende volk (mithin auch für uns) am anfang aller Neuen Dichtung steht" (the poetic · tone movement shape: everything through which Dante stands at the beginning of all modern poetry for every people that is to be considered [therefore, for us too]) (SGSW 10/11:5). In a word, he wished to channel Dante's voice.

The fulfillment of that wish entailed linguistic innovation. Dante's centrality to the development of vernacular poetry might suggest as much. But Dante's vernacular did not signify for George anything like a democratization of poetic language. It denoted a renewal of language's formal possibilities. George was less focused on the contrast of the vernacular to Latin than on Dante's determining the criteria of a *volgare illustre* (illustrious vernacular). Like Dante's poetry, he once explained, his idiosyncratic-sounding lyrics were not the fruits of a new language—"es waren uralte Worte, die noch da waren" (they were ancient words, still present).[8] It was the old made new, though one ought not underestimate just how new. As a child, George had imagined forging a *lingua romana*.[9] Ultimately, he cultivated a peculiar use of syntax, diction, punctuation, and typography. Formal innovations like these enabled the immurement of himself from a philistine public; he wished to use a language that "die unheilige menge sich nie bedienen würde" (the unholy masses would never make use of) (SGSW 17:52). George's disdain for the masses was tied to his estimation of Dante, as one of his disciples, Ernst Morwitz, once explained: specifically, George had drawn inspiration from two episodes in which Dante had placed unintelligible articulations into the mouths of the damned.[10] On occasion, he, too, rendered similarly inscrutable verses (SGSW 6/7:116–117). The translation of the *Commedia*, though not unintelligible, reflects George's refashioning of language to such ends. It was an occasion for the renewal of his powers of lyrical expression, but it likewise kept the bourgeois reading public at bay.[11] Vossler, at any rate, could confirm as much. He found George's German more challenging than Dante's Tuscan.

Techniques of exclusionary language signal one of the primary motivations behind George's Dante: the Italian poet was a weapon in George's war on the bourgeois public. The effort to shape Dante's voice in esoteric verse was indeed a strategy of defense that accompanied a generally bellicose program of reception. Another marker of the same impulse was George's habit of trying to topple commonplaces of *dantismo*, for example, the notion that Dante was synonymous with the crest of the European Middle Ages. He declared instead that Dante was the cornerstone of the Italian Renaissance, the signpost of a new age.[12] A defensible view, perhaps, save that he went so far as to try expunging the *Commedia* of its Christianity. Dante had something Christian about him in the way that Plato did, George explained. Incidental but not integral, his Christianity reflected the commitments of readers more than those of the poet. Sometimes, the effects of such an idiosyncratic stance could be illuminating. The alignment of Dante with the Renaissance, for example, led George to regard Dante as a poet of particulars rather than universals. Freed from the constraints of allegory, Dante emerged as an early devotee of human form and individualism.[13] More often, however, and more to the point, George's program amounted to a de facto annexation of Dante from the reading public. Again and again, his Dante reflects an imperious condescension to modernity.

It comes as small surprise, then, that in an age when Dante figured as a lodestar for Neo-Romantics and Modernists, there surfaced contests over his reception. Particularly acrimonious was that between George and Borchardt. The aversion of the latter to the gothic, the Christian, and the medieval rankled the former. Borchardt disparaged George's translation as a travesty for its Petrarchan style (GW, *Prosa II*, 506). To be sure, the enmity predated these matters. It resulted in part because of George's jealous guardianship of his Kreis. He once forbade a young disciple from interacting with Borchardt. To Borchardt, who had pinned a portrait of George on the wall of his apartment, the discovery of this act of exclusion was too much.[14] He sent George a letter whose temerity—they had never met or corresponded—is striking.[15] He affected the tone of a knight whose honor had been impeached. The letter went unanswered, and Borchardt's status as persona non grata was sealed. But the tension involved more than a clash of personalities. It followed the course of the poets' engagement with Dante.

That course began with what George perceived to be an act of aggression. In 1905, Borchardt sent copies of his own *Commedia* translations to two of the leading *Georgianer*, Friedrich Wolters and Berthold Vallentin. Possibly it was a show of rivalry, as Osterkamp suggests; maybe it was an attempt at ingratiation.[16] Whatever his intent, Borchardt was treading on the territory of the *Meister* (master), so called by his disciples. To add insult to injury, Borchardt failed to conform to rudimentary stylistic principles set forward by George. He had opted instead for an archaic rendition of his own contrivance. Borchardt garnered only scorn from George's disciples, who rejected his subsequent invitations to collaboration.[17] The harshest criticism came in 1910, when George's closest disciple, Friedrich Gundolf, proclaimed George the spiritual leader of German letters. He repudiated Borchardt's earlier pronouncements on Hofmannsthal and George, claiming that no living poet was comparable to his Meister. More injuriously, he contended that Borchardt would be nothing, were it not for his attachment to Hofmannsthal.[18] By contrast, George was "der wichtigste mann des gegenwärtigen Deutschland" (the most important man in contemporary Germany) and the "führer in einem nicht mehr vermeidbaren geisterkrieg" (leader in a spiritual war that is no longer avoidable). As the judge of his age, Gundolf wrote, George was the contemporary equivalent to Dante (21).

Thus it was that the essay's most explosive attack was leveled precisely at Borchardt's Dante. The attack was lodged in a footnote—the only one in Gundolf's thirty-page essay, a minuscule monument to Borchardt's insignificance. Borchardt practiced "angewandte philologie" (applied philology), Gundolf wrote, a workmanlike exercise in the reconstitution of old forms. Borchardt's translations of the *Commedia*, he explained, were "das stationäre Deutsch der russischen Juden" (the static German of Russian Jews) (33). The essay enraged Borchardt, an elitist poet-scholar who had tried perpetually to escape his roots as the son of German-Jewish merchants. It was a doubly galling barb coming from Gundolf, a German Jew who had changed his name from *Gundelfinger.* In a blistering retort, published in the *Süddeutsche Monatsheft*, Borchardt unleashed bilious attacks on the George-Kreis, including allusions to its homosexuality. Max Weber, by no means a friend of George, declared the article an "unverzeihliches Geschehnis für die Öffentlichkeit" (inexcusable affair for the public).[19] Ironically, George's *dantismo* had once portended great things to Borchardt: above all, a return of Romanticism to Germany. Just a few years later, the germanification of Dante had led to a maelstrom.

The quick souring indicates just how fraught the reception of Dante had become in the span of a century. He was no longer the barbarous Catholic of the dark ages, as when the Schlegels rehabilitated him. Now, when Romanticism had become the golden age of the German spirit, Dante was the guarantor of its sanctity. So inseparable was Dante from the *Romantik* that he had begun to assume a Germanic hue. Indeed this was the case already among late German Romantics, who conceived of Dante as one of their own. Peter Cornelius, for example, who had been commissioned to paint frescoes of the *Commedia* in Rome's Villa Massimo, had an elaborate rationale for the repatriation.[20] Yet the effect worked in the other direction, too. Dante had left an indelible impression on German Romanticism. Its reclamation could not occur without his resurrection. As already noted, a reckoning with Dante proved integral to the Neo-Romantic projects of Hauptmann and Borchardt. Dante and the *Romantik* perdured in a symbiosis.

Eventually, Borchardt undertook the regeneration of that symbiosis, which entailed the creation of a German *dolce stil novo*.[21] The need for such a style had its origins in the history of the German language. Martin Luther's codification of a school-bookish grammatica—systematized for poetry by Martin Opitz—had alienated the *Volk* from the organic roots of its literature. With its discovery of Dante, Romanticism had begun to counteract such forces. Yet its success was interrupted by its migration abroad. By resuming the Romantics' work of philological excavation and linguistic renewal, Borchardt believed himself capable of forging a sweet new style. To this end, he collaborated with Insel Verlag on two series of publications: a collection of texts from Romantic Germany, ca. 1750–1850, and a sixteen-volume library of medieval German texts. He would translate the latter, but not into Modern High German. After all, rendering them in Luther's German would have defeated the purpose of the project. Instead, he planned to compose an intelligible, medieval German. As to this choice, he wrote: "nur wer sie [das mittelalterliche Deutsch] uns zurückgewinnt, ist für die Aufgabe, die deutsche *Vita nuova* zu schaffen, reif" (only he who wins it [medieval German] back for us up to the task of creating a German *Vita nuova*) (GW, *Prosa I*, 324–325). In an ironic twist, Borchardt's inability to finish a novel, modeled on the *Vita nuova*, prompted editors at Insel to break their partnership. It was a disappointment, to be sure, but it prepared the way for Borchardt's eventual renewal of the German vernacular. It gave him the opportunity to finally translate the *Commedia*.

By Borchardt's account, the uniqueness of his translation was the result of a dramatic intellectual transformation. In 1904, he had begun to alternate between reading medieval German texts and, for the first time in earnest, the *Commedia*. The reading became an obsession that drove him to the recesses of early European literature: medieval Tuscan and Provencal, Middle High German and Old High German, Old French and Old Catalan, Middle English, and Old Norse. The intensity of his study gave him medieval eyes, which altered his view of the *Commedia*. "Ich hatte . . . ein Riesenwerk der Poesie seines literarischen Charakters entkleidet, indem ich aus seinem Nachfahren mich zu seinem Vorfahren gemacht hatte" (I had divested an enormous work of poetry of its literary character inasmuch as I made myself, its descendant, into its ancestor) (GW, *Prosa II*, 485). He claimed not to see the *Commedia* as Boccaccio did, but as Dante's predecessors might have, had they survived to read it. Few could make a similar claim.

Hyperbolic or not, Borchardt's reincarnation as a medieval reader suffused him with unusual authority—as a scholar and as a translator. For one thing, he was able to refine modern philologists' claim that the fourteenth century was a fruitless gap in the development of German (492). He depicted it instead as a crisis in the whole of European literary history, provoked by the floundering of Provençal, which had been intertwined with several European literary traditions (492). In this moment of crisis, a savior emerged in Italy. Dante's "rettende und gewaltige Tat" (salvific and powerful deed) may not have been comprehended until the age of Romanticism, but in the fourteenth century, it established Italy as a "geistiges Festland" (intellectual terra firma) (504). Germany lacked such a savior. Luther had only cobbled together an Esperanto that severed Germans from the language of their forebears (GW, *Reden* 248). The language of Borchardt's translation, more than two decades in the making, was an almost unthinkable attempt to rewrite this history. He imagined his translation would fill the gap of the fourteenth century as the *Commedia* had for Italy:

> Wie das heiße Blut hinsagt, es könne für die Geliebte stehlen, mit solchen Blicken, um ihm für mein Vaterland etwas uns zu Unrecht Versagtes zu entwenden, las ich nun wieder Dante in einem dunklen Spiele, mir halb vortäuschend, Geschehenes

> könne noch ungeschehen gemacht werden, und Ungeschehenes immer noch geschehen. Fast ohne daß ich wollte oder es hindern konnte, . . . antwortete mein Ohr hier oder da auf einen Vers der Comedia deutsch. (GW, *Prosa II*, 506)
>
> (Just as hot-blooded passion whispers that one can steal for his lover, so it was that I read Dante in a secret game, envisioning I would take for my fatherland something that it had been unjustly denied. I half pretended to myself that things that had transpired could be undone, and that what had never transpired could still be actualized. Almost against my will, or my ability to hinder it, . . . my ear responded to this and that verse of the *Commedia* in German.)

Borchardt writes as if the translation came to him by providence. *Dante Deutsch*, the culmination of his medievalizing transformation, looks like the inexorable fulfillment of Germany's spiritual heritage.

Yet the sweet new style was anything but providential. It was the hard-won fruit of an immersion in the Middle Ages—and one might question just how sweet it was. Like George's Dante, it was a challenge to read. Consider, for example, the lines spoken to Dante in paradise by his ancestor, Cacciaguida:

"Unlauterm gewissen" sprach der teure,
    "durch eigen schanden und durch ander schindig,
    gelte immerhin dein sprechen ungeheure.
Dem ung'achtt, weder lügen halber lindig,
    sag alles dein Gesicht und ungescheuet:
    und lass sich kratzen wo ihn jückt, der grindig.
Denn, wie dein stimme ihnn schweret oder dräuet
    bei erst imbisse: leibhaftige nahrung
    beleibt nach ihr, alsbalde sie verdäuet." (GW, *Dantes Comedia Deutsch*, 394)

(Then [he] made reply: "A conscience overcast
    Or with its own or with another's shame,
    Will taste forsooth the tartness of thy word;
But ne'ertheless, all falsehood laid aside,
    Make manifest thy vision utterly,
    And let them scratch wherever is the itch;

For if thine utterance shall offensive be
At the first taste, a vital nutriment
'Twill leave thereafter, when it is digested.") (Longfellow)[22]

Whereas George's language had been identifiably modern (see below for comparison), Borchardt's sounded ancient. It represented what German might have sounded like had its medieval forms blossomed in the fourteenth century. It was an uncannily convincing artifice, conceived as a "Weiterschreibung, Umschreibung, organische Anpassung" (continuation, reformulation, organic assimiliation) (GW, *Prosa II*, 510). Hovering somewhere between medieval dialects and the standardized language of Luther, it had been drafted on the basis of Borchardt's exposure to dialects around Basel. It was a philological marvel, to be sure, as well as an act of resistance to the currents in nineteenth-century philology. With a spate of translations of Hartmann, Wolfram, Gottfried, et alia into Modern High German, modern scholars had entrenched the gulf between Germans and their roots. Borchardt's Dante was an effort to annihilate it.

In this respect, too, *Dante Deutsch* signified an unrealizable aspiration: the creation of a new mythology. Borchardt never wrote of his affair with Dante as a project of myth. He held fast to the rhetoric of historical time (if not to its concepts). *Dante Deutsch*, then, never bore the epithets of myth. Yet it ought not escape comprehension as such. Born of a desire to initiate "das größte Programm . . . seit den Anfängen der Romantik" (the greatest program . . . since the beginnings of Romanticism), it was the defining project in a life that was bent on realizing the ultimate aspirations of Early German Romanticism (GW, *Reden* 250). Like Romantic mythology, it endeavored to erase historical time and to realize a new present: an abolition of the interregnum that separated the nation from the golden age of its past. It was devoid of the language of reason and enlightenment—Borchardt saw them as anathema to the *Romantik*—but it aimed all the same at the spiritual-intellectual salvation of the *Volk*. It did so, moreover, by means of poetry. Yet, as in Hauptmann, the truly salvific instrument was not poetry per se, but language. Conceived by Romantics as a religion of the senses, an aesthetic garment for the ideas of reason, myth was now determined by the forms of language.

Borchardt's Dante was neither the success he had hoped for (how could it have been?) nor the failure one might expect. Praise arrived from unlikely corners. Made dizzy by George's translation, Karl Vossler wrote that Borchardt was unparalleled in his feel for the "sprachlichen Dichter-Pathos" (linguistic poet-pathos) of Dante.[23] Ernst Robert Curtius, despite an erstwhile proximity to the George-Kreis, highlighted the merits of Borchardt's translation and commentary.[24] It even earned a review in T. S. Eliot's *Criterion* (1927), despite the solipsism of its national focus.[25] Borchardt's project retains significance today for the theory and history of translation, but it looks less like a landmark than a curio.[26] Despite lofty ambitions, Borchardt seems to have intuited such a fate: in a pre-emptive response to the public's eventual bewilderment, he had declared himself in league with the dead, not the living (GW, *Prosa II*, 520). The public would not be the arbiter of his success.

Ideals carried Borchardt only so far. Tragic exigency caught up with the impecunious German Jew who promoted a conservative revolution. In 1933, as anti-Semitic legislation made it nearly impossible for him to publish, his translation took on new meaning. Conceived as a lifeline for Germans' dormant Romanticism, it became a lifeline for its author—or so it looked to be. Borchardt tried deploying the translation to secure his fate in Italy. Having won an audience with Mussolini, he presented it to him as a gift. Mussolini could not read its German, but he deciphered the prefatory pages, where Borchardt had composed an "Ehrentafel" (table of honor) to venerable Germans who had advanced the study of Dante: Augustus Wilhelm Schlegel, Johann von Sachsen, Schelling, Hegel, Karl Witte, Alfred Bassermann, Friedrich Schlosser, Adolf Gaspary, Vossler, and George. Mussolini marveled: "Und sie alle Dantisten!" (And all of them *Dantisti*!) to which Borchardt replied, "Wir sind ein Volk von Dantisten" (We are a people of *Dantisti*).[27] It is a claim whose sincerity is complicated by the "Ehrentafel" itself. Less a *Volk* than a lineage, the paratext to *Dante Deutsch* represents Borchardt as the final heir of A. W. Schlegel, his translation the crowning achievement of German Romanticism. He had conspicuously surpassed the position of Stefan George. Along with the plea to Mussolini, the act of self-promotion indicates the fraught stakes of Dante in the century since the birth of the *Frühromantik*. In addition to a new mythology, Borchardt seemed to promise—to those who would have it—a myth of the self. Stefan George would have both.

A DANTE AMONG *DANTISTEN*

The early literature of the George-Kreis is littered with unsettling comparisons of George to Dante. Unsettling because, even down to physiognomic minutiae, George's peers saw a fateful unity between Dante and their Meister. Consider, for example, Karl Bauer's portrait of Dante, to which he has assigned the features of George (figure 5.1).

fig. 5.1. Karl Bauer, Portrait of Dante with Features of Stefan George, 1918. Stefan George Archiv in the Württembergische Landesbibliothek, Stuttgart.

Among the earliest to make such a comparison was Marie von Bunsen, who witnessed George's first public reading at the Lepsius salon in 1897. Not only might George's manner induce one to imagine that, like Dante, he had been to Hell and back; his profile also bore a striking resemblance to the depiction of Dante in Giotto's fresco in the Bargello chapel of Florence, she pointed out.[28] Similar comparisons were repeated frequently by members of the Kreis, as well as by outsiders—like Bunsen—who came into contact with George. Robert Boehringer once wrote that the hunch in the back of his aged Meister reminded him of how Boccaccio had written of the same feature in Dante. It was as if the poets' heads weighed too heavily to hold them upright.[29] George's publisher, Georg Bondi, described a time when he and his wife glimpsed George and Gundolf from afar; he said to her, "Entweder kommen dort Dante und Vergil oder George und Gundolf" (Either that's Dante and Virgil on their way, or George and Gundolf).[30] These observations reinforce the truth of an insight we noted earlier: by a certain point, the textual corpus of George looked inseparable from Dante. That linkage now encompassed his actual corpus, as well.

Indubitably, George's resemblance to Dante was encouraged. The comparisons of the poets, which agglomerate to a mass of apocrypha, reinforce a vision of George that was advanced in the public scholarship of his disciples: the poet as the judge of the age. Foremost among such heralds was Friedrich Gundolf, a superstar of the academy, whose bestselling study of Goethe paved the way for a monograph on George.[31] There, in a chapter on George's origins, Gundolf brings a discussion of the poet's formative intellectual influences to a rhetorical crescendo, explaining that in Dante George had found "das erhabene Gleichnis seines eigenen Berufs und bis ins Körperliche hinein der eigenen Art" (the sublime likeness of his own calling and of his own type—even in the body) (53). That is, quite apart from the poetry, George learned the art of *being* a poet from Dante. It was from him that George had acquired the stylized habitus that shaped his life and governed the Kreis. Gundolf's characterization, which we may assume George shared, emerges from Dante's status as an exile:

> Der richtende Seher . . . der erschütterte Minner mit der neugeweihten Sprache, allfühlend und unbestechlich, glühend und gerecht, hassend aus Liebe und verachtend aus Ehrfurcht, einsam und mißkannt, doch stolz in der Fülle des Herzens, der einzigen Sendung gewiß—dies hehre Gesicht leitete ihn von früh mit leiser Zauberkraft, wie nur das geheimverwandte und das unerreichbare Wunschbild uns leiten können. (52–53)

> (The judging visionary . . . the shattered singer with newly consecrated language, all-feeling and incorruptible, fiery and just,

> hateful and contemptuous from his love and his reverence, lonesome and misunderstood, but proud in the fullness of his heart, certain of his one mission—this noble visage led him from early on with quiet, magical force, as only mysterious and unattainable ideals can lead us.)

This is a vision of the poet not as a dandy, as one was wont to regard George around 1900. Instead, it is a promulgation of Dante's—and by extension, of George's—prophetic-poetic mission to consecrate a holy new language. Maintaining an arm's length from the world, he could use this language to judge it.

George was the impetus for such comparisons. As with the utterances of his disciples, his stylization after Dante ran a gamut from physical resemblance to poetic self-understanding. It encompassed, too, most of his poetic projects in the twentieth century. He had learned Italian as an adolescent, and probably read Dante early on, but his identification with him first surfaced in the *Commedia* translations. He ascribed prodigious significance to them: "Soviel ist gewiss dass jezt ein toter schatz vom grössten reichtum gehoben ist" (This much is certain: a dead treasure of the greatest value has been raised).[32] He viewed it as formative for the German language, which is to say, the project shared an affinity with Dante's poetic-linguistic renewal.[33] That such an affinity was felt on the level of his person is evident from the manner in which he recorded his translations, as if they were illuminated medieval manuscripts—in blue and red ink, with an occasional initial majuscule and marginal adornment.[34] George's identification with Dante entailed that the *Commedia*, along with a handful of other texts, became required reading for newcomers to the Kreis.[35] More explicit signs of his Dantean transformation appeared in the years of his work on the translations. In 1904, he attended a masque of poets in the underworld and dressed as Dante. There, too, he read from his *Commedia*.[36] Later, he sat for portraiture studies in which his and Dante's profiles were compared.[37] The record of his approximations to Dante is vast. If Hauptmann wished to supersede Dante, and Borchardt wished to possess Dante, then George wished to be Dante.

Though his acts of emulation spanned decades, there is a pregnant moment from which the Dantean mythology of Stefan George was born. In 1907, he published *Der Siebente Ring* (*The Seventh Ring*), his largest volume of poems and an inflection point in his stylization as a poet. Until then, he had been known as a dandy. Tutored by French symbolists, he was known as an aesthete who kept his distance from the world. By reckoning with his age, and with his contemporaries, the new volume struck a new pose. Indeed, it opens with a cycle of *Zeitgedichte* (*Poems of Our Times*), in which George curates poems on actual personages: himself, for example, as well as Goethe, Nietzsche, Boecklin, and Dante, among others. In the first of these, "Das Zeitgedicht" (The poem of our age), he speaks as himself for ostensibly the first time in his oeuvre. His voice evinces a prophetic tone the likes of which is not discernible in his earlier poetry. In this voice, he chides the public for misunderstanding him as an aesthete:

Ihr meiner zeit genossen kanntet schon
Bemasset schon und schaltet mich—ihr fehltet.
Als ihr in lärm und wüster gier des lebens
Mit plumpem tritt und rohem finger ranntet:
Da galt ich für den salbentrunknen prinzen
Der sanft geschaukelt seine takte zählte
In schlanker anmut oder kühler würde ·
In blasser erdenferner festlichkeit. (SGSW 6/7:6)[38]

(You my contemporaries knew me already
Measured me already, chastised me—you erred.
When you, clamoring with savage appetite for life,
Ran with clumsy step and coarse finger:
Then was I deemed the chrism-drunk prince,
Who swayed gently and counted his beats
In slim grace or cool dignity ·
In wan festivity far from this earth.)

Years later, Robert Boehringer characterized the assessment of the young George as an aesthete as one more mark of fate he shared with Dante, whose *Vita nuova* belied the religious-political force of the *Commedia*.[39] Yet the classification of George's early poetry as aestheticizing was not far from the truth. It just happened to contrast with the image that George began to assume after 1901 (As if anticipating this objection, George writes: "Ihr sehet wechsel · doch ich tat das gleiche" (You see change · but I did the same) (SGSW 6/7:7). Thus in the same poem he is quick to allude to a youth full of "rauhen Werken" (rough deeds) and "qualen" (torments) of which the public knew nothing. He had lured readers to a "wunderberge" (magic mountain) and sung enchanting tones, only to seize the fanfare and lead their way "wieder ins gedräng" (back into the crush), as if charging into battle. The pugnacious rhetoric overshadows something more significant: for the first time, George had begun to reckon with his age.

Whence the impetus? The volume's second poem presents a clue: "Dante und das Zeitgedicht" (Dante and the poem of our age). Of the various *Zeitgedichte*, it is the only one in which the subject of the poem speaks for himself. George felt closer to Dante than to any other poet; presumably, it was not so far a stretch to conjure his voice. Indeed there are clear tonal affinities between the two voices of the *Zeitgedichte*: like George, Dante emerges as a battle-hardened hero. Amid the disgrace of "falsche führer" (false leaders), he describes a mission to help where "das heil erschien" (salvation appeared) (SGSW 6/7:8). Like George, he is misunderstood: righteousness earns him only exile and impoverishment. The public's failure to understand his person applies in equal force to his poetry. When his poetry has finally won renown, the public reserves its acclamation for the *Inferno*. It marks them as fools:

> O toren!
> Ich nahm aus meinem herd ein scheit und blies—
> So ward die hölle · doch des vollen feuers
> Bedurft ich zur bestrahlung höchster liebe
> Und zur verkündigung von sonn und stern. (SGSW 6/7:9)
>
> (Oh fools!
> I took from my hearth a spark and blew—
> Thus appeared the inferno · but it took the full fire
> To radiate the highest love
> And to proclaim the sun and stars.)

Like George, the unity of whose poetry the public fails to apprehend, Dante is the victim of perpetual misreading. Ironically, George may have been one such reader: he translated fewer episodes from *Paradiso* than from either of the poem's other canticles. But the point of the *Zeitgedicht*, as is evident elsewhere in his fixation on Dante, was to seize the Italian poet and wield him in the "Geisterkrieg" of which Gundolf had written. With Dante in hand, he was able to mow down his contemporaries.

George's position vis-à-vis the present age marked an important departure from his earlier poetry. He was never a popular poet, to be sure, but in the preface to *Das Jahr der Seele* (*The Year of the Soul*) (1897), he had struck a posture of identification. To his readers, he confessed: "selten sind sosehr wie in diesem buch ich und du die selbe seele" (seldom have you and I been the same soul so much as we are in this book) (SGSW 4:7). One decade later, *Der siebente Ring* reversed that posture and proclaimed a world of difference between the poet and his age. The curious presence of the *Zeitgedichte*, an uncommon genre that would seem to suggest the poet's immersion in the present, does just the opposite: it stages the scene for a sequence of judgments that expose the poet's remove from his contemporaries. Some were laudatory and some were critical, but together they had the effect of confirming what Gundolf later wrote: George was, like Dante, the judge of his age.

If Dante supplied rhetorical instruments to write of the age, they were useful only because George believed himself to have transcended it. This conviction lay at the heart of *Der siebente Ring*. The new volume was the realization of a new mythology that came to govern the Kreis for years to come. It was the gospel of a new god, who George believed had graced his cenacle with its presence. He proclaimed to his disciples:

> In eurem schleppenden und kalten jahre
> Brach nun ein frühling neuer wunder aus ·
> Mit blumiger Hand · mit schimmer um die haare
> Erschien ein gott und trat zu euch ins haus. (SGSW 6/7:99)
>
> (Into your sluggish, cold year
> There broke through a spring of new marvels ·
> With florid hand · with a shimmer around his hair
> There appeared a god and he came to visit you.)

The advent of the new god—an echo of Hölderlin's Dionysus—marks a transfiguration of time: it transforms the winter of the present to an eternal spring.[40] Repeatedly, George represents the god's coming as the advent of a new spring: "Nun wird es wieder lenz" (It's spring again) (SGSW 6/7:92). Organic and biological metaphors permeate George's poetry, but here, and throughout the volume, they denote the inbreaking of mythic time. The interminable waiting of the present has, miraculously, reached its conclu-

fig. 5.2. George (*second from left*) in Dante Costume, with Arm around Maximilian Kronberger, 1904. Stefan George Archiv in the Württembergische Landesbibliothek, Stuttgart.

sion (SGSW 6/7:90). Images of circles, ubiquitous in the ornate illustrations of the volume, illustrate the point: the line of history has curved round to its origins. The age of myth is at hand.

The volume's repertoire of intricate symbols belies, however, the very real origins of what became its foundational myth. It emerged from George's relationship to a teenage devotee, Maximilian Kronberger, who died of meningitis just days after his sixteenth birthday in 1904. Kronberger esteemed George as a mentor and tutor, but there was something unseemly about their contact. George brought the boy to the poets' masque where he dressed as Dante (figure 5.2), for example, and he seems to have had him photographed in the nude.[41] Kronberger's parents harbored reservations about George.[42] After all, their first meeting in 1902 occurred only after George, a full twenty years the boy's senior, had stalked him for several days through the streets of Munich.[43] In short: their encounter was staged, their relationship characterized by artifice. One meaningful sign of this is legible in a memorial of George to the boy:

> Wir hatten eben die mittägliche höhe unsres lebens überschritten und wir bangten beim blick in unsre nächste zukunft . . . als die plötzliche ankunft eines einzigen menschen [Kronberger] in der allgemeinen zerrüttung uns das vertrauen wiedergab und uns mit dem lichte neuer verheissungen erfüllte. (SGSW 17:62)
>
> (We had just passed the midpoint of our life and were anxious at glimpsing our immediate future . . . when the sudden arrival of a single person [Kronberger] in this general disarray infused us once again with faith and filled us with the light of new prospects.)

Just thirty-three at the time of the meeting, George had not in fact passed the midpoint of his life, as the Bible measures it (Psalm 89 [90]:10). More likely, he intended to align his biography with the life of Dante, whose *Commedia* began, after all, with a middle-aged pilgrim in crisis (*Inf.* 1.1–3). Indeed, even the manipulation of age was a device that Dante had employed in the *Vita nuova* for poetic purposes. He claimed to have met Beatrice at the age of nine and to have seen her for the second time at age eighteen. In Dante's Ptolemaic cosmology, these multiples signified a connection to the third planet from earth (i.e., Venus, the goddess of love). In the memorial to Kronberger, George's manipulation of dates is no less deliberate. As a memorial to his deceased beloved, it replicates the function of the *Vita nuova*.

Yet the fullest formal expression of Kronberger's centrality to the Kreis came, quite literally, in the center of *Der siebente Ring*. In the volume of seven cycles, the central cycle, "Maximin," bears Kronberger's name and is devoted to the proclamation of his advent among the members of the Kreis. One of their number, Ernst Morwitz, surmised that the volume's cycles were modeled on the concentric rings of a tree, suggesting that "Maximin" was integral to the growth of the circle's mythology.[44] There was no ambiguity, at any rate, as to how George evaluated the boy: "Dem bist du kind · dem freund. / Ich seh in dir den Gott / Den schauernd ich erkannt / Dem meine andacht gilt" (To him you are a child · to him a friend. / I see in you the god / Whom shivering I recognized / To whom I am devoted) (SGSW 6/7:90). Kronberger was a deity in the flesh.

Together with the history of the affair, George's fusion of religious adoration and eroticism presents an interpretive challenge: how to approach a forty-year-old poet's deification of a dead Gymnasiast, particularly when its impetus was undeniably erotic? Presumably, the question did not occur to George, whose poetry was addressed largely to an audience of obsequious disciples. One critical approach would involve situating George's treatment of Kronberger in a tradition of poets who use religious language to exalt their lovers. There are prominent examples of such a tradition: Dante and Beatrice, Petrarch and Laura, or Shakespeare and the addressee of his sonnets.[45] However, such an approach fails to reckon with two striking phenomena: (1) the literalness of George's deification and (2) the promulgation of that deification to a circle of men who knew the deity. Another tack, adopted by Ernst Morwitz, would effectively de-sexualize the affair. Morwitz thus cited a tradition of English commemorative poetry based on platonic male relationships, explaining its spiritual proximity to Germans ("wohl einer germanischen Grundeinstellung entsprechend") (corresponding probably to some standard Germanic attitude), and places George among the likes of Milton and Tennyson.[46] If the latter of these approaches seems disingenuous, and the former inadequate, it is because each of them overlooks the mythicized homoeroticism of the "Maximin" poems.

Esotericism enabled George, who once said that Thomas Mann knew nothing of the silence in which homosexual love was to be enveloped, to promulgate a homoerotic poetics.[47] The two formal symbols of *Der siebente Ring*, the circle and the seven, bear this out. The ubiquitous images of the circle instantiate the esoteric quality of the poems by presenting readers at each turn with the shape of closure. The cycles are self-contained, they do not interact with external phenomena, and they constitute each other's existence.[48] This reflexivity finds visual expression in the lavish adornment of the book by George's friend, Melchior Lechter, who prefaced each of the seven cycles with illustrations of a particular circle, the ouroboros (i.e., the mythical snake found in alchemical texts that consumes its tail) (figure 5.3). Whether George knew that A. W. Schlegel had once described Dante's *Commedia* as being circumscribed by "d[er] ringförmige[n] Schlange der Ewigkeit" (the ringformed serpent of eternity) is hard to say (KAV 2/1:153). No doubt it would have resonated with his self-stylization in the volume.

The volume's esotericism depends likewise on a program of numerology that is centered on the number seven. Published in 1907, *Der siebente Ring* was George's seventh volume of poetry, appearing seven years after his previous book of poems, seven years before his next, and twenty-one years

fig. 5.3. Ouroboroi in *Der siebente Ring*, 1907. Beinecke Rare Book and Manuscript Library, Yale University.

before his final volume of poems.[49] The collection consists of seven cycles. Each of them comprises a number of poems that is a multiple of the number seven. The book's centerpiece, "Maximin," is a seven-letter contraction of the name *Maximilian*. Careful readers have responded to the numbers with a dose of skepticism: the number functions as a red herring that can symbolize nearly anything.[50] There is likely some truth to this. On the other hand, keeping in mind how intently focused George's production was on the audience of his disciples, the semiotic range of this heavy-handed numerology narrows. Lorenzo Bianchi and Claude David suggested insightfully, for example, that the formulation of a seventh ring might well refer to either the seventh ring of Dante's *Purgatorio* or *Paradiso*.[51] There is good reason to take seriously this thesis, for in his later poetry, George's preoccupation with numerology gestures more pointedly toward Dante. His next volume, *Der Stern des Bundes* (*The Star of the Covenant*), for example, was structured as a triptych of one hundred poems, mimicking the one hundred cantos of the *Commedia*'s three canticles. As noted already, George's manipulation of his age in the memorial to Kronberger imitated a Dantean practice of numerology. In short, there are cogent reasons to think that George's numerology derives from the *Commedia*.

That does not mean there is not further light to shed on the semiotic field in which his esoteric program unfolds. By settling on Dante as its source, the text opens itself to further possibilities. Indeed, it yields at least one compelling new possibility: namely, that George's sevens are an allusion to the seventh ring of the *Inferno*. It is precisely there, after all, in the seventh circle of Hell, where Dante encounters not just sinners of a broadly sexual nature (as on Mount Purgatory), but sinners who have engaged in male–male love. The most prominent among them is Brunetto Latini, a former teacher of Dante. Before he recognizes his pupil, Latini eyes him up and down as men are wont to do "sotto nuova luna" (under the new moon), grabbing his hem and exclaiming, "Qual maraviglia!" (What a marvel!) (*Inf.* 15.19–24). When he realizes he has accosted his former student, Latini exclaims, "O figliuol mio" (Oh my son) (*Inf.* 15.31), an epithet that he repeats six lines later. Before the end of the canto, Dante reflects on Latini's "buona imagine paterna" (kind paternal image) (*Inf.* 15.83). The focus on Latini's paternal character is of special significance with respect to his sexuality, for it suggests how—despite its reproductive limitations—it could generate progeny. To that end, for example, Dante says to Latini, " m'insegnavate come l'uom s'etterna" (you used to teach me how man makes himself eternal) and promises in return to narrate Latini's message for eternity, thus immortalizing him in the *Commedia* (*Inf.* 15.85). The relationship is thus inverted, with Dante, the son, now authoring an eternal life for Latini. The son becomes the father to his father.

The pertinence of the episode to the self-understanding of the George-Kreis is unmistakable: in such a *Männerbund* (men's confederation), where members were bound by a spiritual ethos, the matter of self-propagation was of dire importance. George, who cultivated multiple circles throughout Germany, laid special emphasis on the recruitment of youthful men. In the circle's pedagogical texts, the urgency of members' self-propagation was laid out clearly. Gundolf's *Gefolgschaft und Jüngertum* (*Fealty and Discipleship*), for example, directed disciples to be the "stoff den er (der Meister) beseelt: seines grossen atems umsetzung · vervielfältigung . . . samen seiner kraft" (material that [the master] ensouls: permutation of his great breath · multiplication . . . seed of his force).[52] In a transformation of the Christian Eucharist, Gundolf wrote that George's blood was to be taken up (*aufgenommen*) in disciples' being (*dasein*) and passed on "in die noch starre oder leere welt" (into the still rigid or empty world) (110). Such a form of reproductive surrogacy enabled George to realize his *geistiges Reich* (spiritual kingdom) in an exclusively male process of self-siring. In Dante's depiction of Brunetto Latini, George had discovered an apt model for such a singular means of reproduction: the male poet, Latini, fathers a son, Dante, who in turn reproduces the father for eternity via his poetry. Even in his translation of this episode from the *Commedia*, George renders "Ser Brunetto" as "Meister Brunetto," awarding him the honorific so reverentially used by George's disciples to address him (SGSW 10/11:28).[53]

Like Latini, whose student could extend his lineage, George used Kronberger as a vessel in which to reproduce himself. In "Einverleibung" (Incorporation), a poem in the central ring of *Der siebente Ring*, George describes himself as the "geschöpf nun eignen sohnes" (creation of my own son) (SGSW 6/7:109).[54] At the end of the poem, he reiterates the inversion in an overladen botanical metaphor, writing there, "Ich empfange von dem keime" (I receive from the germ). This paradox was expressed again, seven years later in *Der Stern des Bundes*, where George confessed: "Ergeben steh ich vor des rätsels macht / Wie er mein kind ich meines kindes kind" (I stand humbly before the power of the mystery / Of how he is my child, I the child of my child) (SGSW 8:14). The representation of Kronberger in *Der siebente Ring* thus functions as a means of transforming a pederastic relationship into a productive one in which the goal of self-propagation is achieved. The special authority associated with this uniquely male reproductive ability was magnified by the deification of Kronberger, which underscored George's divine sonship.

The mythic advent of Maximin shored up the overarching myth under which the George-Kreis understood its identity: the spiritual Reich of a secret Germany. When George published *Der Stern des Bundes*, the new volume read like the handbook of a secret society whose existence had been occasioned by Maximin's incarnation. The first cycle of poems, "Eingang" (Entry), explored the effect of the deity on the composition of the circle. When Maximin was present, the disciples did not know that they knelt before the one in whom the "geburt des gottes sich vollzog" (birth of a god was fulfilled) (SGSW 8:9). Now, they recognized him as the *Stern* of their *Bund*, who through his incarnation had banished their darkness and quelled their longing (SGSW 8:9). So transcendent was Maximin that, in his name (*Gott*), George could write in the volume's closing poem, "Gottes land ist uns bestimmt / Gottes krieg ist uns entzündet" (God's land is destined for us / God's war has been sparked for us) (114). George had used *Der siebente Ring* to unite the circle in a common mythology; *Der Stern des Bundes* exploited that mythology and articulated the political objectives of the new spiritual state. In addition to supplying George the means of peopling his male *Reich*, the deification of Maximilian Kronberger granted divine authorization to its fantasies: the *Geisterkrieg* of which Gundolf had written would be launched under the aegis of the new god.

Unsurprisingly, Dante does not disappear from the increasingly misanthropic posture of the Kreis; instead, George conjures once again the combative Dante whom he had already exploited. He summoned the authority of that Dante for his notorious poem of 1917, "Der Krieg" (The war). It is a long, ugly piece in which George maintains his indifference to the global conflict: "Was ist IHM mord von hunderttausenden / Vorm mord am Leben selbst?" (What matters to HIM the murder of hundreds of thousands / When life itself is murdered?) To be clear: the figure of indifference is George, the *Seher* of the same stanza, whose spiritual aloofness rendered him unfeeling in the face of his contemporaries' destruction. What mattered their deaths to the poet of the secret Germany, the man who was building a spiritual empire? The balefulness of the poem was no secret to the poet. He justified it as prophecy, drawing on the *Commedia* to do so. Thus, in a pre-emptive authorization for the cruelty to follow, he appends an epigraph that is spoken to Dante by his ancestor, a twelfth-century crusader:

> . . . WEM DAS GEWISSEN DROHE
> MIT EIGNER ODER FREMDER SCHANDE DRUCKE
> EMPFINDET DEINE WORTE WOL ALS ROHE.
>
> DEM OHNGEACHTET HALT DICH FREI VON SCHMUCKE
> UND GANZ ERÖFFNE DAS VON DIR GESCHAUTE.
> LASS ES GESCHEHN DASS WEN ES BEISST SICH JUCKE.
>
> WENN AUCH BESCHWERLICH WERDEN DEINE LAUTE
> BEIM ERSTEN KOSTEN: WIRD LEBENDIGE ZEHRUNG
> MAN DRAUS ENTNEHMEN WENN MAN SIE VERDAUTE.
> DANTE · GÖTTLICHE KOMÖDIE · HIMMEL XVII
>
> (. . . ONE WHOSE CONSCIENCE THREATENS
> WITH ITS OWN OR WITH ANOTHER'S IGNOMINY
> WILL FEEL YOUR WORDS TO BE HARSH.
>
> NONETHELESS KEEP YOURSELF FREE OF ORNAMENT
> AND LAY OUT IN ITS ENTIRETY WHAT YOU HAVE SEEN.
> MAY HE WHO IS BITTEN FEEL THE ITCH.
>
> EVEN IF YOUR TONES ARE TROUBLESOME
> AT THE FIRST TASTE: LIVING NOURISHMENT
> WILL BE TAKEN FROM THEM, WHEN THEY ARE DIGESTED.
> DANTE. DIVINE COMEDY. PARADISE XVII.)[55]

Dante's ancestor, Cacciaguida, speaks these words in the sphere of Mars (*Par.* 17.124–132). His speech, along with a record of similar encounters, contributed to the persuasive realism of Dante's prophecy. In this case, that prophecy appears sanctioned by the heavens. Having long regarded himself as an oracular figure, George adopted the same rhetorical posture and deployed it in a pulverizing takedown of his enemies. Given that his enemies were simply bourgeois philistines, and not political opponents who had actually exiled him, it is difficult to regard his *Sendung* (mission) (Gundolf's word) as in any way equivalent to that of Dante.

Yet this did not stop disciples from enlisting. In fact, the linkage of George to Dante remained a selling point for proselytizers like Gundolf throughout the 1920s. Between 1922 and 1925, for example, Gundolf delivered readings of George's Dante translations to auditoriums with as many as seven hundred auditors.[56] Each reading came with a word of introduction, in which Gundolf acknowledged the fervor of contemporary interest in the Florentine poet, declaring that "Dante geht uns heute näher an als je zuvor . . . dringlicher, herzlicher als er selbst die Romantiker anging" (Dante is more relevant to us than ever before . . . more urgent, more precious than he was even to the Romantics).[57] He explained to his audience that, for several reasons, the age was ripe for Dante: the war had primed the German youth to ponder their fate; Nietzsche had fended off the philistinism of the nineteenth century, and most importantly, Stefan George had renewed the poetic language of Germans. He displayed a "mysterious attunement" to Dante: "Unter den Ewigen fordert keiner strenger von uns als Dante und kein Heutiger hat seinen Anspruch so vernommen, erfüllt und erneuert wie George" (Among the timeless there is none who demands as much of us as Dante. No man of today has taken up that demand, fulfilled it, and renewed it like George has) (39). Rhetoric of this sort, dating back to the 1890s, persisted if it did not indeed proliferate in George's later years. Karl Bauer, a painter and acquaintance of the poet, believed the physiognomic resemblance to Dante only intensified as George aged.[58]

Neither the centrality of myth to the George-Kreis nor its devotion to Dante is a secret: it is time to recognize their bond. After all, it was also no secret to the members of the Kreis or to their contemporaries. Young acolytes of the circle, including Ernst Robert Curtius and Kurt Hildebrandt, reflected on the matter in their later years. Each of them identified a mythic enterprise that began with *Der siebente Ring* and extended into the subsequent volumes of George's poetry. Writing that the fantastical in Dante belonged to the terrain of myth, Curtius asserted that "ein Dante verwandter Herrschafts- und Formwille" (a Dante-related will to govern and shape) drove the last three volumes of George's poetry.[59] For Hildebrandt, it was the myth-building enterprise that lured him to the circle in the first place. Born of the encounter with Kronberger, sealed in the poetry of the *Bund*, and climaxing in the idea of a new Reich, the circle's mythology represented a new manifestation of Dante's *Weltmythos*.[60] Even in the early days of the Kreis, a contemporary like Rudolf Alexander Schröder, a translator and friend of Borchardt, could see what was taking place. He wrote to Hofmannsthal about the use of Christian mythology in George, warning that it had only once found grand poetic expression, in Dante, and "dieses ungeheuerliche, ja unmenschliche Werk (*Commedia*) sollte gewiss in unsern Zeiten keine Nachahmer finden, oder Leute, die ohne zu wissen was sie thun mit dem gefährlichen Feuer seiner Symbole spielen" (This enormous, indeed unhuman work should certainly find no imitators in our age, or people who play unknowingly with the dangerous fire of its symbols).[61] Such fire could not have burned George, Hildebrandt believed, for fire was the Meister's "Weltsubstanz" (world substance), comparable not just to Heraclitus's elemental fire, nor to the lover's fever in Plato's *Phaedrus*, but also to the purifying fire of the *paradiso terrestre*.[62] George forged his mythology in the fires of Dante.

Schröder's comments on the untimeliness of George's Dante recall the observations from the outset of the chapter. Myth is never of the present. The generation of its presence relies on manipulations of time, which rely in turn on rites and symbols of purification and renewal. Dante figured among the latter of these for George, the telos of whose myth was never Dante himself, but rather an extratemporal alternative to the intellectual-spiritual dissolution of the present—a *geheimes Deutschland*, a *geistiges Reich*. This meant that, writing in 1965, when for all intents and purposes that myth had evaporated, Hildebrandt could still cling to its meaning:

> Bleibt Dantes Werk nicht der größte Mythos des Mittelalters, obwohl Dante in seinem geistig-politischen Werk vollkommen gescheitert ist? Ohne das Mythische, die Transparenz des Ewigen, ist nicht nur das Dichterische auf eine geringere, belletristische Ebene gerückt, ist das Wesentliche in Georges Dichtung unverständlich. (14)
>
> (Does Dante's work not remain the greatest myth of the Middle Ages, even though Dante failed utterly in his spiritual-political work? Without the mythical, without the sheen of the eternal, not only does the poetic in George move to a lowlier, belletristic level but the essence of his poetry becomes incomprehensible.)

His habitus, his prophecies, his judgments, his language, his model of self-propagation—to George, these all attested to the distance Dante maintained from his age. They were vital instruments in the creation of his mythology.

CHAPTER SIX

Thomas Mann and the Demythologization of Dante

OUR ITINERARY BEGAN with an acknowledgment of Dante's pride—and the insistence that to recognize it as such is not a mark of ungenerous reading. That observation, together with the introduction's survey of debates around the *Commedia*, underscored how uniquely interwoven are the poet and his poem. The force of that truth has been borne out by the waystations where we have sojourned. A mythology around the model of the *Commedia* became engrossed in the matter of its legitimation. Sometimes the poetry languished ("Das himmlische Bild") and sometimes it flourished (*Heinrich von Ofterdingen*), but almost always, its creation went hand in glove with a mythologization of the poet.

The troubling outcome of this shift in mythological foci is clear: it thrust a project of enlightenment into darkness. The heirs of the *Romantik*—those who would rehabilitate it in the new century—seized not on the project of reason but on the Romantics' mythologization of that very project. Thus Dante, who gave no reason to believe he conceived of his poem in the terms of myth, persisted as a mainstay in the quest to realize it. Now, though, rather than take its cues from reason, the project was governed by preoccupations with language, rhetoric, and form. Fascism and Nazism were not the results of such quests, but their proximity, which is conspicuous in Hauptmann, Borchardt, and George, is remarkable. Each of these rehabilitations of Dantean myth lent intellectual and cultural legitimacy to the authoritarianism that emerged in the first half of the twentieth century.

The first and perhaps only person who recognized the centrality of Dante to such authoritarian myths was Thomas Mann. That he should be the one to arrive at that conclusion makes a certain sense: he was a critic (and friend) of Gerhart Hauptmann and Stefan George. Mann's early opposition to democracy (cf. *Betrachtungen eines Unpolitischen*) (*Reflections of a Nonpolitical Man*, 1918) is no secret, but neither is his conversion to and embrace of it. That conversion to democracy is at the root of his criticism of Stefan George, with whom he otherwise shared important similarities. Above all, they were gay writers who, despite political differences, believed during the Weimar era that Germany's future depended on a homoerotic inflection of society. Through a hermeticized poetics, George spiritualized the features of male–male love for the structure of his *geistiges Reich*. Mann, on the other hand, spoke openly about the significance of male relationships for the "official" Germany as it came to emerge in the new republic. His 1922 speech "Von deutscher Republik" (On the German Republic), delivered on the occasion of Gerhart Hauptmann's birthday, appealed to two poets, Novalis and Walt Whitman, and argued that it was love—and "nicht in irgend einem verblasenen, anämischen, asketisch mitleidigen Verstande" (not in some nebulous, anemic, ascetically sympathetic sense)—that constituted the basis of those poets' humanity and socialism (GkFA 15.1:550). The love that imbued the humanity of their political approach, he goes so far as to say, was that which one found in the phallic emblem of Whitman's *Calamus* poems.[1] Mann did not share George's reservations. In fact, he argued that erotic love generates the bonds between the members of the democratic body. He insisted even on the corporeal dimension of this love, expressing it alternately as "Sympathie mit dem Organischen" (sympathy with the organic) and "Biologie als Verliebtheit" (Biology as passion) (551). This focus on the body as organic matter culminates in the pronouncement (of Whitman's claim) that the body is not part of the soul—it is the soul. And its king, no, its president—Mann corrects himself—is Eros (553). George had sublimated homosexuality in esoteric symbols, but Mann openly proposed a republic of erotic connections among men.

Clearly, these opposed visions were a source of tension—political, aesthetic, and personal. Mann understood his ethics of eroticism to emanate from a democratic ideal of equality. To witness the relations among members of the George-Kreis, then, was to cognize a fundamentally different politics, which Mann acknowledged: "man sagt, daß Beziehungen solcher Art den geheimen Kitt monarchistischer Bünde bilden" (one says that relations like this form the mysterious cement of monarchical leagues) (554). Sublimation of this sort had no place in the new republic, which would thrive on eros (555). Any concept of social being that dismissed the body as readily as that of George's *Reich* could not fathom the corporeality of *Verliebt-*

heit. George's circle, in short, could not fathom democracy. Mann stopped short of launching a full-scale attack on the Kreis in the 1922 speech. He had friends among the circle.[2] Furthermore, why invite the sort of rejoinders that had mired Borchardt in controversy? The wisdom of another democratic writer, Mark Twain, seems to have applied: "Never wrestle with a pig. You both get dirty and the pig likes it."

Yet the speech on the Republic was by no means Mann's last word on the matter. The novel that won him the Nobel Prize, *Der Zauberberg* (*The Magic Mountain*, 1924), was a subtle but incisive appraisal of the undemocratic mythic cult of the Kreis.[3] Adopting the *Commedia* as an intertext, it co-opted George's weapons and turned them against him. Most conspicuously, the critique surfaces in the novel's replication of the idiosyncratic numerology that structured *Der siebente Ring*. To summarize, the novel is divided into seven chapters and spans seven years, 1907 to 1914. Each of the patients at the sanatorium eats at one of the seven tables in the refectory, and each of them takes his temperature for seven minutes every day. The band that performs at the sanatorium on Sundays plays seven-minute pieces. The romantic interest of Castorp, Clawdia Chauchat, resides in room number seven, while Castorp occupies room thirty-four, whose digits add up to seven. When they have sex, Castorp—whose name is seven letters long—is in "siebentem Himmel" (seventh heaven) (GkFA 5.1:932). The narrator notes that Castorp's circle of friends comprises seven people, though one of them, Naphta, commits suicide just before a duel held at seven o'clock in the morning. He was to square off against Ludovico Settembrini, whom Castorp at one point calls "Herr Septembrini," thus underscoring the number seven internal to Settembrini's name (90). The numerology that George had used to mystical effect is now repurposed: its mundane application to the lunchroom, to a daily medical procedure, to a grisly death, and above all, to a sexual encounter, inverts George's technique by vulgarizing it in a codification of the body's organic states, processes, and activities: consumption, sickness, death, and sex. Mann's description of Castorp's ecstasy in "siebentem Himmel" is especially artful, for besides instantiating the numerology, the formulation parodies precisely the spiritualization of sex. But it is not the most significant of the novel's sevens.

Herr Settembrini, a living embodiment of the numerology, is a decisive figure in Mann's critique of George. In him, we recognize Mann's effort to leverage the Dantean program of the George-Kreis. The Italian humanist traces his spiritual lineage back to, of all people, Brunetto Latini—the obscure scholar whose model of bodiless propagation had formed the basis of George's central mythical document, "Maximin."[4] In a description of his forefathers, Settembrini claims to represent the union of his grandfather's political activism and his father's learning, linking this combination of values with Brunetto Latini:

> Ob, fragte Settembrini, seine Zuhörer je von Herrn Brunetto gehört hätten, Brunetto Latini, Stadtschreiber von Florenz um 1250, der ein Buch über die Tugenden und die Laster geschrieben? Dieser Meister zuerst habe den Florentinern Schliff gegeben und sie das Sprechen gelehrt sowie die Kunst, ihre Republik nach den Regeln der Politik zu lenken. (243)

> (Had anyone, Settembrini asked his listeners, ever heard of Herr Brunetto, Brunetto Latini, chronicler of Florence in 1250, who had written a book about the virtues and vices? Apparently this master had first given the Florentines polish, having taught them speech as well as the art of guiding their republic according to the rules of politics.)

Repeated nearly verbatim at another juncture in the novel (535), the account emphasizes Settembrini's humanist heritage, his association with the West, and above all his connection to Dante's teacher. Settembrini so closely resembles Latini, a medieval encyclopedist, that he contributes regularly to an international encyclopedia. But he is a figure who, despite a sympathetic demeanor, often merits our skepticism. Conceiving himself as a "disembodied intellect"[5] Settembrini states in no uncertain terms that "innerhalb der Antithese von Körper und Geist bedeutet der Körper das böse, das teuflische Prinzip, denn der Körper ist Natur, und die Natur . . . ist böse" (in the antithesis of body and spirit, the body signifies the evil, the devilish principle, for the body is nature, and nature . . . is evil) (379). This outlook, antithetical to that of Mann, propels much of Settembrini's action. It leads to intense debates with his adversary, Leo Naphta, a Jewish Jesuit whose nickname as a boy, not incidentally, was *Leib* (body). It animates his scholarly work too, with Settembrini planning an international conference on the topic of cremation. Settembrini embodies the wish for disembodiment.

He is, accordingly, at odds with anything like an eroticism of the flesh. Indeed, he figures as a foil to Clawdia Chauchat, an alluring Russian patient who engages in illicit affairs. She and Settembrini enter the novel at nearly the same point, with the narrator alluding to their symbolic opposition:

> Was oder wer aber befand sich auf dieser anderen, dem Patriotismus, der Menschenwürde und der schönen Literatur entgegengesetzten Seite, wohin Hans Castorp sein Sinnen und Betreiben nun wieder lenken zu dürfen glaubte? Dort befand sich . . . Clawdia Chauchat,—schlaff, wurmstichig und kirgisenäugig. (245)
>
> (What or who found themselves on this other side, to which Hans Castorp believed he might now guide his thoughts and deeds? Who opposed patriotism, human dignity, and fine literature? There was . . . Clawdia Chauchat,—languid, worm-eaten, and Kyrgyz-eyed.)

Chauchat's sexuality is doubly significant: insofar as the narrative repeatedly configures her as a reincarnation of Pribislav Hippe, a boy who had attracted Castorp in his youth, her sexual encounter with Castorp represents a fulfillment of his homosexual desire. Chauchat affords the realization of a sensual eros.

At the moment of sharpest opposition between Settembrini's spiritualism and Chauchat's sensualism, the former appraises the sins of the latter by making recourse to Dante. Like George, whose appeal to Dante had sanctioned a practice of spiritual propagation, Settembrini invokes the *Commedia* to censure Castorp's carnal affair with Chauchat, a married woman. He admonishes his young friend: "Fürchten Sie nicht den Wirbelsturm des zweiten Höllenkreises, der die Fleischessünder prellt und schwenkt, die Unseligen, die Vernunft der Lust zum Opfer brachten?" (Don't you fear the cyclone of Hell's second circle, which shoots and tosses the carnal sinners, those unfortunate souls who sacrifice reason to lust?) (539). Settembrini alludes to the cyclones that whirl about the adulterers in the second circle of Dante's Hell. There Dante met Francesca, whose affair with Paolo had violated her matrimonial bond to Paolo's brother. She, her lover, and other adulterers now find themselves subjected to violent gusts, a contrapasso that signals their failures of constancy (*Inf.* 5). Castorp and Chauchat commit adultery too, but it is the carnal nature of their affair that prompts Settembrini's admonition: he refers to the inhabitants of the second circle not as *Ehebrecher* (adulterers) but as *Fleischessünder* (sinners of the flesh).

The warning proves prescient, for in one of the novel's climactic moments, Castorp suffers that exact punishment. In the chapter "Schnee" (Snow), which was once intended to be the novel's conclusion, he leaves the sanatorium to ski but is caught in a violent snowstorm. Winds hurl snow with such force that Castorp cannot find his way forward. In an account of such storms, the narrator offers an image of the chaos in which Castorp finds himself:

> Die nichtige Atmosphäre geriet in Aufruhr, sie war so ausgefüllt von Flockengewimmel, daß man nicht einen Schritt weit sah. Böen von erstickender Stärke versetzten das Gestöber in wilde, treibende, seitliche Bewegung, sie wirbelten es von unten nach oben, von der Talsohle in die Lüfte empor, quirlten es in tollem Tanz durcheinander,—das war kein Schneefall mehr, es war ein Chaos von weißer Finsternis, ein Unwesen. (711)[6]
>
> (The idle atmosphere would rise up in turmoil, fill up with such squalls of snow that one couldn't see a step forward. Gusts of suffocating power drove drifts into wild, driving, sideward movement; they whirled them from bottom to top, from the depth of the valley into the air above; they beat them together in a mad dance,—it was no snowfall anymore, it was a chaos of white darkness, a demonic state of affairs.)

Like Paolo and Francesca, Castorp loses his way in the storm and roams from one place to another in a series of circles. But his wandering, it turns out, is not the consequence of a carnal affair, as Settembrini had suggested; rather, he is confused by how to navigate the poles of Settembrini's intellectualism and Chauchat's sensuality. The narrative indicates this in quite literal terms by describing the fluctuations of Castorp's perception: one minute, he sees in the snow his imminent destruction and is reminded of Settembrini's warning; the next minute, the greenish-blue reflection of the snow reminds him of Chauchat's lovely eyes. A microcosm of the novel, Castorp's wandering is an effort to reconcile body and soul.

Just as in Castorp's changing allegiances between Settembrini and Leo "Leib" Naphta, it is the uncertainty over how to square the corporeal and the spiritual dimensions of his existence that leads to such confusion. The antinomy leads to a consequential remark in which the voice of the narrator reflects the thinking of Mann: "Liebe kann nicht unkörperlich sein in der äußersten Frömmigkeit und nicht unfromm in der äußersten Fleischlichkeit, sie ist immer sie selbst, als verschlagene Lebensfreundlichkeit wie als höchste Passion, sie ist die Sympathie mit dem Organischen" (Love cannot exist in the utmost piety as incorporeal; it cannot help but exist as impious in the utmost carnality: it is always itself, both as canny vitality and as highest passion—it is sympathy with the organic) (907–908). Echoing the words of Mann's speech, without actually broaching the matter of politics, the narrative affirms the legitimacy of the body in the experience of love. By the end of the novel, when the narrator bids Castorp adieu and alludes to his "Abenteuer im Fleische und Geist" (adventures in the flesh and spirit), readers catch a glimpse of the political import of love. It surfaces in the narrator's final question: "Wird auch aus diesem Weltfest des Todes, auch aus der schlimmen Fieberbrunst, die rings den regnerischen Abendhimmel entzündet, einmal die Liebe steigen?" (Will love ever rise from this cosmic fest of death, from this awful, feverish season, which sets ablaze the rain-drenched, twilit sky?) (1085). Will there ever rise from the catastrophe of war, in other words, a society bound by love? Mann at least saw the potential of its realization in the fledgling Republic.

What at any rate would not suffice was a *Reich* that suppressed the legitimacy of the flesh in the name of the spirit. With its mysticizing rituals, the imperial cult around George's imperious person was no model for the future. Mann's aversion to such a cult underpins his depiction of Mynheer Peeperkorn, another patient in the sanatorium. Peeperkorn arrives at the sanatorium as the traveling partner of Chauchat. Having left the mountain after her tryst with Castorp, she returns with Peeperkorn during the season of Advent. But it is he, not she, whose person recalls the Messiah of the season. The insistent use of his title, Mynheer, is one sign of his lordly persona, but not the only one. His surname, too, points to an affinity with Christ—it is a rough paraphrase of bread and wine.[7] Furthermore, the Dutchman has a clerical air about him: his vest grants him the semblance of a priest. Yet for all his sacred trappings, Peeperkorn will not resolve Castorp's spiritual confusion. He amounts only to a "Veranstalter geistiger und pädagogischer Konfusion" (source of spiritual and pedagogical confusion) (828).

This would-be Messiah, like Stefan George, represents an unholy union of spiritualized sexuality. Referred to repeatedly by his mighty head—a big, bulbous thing that swells and reddens—Peeperkorn is a phallus personified as a priest. The conjunction, of course, is ironic, for a priest is celibate. That irony cuts to the core of Peeperkorn's identity: for all the apparent virility of his person, he seems to be sterile (914). But as George does, Peeperkorn finds other means of reproduction. He does not have a *Bund* per se, but Chauchat and Castorp are obsequious devotees who commit themselves to a cult of his person. Chauchat asserts that she would not be a woman if she were not willing to suffer "Erniedrigungen" (humiliations), which Castorp affirms in a telling statement: "die Frau kann von der Höhe ihrer Erniedrigung herab zu denen, die kein Königsformat haben . . . geringschätzig sprechen" (woman can, from the height of her humiliation, condescend to those who lack royal bearing) (905–906). Castorp, however, suffers similar humiliations, which is to say that these remarks, though directed at Chauchat, reveal his emasculation at the hands of Peeperkorn. In their subservience, the two former lovers recognize each other as equals under one monarch; after a period of hostility, they come to terms with each other by forming a "Bündnis . . . für ihn [Peeperkorn]" (alliance for him) (906). Peeperkorn and his lackeys are parodies of George and the members of his Kreis, their most awful affinity a sublimated sexuality of subservience.

Of all places, the parody of the George circle's mystificatory stylings reaches its height in the only numbered chapter of the novel: *Vingt et un* (twenty-one), another multiple of seven.[8] Peeperkorn stages a re-enactment of the Last Supper in which he serves bread and wine to twelve patients of the sanatorium. Embracing his religious persona, he exhorts his tablemates in ridiculous fashion to cherish their omelets as "Gottesgabe" (godsend) (852). Many tire quickly of the bacchanalia, and Peeperkorn rouses them with a reminder of the disciples' sleepiness at Gethsemane. But Hans Castorp proves himself worthy of his name. Like the disciple John, who stays with Christ as he hangs from the cross (John 19:25), Castorp accompanies Peeperkorn to his room, where he will soon die by suicide. As an evangelist to this new god, Castorp debases himself one time after another. He comes to imitate the speech of his master, as George had demanded of his disciples; he employs it even when he defends Peeperkorn to the model of humanistic rhetoric, Settembrini. Like the Georgianer, who were compelled to renounce romance with women, Castorp transfers his attraction to Chauchat to Peeperkorn. It is an act of emasculation, which is underlined by his connection to the disciple, John, a traditional figure of effeminacy. As Castorp states "Ich bin gar nicht männlich auf die Art, daß ich im Manne nur das nebenbuhlende Mitmännchen erblicke,—ich bin es vielleicht überhaupt nicht" (I am not at all manly in the sense that I glimpse only a mere rival in my fellow man,—perhaps I am not manly at all) (885–886). Mann's implication is clear: there was no manliness in George's *Männerbund*.

How could the new Republic flourish in the absence of an authentic masculinity? In short, Mann believed that it could not. The danger of George's circle was the threat of monarchy. Peeperkorn, referred to metonymically by his "majestätisches Haupt" (regal head), functions as a monarch among the patients of the sanatorium. When Settembrini and Naphta tangle over politics, Peeperkorn silences their discussion by calling attention to an eagle that soars above their heads. Describing it as "Jupiters Vogel, der König seines Geschlechts" (Jupiter's bird, the king of its kind), he effectively ends the debate: there is no place for disagreement in the presence of an autocrat (896). That truth dawns on Castorp when, in a rare moment, he risks disagreement with Peeperkorn. The matter was ostensibly trivial: does tobacco constitute a legitimate pleasure? But the contradiction of Peeperkorn was significant: "Was redete er da? War es nicht der demokratischen Unverschämtheit genug, 'einer von uns beiden' zu sagen, wo es sich um eine Persönlichkeit und um ihn handelte?" (What was he talking about? Wasn't it shamelessly democratic enough to have said, 'one of the two of us,' when it came to a personage and him?) (857). Castorp recognizes his mistake, for Peeperkorn begins "sich von der Lehne aufzurichten, höher und höher, zu voller Größe, während zugleich sein majestätisches Haupt rot anschwoll" (to rise from the backrest, higher and higher, to his full height, all the while that his regal head swelled red) (857–858). Summoning the force of his sexual potency, Peeperkorn frightens Castorp into retraction before disaster strikes. But what was his transgression? Castorp had contradicted the divine figure, he had spoken of an "us" as if they were equals. The rift runs deeper yet, for Castorp's smoking is not just any pleasure—it is a homoerotic pleasure, for he is always handling his cigars as if they were phalluses. Peeperkorn's anger, then, is directed not just at a democratic argument, but at a democratic argument that maintains the legitimacy of male eroticism. Suppression of the flesh worked in tandem with the impulse toward monarchy.

The mythology around George implodes, symbolically anyway, in Mann's depiction of Peeperkorn's suicide. Using a tool made of steel, gold, and ivory, which has been fashioned in the form of a fanged snake, Peeperkorn injects himself with fatal venom. A snake has bitten a salesman of snake oil, one phallic object has wounded another. The symbols are pointed in more ways than one, for in the image of the serpentine phallus biting the phallus, Mann replicates the reflexive symbol known as the ouroboros—the emblem that was omnipresent in Stefan George's *Der siebente Ring*.[9] Corporeal eroticism, exemplified by the figure of the phallus, was as deadly to the monarchical constitution of George's Kreis as the venom of a cobra. Homoerotic love, carried through to corporeal expression, was fatal to the myths of empire that plagued the Republic. In this respect, Peeperkorn's death bears pedagogic value. As Mann had said in the speech on the Republic: "wer sich für das Organische, das Leben, interessiert, der interessiert sich namentlich für den Tod; und es könnte Gegenstand eines Bildungsromanes sein, zu zeigen, daß das Erlebnis des Todes zuletzt ein Erlebnis des Lebens ist, daß es zum Menschen führt" (He who is interested in the organic, and in life, interests himself in the matter of death; indeed it could be the object of a Bildungsroman to show that the experience of death is ultimately an experience of life, that it leads to the human person) (GkFA 15.1:558).

If *Der Zauberberg* is a bildungsroman, however, its hero is not Castorp. It is the young Republic that was coming of age in the 1920s. Its most important lesson was to be wary of myth. Castorp had failed to learn this lesson, despite the egregiousness with which it was conveyed to him: "Indem Sie aus der Persönlichkeit ein Geheimnis machen, laufen Sie Gefahr, der Götzenanbetung zu verfallen. Sie venerieren eine Maske. Sie sehen Mystik, wo es sich um Mystifikation handelt" (By making a mystery of the personage, you run the risk of idolatry. You venerate a mask. You see mysticism, where there is only mystification) (883–884). Settembrini's admonition expresses precisely the danger that Mann had discerned in the veneration of Stefan George. The mythologization of *Persönlichkeit* lent itself to debasement, subservience, and an elitist politics of monarchy. There was a remedy to ward off these dangers, and in this respect, "Von deutscher Republik" may be read as an answer to the final question of the novel: yes, it affirms, love can rise from the prolific death of war. But it requires the body of democracy, bound by real love—not its sublimation in myth. Tragically, Castorp was not the only one who failed to learn this lesson. Mann had to address it again, from the other side of another catastrophic war.

This time around, he wrote in the key of mourning: *Doktor Faustus* is a tragedy rather than a bildungsroman. Ostensibly the biography of a composer, Adrian Leverkühn, a friend of the narrator, the novel uses its subject as a personal metonym for the self-wrought destruction of Germany. At its heart is a deal with the devil, the record of which emerges from one of Leverkühn's secret documents. It describes how, while sojourning in Palestrina, he was visited by Lucifer. For Leverkühn's soul, and on the condition that he will renounce the possibility of love, Lucifer promises a twenty-four-year span of musical genius. The terms of the agreement reveal the unique music that the devil promises Leverkühn:

> Du wirst führen, du wirst der Zukunft den Marsch schlagen. . . . Nicht genug, daß du die lähmenden Schwierigkeiten der Zeit durchbrechen wirst,—die Zeit selber, die Kulturepoche, will sagen, die Epoche der Kultur und ihres Kultus wirst du durchbrechen und dich der Barbarei erdreisten, die's zweimal ist, weil sie nach

> der Humanität, nach der erdenklichsten Wurzelbehandlung und bürgerlichen Verfeinerung kommt. Glaube mir! Sogar auf Theologie versteht sie sich besser, als eine vom Kultus abgefallene Kultur, die auch im Religiösen nur eben Kultur sah, nur Humanität, nicht den Exzeß, das Paradox, die mystische Leidenschaft, die völlig unbürgerliche Aventüre. (GkFA 10.1:355)
>
> (You will lead, you will strike a path into the future. . . . It's not enough that you will break through the obstacles of the age,—you will break through the age itself, this cultural epoch, this epoch of culture and its cult. You will venture a barbarism that is doubly barbarous, since it follows humanitarianism, that most conceivable root canal and bourgeois refinement. Believe me! Barbarism even understands theology better than a culture that has fallen away from the cult, a culture that saw in religion, too, only culture, only humanity—not the excess, the paradox, the mystical passion, the utterly unbourgeois occurrence.)

The pledge of Durchbruch is not merely that of a breakthrough to success. It is more fundamental: Leverkühn will have the force to break through the veneer of bourgeois culture and access the "barbaric," a primordial realm in which art has not yet been ossified by philistinism. It is a notion that overlaps specifically with the antibourgeois impulses of the George-Kreis. Simultaneously, it evinces that more general tendency of myth to transcend the present. The devil promises the fulfillment of a new mythology.

It is safe to presuppose the Romantic origins of that promise; the novel, after all, makes no secret of the Romanticism that underpins Leverkühn's attempts at a mythology. Apart from a propensity to cull from (medieval) romantic legends, he propounds a philosophy that is steeped in Romantic aesthetics. In an eloquent speech, he explains the difficult task of the composer: to create intellectual music while distilling it for a popular reception. His artistry may be complicated, but his music should result in "Einfachheitswirkung" (the effect of simplicity) (467–468). Aimed at engendering a community of recipients (rather than an audience), what Leverkühn outlines is the recapitulation of the social agenda from the Romantics' new mythology. That project had pointed to a utopian future, which Leverkühn, too, presumes. Thus he tells friends, in a catastrophic misreading of the future, that the conjoining of art and the *Volk* will result in "eine neue Unschuld, ja Harmlosigkeit" (a new purity, indeed innocence) (469). It is a repetition of

Romantic portents, though in this case, it is predicated on the word of the devil. Indeed, Leverkühn echoes the words of Lucifer: "Wem also der *Durchbruch* (emphasis added) gelänge aus geistiger Kälte in eine Wagniswelt neuen Gefühls, ihn sollte man wohl den Erlöser der Kunst nennen" (He who manages a breakthrough from the spiritual cold into a brave new world of feeling—we should call him the redeemer of art) (468). The statement betrays the divergence of Romantic myth from its self-appointed aspirations: the utopianism of myth devolves quickly into a cult of the person.

We know that lesson from the *Zauberberg*, and this time, too, its instruction is signaled by means of numerology. Leverkühn's "breakthrough"—the crescendo of his life and of the novel—occurs in chapter XXXIV. The chapter's significance is demarcated in an obvious way: with three parts, it is the only chapter in the entire novel that has been divided. This is particularly striking, for throughout the novel, the narrator frequently apologizes for the length of his chapters, at one point claiming that the breaks exist only for the reader's benefit. The claim may be true, though not for the reason we think: the chapter breaks are not an occasion for respite so much as they are for reflection. That is to say, it is a provocation to reflection that one chapter includes three sections, each of which is headed by the numeral XXXIV. Why not have labeled them chapters XXXIV, XXXV, and XXXVI, as the confession of their arbitrary character would suggest? The narrator demands reflection on the matter, calling attention to it again at the start of chapter XXXV, where he refers to "die neue Ziffer" (the new number) at the head of the chapter (550). Earlier, he had claimed "Zahlenmystik ist nicht meine Sache" (numerology is not my thing) (164), yet it looks to be exactly his thing: in a narrative in which forty-six other chapters do not repeat themselves, the one chapter that does repeat itself comprises numbers that were of significance to Leverkühn. On his wall had hung an image of Albrecht Dürer's engraving, *Melencolia I*, which includes a "magic" square of numerals in four rows and four columns. The sum of four numbers in any direction of the square is always thirty-four. *Zahlenmystik*, as it was in the *Zauberberg*, is a significatory device in *Doktor Faustus*.

The numerological operations in the new novel point up the resumption of the former critical program. It will have occurred by now, however unbelievably, that apart from the return to numerology as a device, we are witnessing a return to the very same numerals—three, four, and most importantly, seven. The operation that is performed by Dürer's magic square, hanging on Leverkühn's wall, mimics the operation of the numbers that had hung on the door of Castorp's room: $3 + 4 = 7$. There are cogent reasons to suppose that despite Stefan George's death in 1933, Mann's numerology evokes yet again the specter of him and his circle.

That thesis finds support in the middle panel in this triptych of a chapter, where the narrator describes his encounters in the mid-1920s with the Kridwiss-Kreis, a circle of male intellectuals. They may not be a "faithful copy" of George and his disciples, as Gunilla Bergsten wrote, but "ideological connections exist."[10] Consider who numbers among their members: Egon Unruhe, a paleozoologist, uses fossils and rocks to demonstrate the scientific veracity of ancient sagas (GkFA 10.1:527). Georg Vogler is the author of a history of German literature, organized by writers' "Stammeszugehörigkeit" (tribal membership). He promotes the image of the writer as the "blut- und landschaftsgebundenes" (blood-and-landscape-bound) product of his point of origin (527). Daniel zur Höhe, another attendee, writes apocalyptic and bellicose poetry, publishing it in small, lavish editions. These men belong to the circle of Sixtus Kridwiss, a printer and graphic artist. Each of them, if not a copy of a member of the George-Kreis, represents some amalgamation of identities from the members of the Kreis.[11] Like the actual Kreis, this one meets at an apartment in Schwabing. More importantly, it is another coterie of rabidly conservative ideologues, whose allegiance to a primal past sours their view of the new Republic. To them, a democratic state is a "schlechter Spaß" (bad joke) (530). Like the members of George's cenacle, these men dismiss the power and authority of the official Germany, scoffing at parliamentarism. They believe, instead, that

> massengerechte Mythen fortan das Vehikel der politischen Bewegung sein würden: Fabeln, Wahnbilder, Hirngespinste, die mit Wahrheit, Vernunft, Wissenschaft überhaupt nichts zu tun zu haben brauchten, um dennoch schöpferisch zu sein, Leben und Geschichte zu bestimmen und sich damit als dynamische Realitäten zu erweisen. (532)
>
> (myths for the masses would henceforth be the vehicle for the political movement: fables, hallucinations, phantasms that need not connect to truth, reason, or science in order, nevertheless, to be generative, to determine life and history, and to establish themselves thereby as dynamic realities.)

This doctrine did not emerge from their Kreis sui generis, our narrator says, but was inspired by Georges Sorel's *Réflexions sur la violence*, "ein sieben

Jahr vor dem Krieg erschienenes Buch" (a book that appeared seven years before the war) (531). Sorel's book appeared in 1908, not 1907, but the narrator's error is suggestive: after all, it was in 1907, not 1908, that a man with almost the inversion of the name Georges Sorel had published a volume of mythical poems that led a like-minded circle of male intellectuals to brace for a *Geisterkrieg*.[12] Kridwiss's circle, hailing a *sacrificium intellectus*, favors the proliferation of myth for the reason that Leverkühn had espoused the union of art and the *Volk*: only through an all-encompassing myth could the present witness the formation of a genuine community (Gemeinschaft). The doing away with reason, as our narrator, Serenus Zeitblom, recognizes with more than a modicum of discomfiture, constituted a repudiation of the Enlightenment. So unnerving were the ideas espoused in the Kridwiss-Kreis that, by sheer virtue of Zeitblom's proximity to it, he suffers visceral effects: "Wird man es verstehen, daß ein Mann bei der Verarbeitung solcher Neuigkeiten 14 Pfund Gewicht verlieren mag?" (Might one understand that at hearing the concoction of such novelties a man could lose fourteen pounds?). Were these men not so giddy over their shocking ideas, he says, he would have lost not fourteen pounds—just seven (538). It is so odd an observation, much like Zeitblom's comments on the numbers of his chapters, that it cannot sustain the weight of its own sense. It points to the numerological hermeneutic of the novel; for just as the *Zauberberg* had used sevens to codify corporeal phenomena as a contrast to George's numerologized kingdom of the spirit, so too does *Doktor Faustus*. Now, however, the sevens suggest something more ominous than in the earlier novel: the apocalyptic yearning of the barbaric Kridwiss-Kreis could (and would) take a physical toll.

No mere *roman à clef*, chapter XXXIV concentrates the novel's sprawling preoccupation with the force of myth. It is the central chapter of *Doktor Faustus*, where the devil's promise to Leverkühn is finally realized: the Kridwiss-Kreis speculates about myth in the middle panel of the triptych, while the outer panels recount its genesis and performance in Leverkühn's mythic opus, the *Apocalipsis cum figuris*. Zeitblom recalls the proximity of Leverkühn's mad oratorio to the intellectual sphere of the Kridwiss circle, saying that he witnessed the "Geburt eines Werkes . . . das gewisser kühner und prophetischer Beziehungen zu jenen Erörterungen nicht entbehrte, sie auf höherer, schöpferischer Ebene bestätigte und verwirklichte" (birth of a work . . . that did not dispense with certain bold and prophetic relations to those disquisitions, but confirmed and realized them on a higher, more generative plane) (514). Whereas the first of the three panels describes the work's origins and sources, the third panel delivers what resembles a formal assessment of the oratorio. Zeitblom describes its techniques and effects. The oratorio's vaguely ancient rhythms, its use of loudspeakers, and above all its vacillation between the most elemental tones of nature and the highest forms of modern music contribute to an overall impression of barbarism (542–550). Zeitblom is at pains to defend the composer from such an accusation, and yet he knows it to be true:

> Und ist es verständlich oder nicht, daß die spät-kulturelle, aus der Atomisierung Gemeinschaft ambitionierende Erneuerung des Kultischen, zu Mitteln greift, die nicht nur dem Stadium seiner kirchlichen Sittigung, sondern auch seinem Primitiv-Stadium angehören? Die ungeheueren Schwierigkeiten, welche jede Einstudierung und Aufführung von Leverkühns Apocalipsis bietet, hängen ja eben hiermit unmittelbar zusammen. (541–542)
>
> (And is it comprehensible or not that the recent cultural renewal of the cultic, aspiring from atomization to community, grasps for means that belong not just to the stage of its taming by the church but also to its primitive stage? The monstrous difficulties posed by any study and performance of Leverkühn's Apocalipsis are directly related to this.)

Leverkühn's oratorio represents the realization of a new Romantic mythology, as it was received and promulgated, anyway, by protofascist intellectuals. In myth, they glimpsed an escape from history and a return to the elemental. Its realization seemed to promise an escape from the philistinism wrought by the expansion of capitalism in the nineteenth century. This meant, of course, that it was not the new mythology heralded by the Romantics. Yet the curvature of their ambitions—leading as it did to the likes of Hauptmann, Borchardt, and George—had implicated them in its consequences.

As with the Romantics and their Neo-Romantic heirs, the *Commedia* figured vitally in the development of Leverkühn's mythology. If Arnold Schönberg was the basis of Leverkühn's technique, then Dante was the basis of his symbolic regime. There are overt signs of this in the first part of chapter XXXIV, where Zeitblom surveys Leverkühn's sources. Important for him was an immersion in the literature of visionaries: Ezekiel, John of Patmos, Mechtild of Magdeburg, Hildegard of Bingen, and the venerable Bede. In the first edition of the novel, there are mentions of Pope Gregory I and Alberich of Monte Cassino, both of whom, Zeitblom remarks, influenced

Dante. In point of fact, virtually all of these figures were important to Dante, as Mann knew well. In his research into the sources for Leverkühn's oratorio he had relied on a review of August Rüegg's *Die Jenseitsvorstellungen vor Dante und die übrigen literarischen Voraussetzungen der "Divina Commedia"* (Conceptions of the afterlife before Dante and the other literary preconditions of his "Divina Commedia"). Bergsten observed that Zeitblom quotes several passages from it in tracing the genesis of the oratorio.[13] For his part, Leverkühn confesses an interest in the accounts of figures who have descended to the dead—figures like Paul, Aeneas, and Dante (517). Zeitblom elaborates the significance of the poem for him in a comparison to Michelangelo's *Last Judgment*:

> Von Dantes Gedicht hat Leverkühns tönendes Gemälde viel, noch mehr von jener körperstrotzend übervölkerten Wand, auf welcher Engel hier in die Posaunen des Untergangs stoßen, dort Charons Nachen sich seiner Last entlädt, die Toten auferstehen, die Heiligen anbeten, Dämonenmasken den Wink des schlangengegürteten Minos erwarten . . . kurzum von dem Gruppen- und Szenenaufbau des Jüngsten Gerichts. (520–521)

> (Leverkühn's sound painting has a great deal from Dante's poem, but more still from that bursting-with-bodies, overpeopled wall on which angels blast the trumpets of doom, and at the same time Charon's boat unloads its cargo, the dead rise and adore the saints, masked demons await the signal of Minos, with his belt of serpents . . . in short, from the *Last Judgment*'s composition of figures and images.)

The statement is loaded because, in the suggestion that Michelangelo influenced Leverkühn more powerfully than Dante, Zeitblom overlooks what nearly every historian of Renaissance painting has noted since the time of Michelangelo: the *Last Judgment* owes its vision to Dante.[14] It is a remarkable oversight because Charon and Minos, whom Zeitblom singles out, are Michelangelo's best-recognized allusions to the *Commedia*. Bernadine Barnes's words sum this up helpfully: "The Charon/Minos group points to Dante like a neon sign, instructing the viewer to use Dante's *Divine Comedy* in some way to give meaning to the *Last Judgment*."[15] Zeitblom may or may not realize it, but certainly Mann did. Just as the *Commedia* supplies meaning to Michelangelo's apocalypse, it supplies meaning to Leverkühn's *Apocalipsis*.

We are confronted, yet again, with a curious elision of the *Commedia* from the itinerary of Romantic mythology. Indeed, the path of the poem (and poet) we have been tracing looks to have been a dark one. Notwithstanding the salvos of Schelling and the Schlegel brothers, the adaptations of Dante and his *Commedia* to Romantic myth have been oddly obscured. Goethe maintained a relative silence on the linkages of his poetry to Dante, while Novalis and George, we are almost inclined to believe, concealed him from view. An ambiguity of Dante's presence haunts the Romantic efforts at generating a Dantean mythology. It persists, we now see, in *Doktor Faustus*. Zeitblom acknowledges a range of influences on the mythic oratorio, including Dante, but he is silent about one obvious feature; namely, the one commonality among all these sources is their contribution to or influence by Dante. The point, of course, is not that Dante is owed a paean of praise, but that his presence is simultaneously registered and suppressed. That ambiguity obtains in Zeitblom's reference to Michelangelo, which would ostensibly divert our gaze from the *Commedia*, all the while that the very referents of the observation evoke the *Commedia*. It is an ambiguity that features in the history at hand. In an apparent paradox, Romantic mythology would both claim and spurn Dante. Hauptmann would be commissioned by Dante all the while that he delegitimizes his vision. Novalis would mold his identity on that of Dante all the while that he does not suffer to utter his name. George would model his image on that of Dante, all the while that his mythology would conceal the centrality of Brunetto Latini and *Inferno* 15. The last of these ambiguities, of course, reveals a difference: it does not avoid Dante so much as it exploits his *Commedia* to secure the hermetic seal of a new mythology. Mann had recognized this and subverted it—the *Zauberberg* attacked George's embrace of myth via an esotericism inflected by Dante. An admonition in 1924, that subversion had become a judgment in 1947. *Doktor Faustus* retains the esotericism of Dantean myth all the while that it holds the George-Kreis to account for the destruction that it has wrought. Leverkühn's *Apocalipsis*, the fulfillment of the primeval mythology anticipated by the Kridwiss-Kreis, was bound to have its origins in the *Commedia*.

The novel's central chapter, XXXIV, is a confirmation of this damning judgment. It intimates as much by the affinity it underscores between Leverkühn's mythic opus and Michelangelo's fresco. The composer cannot escape his impending damnation. But again, a Dantean esotericism underwrites the hermeneutic program of the novel: it confirms what we suspect. Chapter XXXIV, singular as we have seen for its numerological oddity, corresponds to a singular oddity in the *Commedia*. Dante's poem of one hundred cantos has just one canto that bears the number XXXIV. *Purgatorio* and *Paradiso* each contain thirty-three, whereas *Inferno* ends in a thirty-fourth. It is there that Dante witnesses the gargantuan figure of Lucifer, frozen in the bottommost pit of Hell. The numerological allusion signals Leverkühn's fate, but it also condemns his precipitous fall. Lucifer had been the highest of the Seraphim—his fall to the pit of Hell an Icarian plunge. Leverkühn's damnation points to the novel's ultimate judgment, which is reserved for a form of aestheticism that would consort with barbarism. Dante had once helped Romantics to visualize a poetics of mythic utopianism; by the time of its co-optation by George, Mann saw such a poetics as fated to infernal damnation. In the end, *Doktor Faustus* is an abjural of the efforts to wring a new mythology from Dante's *Commedia*.

This is not to say it could not be a symbolic touchstone for German national culture, just that its meaning for Germans, as Mann saw it, was vastly different from that which Romantic mythologists had envisioned. No longer a model for the future, the *Commedia*, and the *Inferno*, specifically, had become a symbolic record of the German past. This is the sense, after all, of the novel's epigraph. Mann cites the opening lines of the second canto of *Inferno*, where Dante foregrounds the painful task that his memory is preparing to undertake (*Inf.* 2.1–9). Mann and Zeitblom are the scribes of a tragic history, which—unlike that of Dante—never escapes the depths of Hell. The heralds of the new mythology, as well as their latter-day heirs, were so enthralled to the future that for them the *Commedia* was a crucible in which to forge a new culture. For Mann, the poem helped account for the past. The challenge to Dante in recounting the events of *Inferno* had become a rhetorical model for writing the German past. The source of myth had become a source of history.

Conclusion

RECOVERED, REPURPOSED, REVERED, and reduplicated, Dante and his *Commedia* shaped the origins of German Romanticism and the attempts at its rehabilitation. Dismissed as a barbarian through much of the Enlightenment, he spoke meaningfully to a young coterie that regarded itself on the brink of historical crisis. For August Wilhelm Schlegel, he modeled how intellect and spirit could overcome barbarism and factionalism. For Friedrich Schlegel and Friedrich Schelling, his *Commedia* marked the beginning of a new age; indeed, the poem seemed to furnish an encyclopedic representation of that age. The way it did so—its strategies of reflexivity, realism, and didacticism—rendered the poem a model for the utopian project of Early German Romanticism: the new mythology. Efforts at the realization of a Dantean mythology were sporadic and disparate. Novalis's *Heinrich von Ofterdingen* used the *Commedia* to enact in literature the philosophy of absolute idealism; Goethe's *Faust II* naturalized an ethics derived from Dante's scholastic theology; Schelling's stanzas had gestured in a similar direction. But in each venture, the creation of myth was beset by the enormity of Dante's authority. Schelling, Novalis, and Goethe reckoned as much with the looming presence of Dante as they did with his poem. The preoccupation with the man became a fixation, and by the time of Neo-Romanticism, an obsession. Gerhart Hauptmann postulated a theory of myth whose realization was predicated on superseding Dante. Rudolf Borchardt believed it was necessary to reclaim Dante for the nation whose Romantics had discovered him; only through such means could the aspirations of German Romanticism be realized. Stefan George, meanwhile, forged a veritable cult at whose center he stood—his authority validated by the adoption of a Dantean hermeticism. Only with Thomas Mann's novels of European modernity, *Der Zauberberg* and *Doktor Faustus*, was the Romantic obsession with Dante recognized and redressed.

It is doubtful that the Romantic-Dantean subtext of Mann's novels was ever known, besides by some few in the circle around Stefan George; but Mann's use of the *Inferno* to interpret the nation's past prefigured a tendency wherein the poem became a harbinger of history. Infernal figurations mark many postwar texts that reckoned with the catastrophic events at the middle of the century. These include the likes of Hermann Broch's *Der Tod des Virgil* (*The Death of Virgil*, 1945), Peter Weiss's *Die Ermittlung* (*The Investigation*, 1965), and Hans Magnus Enzensberger's *Der Untergang der Titanic* (*The Sinking of the Titanic*, 1978). There was indeed a veritable "Lagerliteratur" (literature of the camps) that arose around the model of the *Commedia*.[1] Franz Werfel's science fiction novel *Der Stern der Ungeborenen* (*The Star of the Unborn*, 1946), almost an exact contemporary of *Doktor Faustus*, blends Romantic and postwar impulses: Dante figures in the novel's utopian thrust and in its reckoning with the events of the war. As distance from the events of the twentieth century grows, new receptions will emerge: they already have in the narratives of W. G. Sebald, Ingo Schulze, and Sybille Lewitscharoff. No matter the ends to which it is put, the *Commedia* remains a reservoir of generative potential.

The poem's proclivity for such receptions demands an ongoing historiography. The failure to produce one results, for one thing, in a misapprehension of how integral to and productive for European modernity its author remains. In March 2021, for example, Arno Widmann of the *Frankfurter Rundschau* published a critique of Dante that could well have been published three centuries earlier.[2] By Widmann's reading, Dante comes off as a not terribly original poet and a judgmental moralist. His humanity is not nearly as capacious and modern as that of Shakespeare. Widmann's assessment was not so provocative as to warrant the response it garnered—statements from representatives of the Italian Ministry of Culture, the Uffizi, the Società Dante Alighieri, and others. Yet its bromides point to what happens when a reception as significant as that of Dante and the *Commedia* is neglected: criticism becomes shallow and knowledge runs in circles.

More disconcerting than the fate of criticism, the case of Dante shows, is how the neglect of a critical historiography creates a vacuum from which manipulations of history emerge. The examples of Hauptmann, Borchardt, and George attest to that danger. Each poet's project depended on either an ignorance of the *Commedia* or an ignorance of its reception, or both. All three failed to observe that, for all his pride, Dante represented himself as an anti-Ulysses; he was a poet who, for all the splendor of his poetry, claimed to restrain the excesses of language (*Inf.* 26.21–22). One may debate the veracity of that claim, but there is no question that Neo-Romantic projects of Dantean myth had no pretension to do so: they sought to absolutize poetry. Their quests to do so were ostensibly aligned with the *neue Mythologie* of the earliest German Romantics, but in their abrogation of the history of Early German Romanticism they transplanted the roots of that first project: instead of bringing forth reason, their projects of Dantean myth promised authority—of language, of poetry, and of the poet.

The co-optation of Dantean myth by Neo-Romantics, to be sure, was not the only outcome of the *neue Mythologie.* Other narratives of Romantic myth emerged in the nineteenth century. Some of their histories, which overlap with the present study, have been traced by Manfred Frank and George Williamson.[3] Nor is the Neo-Romantic corruption of Romantic myth the only outcome of Jena's preoccupation with a Dantean mythology. Friedrich Schlegel and Friedrich Schelling moved in different directions in the years after the dissolution of the Early Romantic period. The former dispensed with the prospect of a new mythology. Its goals of cultural and aesthetic unity retained their appeal, to be sure, but the end of Romantic theory brought with it a new realism: it would be easier to leverage the corpus of medieval Christian mythology than to generate something new. In this respect, then, the scenes of *Paradiso* on the plaster ceiling of Rome's Villa Massimo—painted by Philipp Veit, the stepson of Friedrich Schlegel—may be read as a translation of the Romantics' Dantean mythology. It was Schlegel, after all, who corresponded with and tutored his stepson in the interpretation of the *Commedia*. Schelling, for his part, explored the workings of myth for the duration of his life. He, too, alighted on a new realism, elaborating in his later lectures that myth was not the artificial product of a single person. The project of 1800, in other words, ramified in more than just one way.

Are the Romantics, then, fit to be exculpated for the fate of their myths? There is no unequivocal answer to the question. Their theorization of myth along Dantean lines did not aim at the outcomes pursued by the heirs of Romanticism in the twentieth century. Neo-Romantics' dwindling esteem for truth and reason would have been a foreign prospect to the Romantics of the eighteenth and nineteenth centuries. Among the most culturally conservative of them—the Lukasbund—there prevailed a simple motto: *Wahrheit* (truth). Yet our itinerary has revealed that attempts at the generation of a reason-bound mythology proved exceedingly difficult. More challenging than the scale of the project was its quest for legitimation. Though they made much of their *Symphilosophie*, this first avant-garde collective pursued the generation of a new mythology individually. Here, the influence of Dante was arguably ruinous: his formidable shadow overtook the movement's basically collectivist impulses. Longing for a new mythology, the Romantics became convinced that, to obtain one, they required a new Dante. The result, to judge by the terms of the Romantics themselves, was a failure: Romantic poetry came unmoored from Romantic theory. Instead of authoring a new mythology, the *Romantik* became a new mythology.

ACKNOWLEDGMENTS

There is a delightful feature of the *Commedia* that I have left all but unremarked: the role of wise and compassionate guides and friends. In the years it took me to write this book, I had no shortage of Virgils.

The collaboration with Bucknell's editorial team could not have been more felicitous. I am especially grateful to Suzanne Guiod for her faith in this project. Pam Dailey's dependability provided me the calm to tie together many loose ends in the final stages of writing and editing.

I was aided in tying together those loose ends by collaborators whose care and commitment are all the more impressive for working amid the constraints of the COVID-19 pandemic. Maik Bozza generously communicated and shared material from the Stefan George Archiv. Adrienne Sharpe of the Beinecke Library made it easy to access holdings when visits were not possible. The team of Interlibrary Loan librarians at Worcester Polytechnic Institute regularly worked magic and never griped about my innumerable requests. Ryan McGinnis overhauled my citations, indexed the manuscript, and created a more readable scholarly apparatus. John Donohue and Diane Ersepke performed a sharp round of copyedits. I am grateful, too, to *The German Quarterly* for permission to reprint portions of my article "Stefan George, Thomas Mann, and the Politics of Homoeroticism," *The German Quarterly* 86, no. 3 (2013): 311–333. It appears in edited form across chapters five and six.

This project is deeply indebted to the global community of Goethe scholars, but especially to those in the Goethe Society of North America. Their passion and care helped shepherd me from a young scholar to the author of the present volume. Jane Brown guided the manuscript in its early stages, and since assuming the reins of the New Studies in the Age of Goethe series, Karin Schutjer has been a steadfast advocate; the book would not have materialized without her encouragement and support. Anonymous reports contributed immensely to the final manuscript, as did the exceptionally honest and generous comments of Marshall Brown. Daniel Purdy and John Smith gave helpful feedback on an early version of chapter three at an Atkins Goethe Conference. Valuable comments on portions of the project came from interlocutors at the Symposium junger Goethe Forscher of the Goethe-Gesellschaft in Weimar.

Friends and colleagues from the University of Pennsylvania contributed intellectually and emotionally in myriad ways to the advancement of this project. My dissertation adviser, Catriona MacLeod (now in Chicago), has guided my path since my first semester of graduate school. Simon Richter has been a stalwart advocate and dear friend. Liliane Weissberg has always prodded me with valuable questions, especially at a colloquium organized by Ian Fleishman. I am grateful to them, as well as to so many others, whose minds and friendship I treasure: Melanie Adley, Florian Breitkopf, Kevin Brownlee, Vance Byrd, Sonia Gollance, Matt Handelman, CJ Jones, Bridget Levine-West, Rita Pasqui, Peter Struck, Nick Theis, Frank Trommler, Maya Vinokour, David Wallace, Kerry Wallach, Leif Weatherby, Caroline Weist, and Bethany Wiggin.

Colleagues at Worcester Polytechnic Institute have been warm and constructive interlocutors. Jim Cocola has provided insightful critical feedback and invaluable advice for the writing process. Kris Boudreau brought me on the tenure track and gave me light to finish this project. Ulrike Brisson, Steve Bullock, David Dollenmayer, Katherine Foo, John Galante, Peter Hansen, Shana Lessing, Aarti Smith Madan, Ryan Smith Madan, Kate Moncrief, Ángel Rivera, Ruth Smith, John Sanbonmatsu, and Yunus Telliel have been invaluable friends and mentors.

I am a German Italian American, and a Catholic too, so it may seem inevitable that I would write a book like *Dante in Deutschland*. But it would not have happened save for the teachers who introduced me to the figures about whom I write. I will remain forever grateful to Cyrus Hamlin, Vittorio Hösle, and Traugott Lawler, whose seminars left indelible impressions.

Ultimately, this book owes its existence to the faith, love, and patience of my family. The decades of schooling that underpin this slim volume were the gift of my parents, Mike and Nana. Their lives of quiet determination and devotion, whether they believe it or not, are exemplary models for how scholarship is accomplished. In the (too) many years of quiet determination it has taken me to write this book, I had the unwavering love and support of my wife, Victoria, and more recently, of our son, Teddy. I dedicate this book to them.

NOTES

Introduction

1. Joan Acocella, "Cloud Nine: A New Translation of the *Paradiso*," *New Yorker*, August 27, 2007, https://www.newyorker.com/magazine/2007/09/03/cloud-nine.

2. Joseph Luzzi, "This Could Be 'Heaven,' or This Could Be 'Hell,'" *New York Times*, April 19, 2013, https://www.nytimes.com/2013/04/21/books/review/dantes-divine-comedy-translated-by-clive-james.html.

3. See the discussion of Rudolf Borchardt in chapter five.

4. Phillippe Lacoue-Labarthe and Jean-Luc Nancy, *The Literary Absolute: The Theory of Literature in German Romanticism*, trans. Philip Barnard (Albany: State University of New York Press, 1988), 8.

5. Robert Hollander, "Dante and His Commentators," in *The Cambridge Companion to Dante*, ed. Rachel Jacoff (New York: Cambridge University Press, 1993), 232; Ernst Behler, "Dante in Germany," in *Dante Encyclopedia*, ed. Richard Lansing (New York: Routledge, 2010), 266.

6. This quote is drawn from the call for papers for that conference. Proceedings of the conference have since been published. See Fabio Camilletti, Manuele Gragnolati, and Fabian Lampart, eds., *Metamorphosing Dante: Appropriations, Manipulations, and Rewritings in the Twentieth and Twenty-First Centuries* (Vienna: Turia + Kant, 2011).

7. Nicholas Halmi, *The Genealogy of the Romantic Symbol* (New York: Oxford University Press, 2011), 134.

8. Leif Weatherby, "The Risk of Theory: Romanticism, Science, Media," *German Quarterly* 89, no. 3 (2016): 352.

9. Halmi, *The Genealogy of the Romantic Symbol*.

10. Lacoue-Labarthe and Nancy, *The Literary Absolute*, 17.

11. Karl Heinz Bohrer, "Friedrich Schlegels Rede über die Mythologie," in *Mythos und Moderne*, ed. Karl Heinz Bohrer (Frankfurt: Suhrkamp, 1983), 52.

12. On Heine, Steffens, and Immermann, see chapter two.

13. Margaret Howitt, *Friedrich Overbeck: Sein Leben und Schaffen*, ed. Margaret Howitt (Freiburg: Herder'sche Verlagshandlung, 1886), 1:100–101.

14. Julius Schnorr von Carolsfeld, *Briefe aus Italien geschrieben in den Jahren 1817 bis 1827* (Gotha: Perthes, 1886), 402. Christian Friedrich Schlosser, the nephew of Goethe's brother-in-law, also lectured on Dante to the German painters who lived at Sant' Isidoro in Rome. One of them, Friedrich Overbeck, deemed the *Commedia* an important factor in Schlosser's conversion to Catholicism; see Howitt, *Friedrich Overbeck*, 1:226, 274.

15. Carlo Massimo contracted Friedrich Overbeck, Julius Schnorr von Carolsfeld, and Peter Cornelius to adorn three rooms of his villa with scenes from Tasso, Ariosto, and Dante. It is unclear why he hired only Germans for the project, but when Schnorr's illness led to the hiring of an Italian painter, it resulted in disappointment among the German artists. Kurt Gerstenberg and Paul Rave, *Die Wändgemälde der deutschen Romantiker im Casino Massimo zu Rom* (Berlin: DVFK, 1934), 21; Carolsfeld, *Briefe aus Italien*, 211. Cornelius, who first managed the planning of the Dante frescoes, intended to frame them within a gothic architecture he would paint on the walls of the Baroque villa. Büttner interpreted this to be an act of German nation formation. Cornelius eventually relinquished responsibility for the frescoes so that he could return to Munich and paint the Glyptothek. Philipp Veit assumed the direction of the project and corresponded about it with Friedrich Schlegel. Frank Büttner, *Peter Cornelius: Fresken und Freskenprojekte* (Wiesbaden: Steiner, 1980), 1:103.

16. Peter Cornelius, the man to whom the project was commissioned, was not an exception to this, but like the early Romantics, he wrote of the *Commedia* in mythological terms. Herman Riegel, *Peter Cornelius: Festschrift zu des grossen Künstlers hundertstem Geburtstage, 23. September 1883* (Berlin: R. v. Decker, 1883), 89.

17. Gerstenberg and Rave, *Die Wändgemälde*, 46.

18. Fritz Strich, *Die Mythologie in der deutschen Literatur von Klopstock bis Wagner* (Bern: Francke, 1910); Manfred Frank, *Der kommende Gott: Vorlesungen über die neue Mythologie* (Frankfurt: Suhrkamp, 1982); Manfred Frank, *Gott im Exil* (Frankfurt: Suhrkamp, 1988); George Williamson, *The Longing for Myth in Germany: Religion and Aesthetic Culture from Romanticism to Nietzsche* (Chicago: University of Chicago Press, 2004).

19. György Lukács, *Die Zerstörung der Vernunft: Der Weg des Irrationalismus von Schelling zu Hitler* (Berlin: Aufbau Verlag, 1954).

20. Manfred Frank, "Wie reaktionär war eigentlich die Frühromantik?," *Athenäum: Jahrbuch für Romantik* 7 (1997): 141–166; Frederick Beiser, *The Romantic Imperative: The Concept of Early German Romanticism* (Cambridge, MA: Harvard University Press, 2003); Stefan Matuschek, "Was heißt 'Mythologisieren'? Oder: Warum und wie sich die romantische Neue Mythologie der Aufklärung verdankt," in *Romantik und Revolution: Zum Reformpotential einer unpolitischen Bewegung*, ed. Klaus Ries (Heidelberg: Universitätsverlag, 2012), 71–82.

21. Hans Robert Jauss, *Toward an Aesthetic of Reception*, trans. Timothy Bahti (Minneapolis: University of Minnesota Press, 1982).

22. Arturo Farinelli, *Dante in Spagna–Francia–Inghilterra–Germania (Dante e Goethe)* (Turin: Fratelli Bocca, 1922); Werner Friederich, *Dante's Fame Abroad, 1350–1850: The Influence of Dante Alighieri on the Poets and Scholars of Spain, France, England, Germany, Switzerland and the United States. A Survey of the Present State of Scholarship* (Rome: Edizioni di Storia e letteratura, 1950); Michael Caesar, *Dante: The Critical Heritage, 1314(?)–1870* (London: Routledge, 1989); Eva Hölter, "Dante's Long Road to the German Library: Literary Reception from Early Romanticism until the Late Nineteenth Century," in *Dante in the Long Nineteenth Century*, ed. Aida Audeh and Nick Havely (Oxford: Oxford University Press, 2002), 225–247.

23. Mirjam Mansen, *"Denn auch Dante ist unser!" Die deutsche Dante-Rezeption 1900–1950* (Tübingen: M. Niemeyer, 2003).

24. Although one fails to find many studies of Dante and the *Frühromantik*, there is some interest in Schelling's reception of Dante. Indeed, this has its own body of literature,

among which are Claudia Becker, "'Im Allerheiligsten, wo Religion und Poesie verbündet'—F.W.J. Schellings Aufsatz 'Über Dante in philosophischer Beziehung' im Kontext der idealistischen Bemühungen um eine neue Mythologie," in *Poetische Autonomie? Zur Wechselwirkung von Dichtung und Philosophie in der Epoche Goethes und Hölderlins*, ed. Helmut Bachmaier and Thomas Rentsch (Stuttgart: Klett-Cotta, 1987), 308–328; Wolfram Hogrebe, "Schelling und Dante," *Deutsches Dante-Jahrbuch* 62 (1987): 7–31; Daniel Whistler, "Schelling's Poetry," *Clio* 43, no. 2 (2014): 143–175; and Flavio Auer, "Schelling über Dantes *Commedia* und Goethes *Faust* als neue Mythologien," *Scientia Poetica* 24, no. 1 (2020): 115–132.

25. Clara Charlotte Fuchs, "Dante in der deutschen Romantik," *Deutsches Dante-Jahrbuch* 15 (1933): 61–131; Erich Auerbach, "Entdeckung Dantes in der Romantik," in *Gesammelte Aufsätze zur romanischen Philologie*, ed. Gustav Konrad (Bern: Francke, 1967), 176–183.

26. There is a third species of history one might identify: the reception of either Italian or medieval literature in a German or German Romantic context. These texts are further afield of the present endeavor, but some are useful touchstones. Among them are Achim Hölter, "Zur Rezeption der italienischen Literatur in der deutschen Frühromantik," in *Deutsche und italienische Romantik: Referate des Bad Homburger Colloquiums in der Werner-Reimers-Stiftung*, ed. Enrico de Angelis (Pisa: Jacques e i suoi Quaderni, 1989), 49–86; Frank-Rutger Hausmann, *"Italien in Germanien": Deutsche Italien-Rezeption von 1750–1850* (Tübingen: Gunter Narr, 1996); Edith Höltenschmidt, *Die Mittelalter-Rezeption der Brüder Schlegel* (Paderborn: Schöningh, 2000); Wolfgang Lange and Norbert Schnitzler, *Deutsche Italomanie in Kunst, Wissenschaft, und Politik* (Munich: Wilhelm Fink, 2000); and Jochen Strobel, "*Blumensträuße* für die Deutschen: August Wilhelm Schlegels produktive Rezeption der romanischen Poesie als Übersetzer und Literaturhistoriker," in *Der Europäer August Wilhelm Schlegel: Romantischer Kulturtransfer—romantische Wissenschaften*, ed. York-Gothart Mix and Jochen Strobel (Berlin: De Gruyter, 2010), 159–183.

27. Giovanni Boccaccio, *Life of Dante*, ed. and trans. G. R. Carpenter (New York: Grolier, 1900), 85.

28. Erich Auerbach, "Dante's Addresses to the Reader," *Romance Philology* 7 (1953–1954): 268–278.

29. Teodolinda Barolini, *The Undivine* Comedy: *Detheologizing Dante* (Princeton, NJ: Princeton University Press, 1992), 6.

30. Charles Singleton, "The Irreducible Dove," *Comparative Literature* 9, no. 2 (1957): 129–135.

31. Benedetto Croce, *La Poesia di Dante* (Bari: Laterza & Figli, 1921).

32. Barolini, *The Undivine* Comedy.

33. Albert Russell Ascoli, *Dante and the Making of a Modern Author* (Cambridge: Cambridge University Press, 2011), 3.

34. George is fascinating for his reluctant ties to Romanticism. From the perspective of myth creation, he is clearly at work on a Neo-Romantic project. The cultivation of a personal mythology within his circle speaks for itself. This, too, is a governing presupposition of Frank; see Frank, *Gott im Exil*. Yet George does not "own" his Romanticism in the manner of Hauptmann or Borchardt. Walter Benjamin contemplated the matter and concluded with the incisive observation that "Jede dialektische Betrachtung der Georgeschen Dichtung wird die Romantik ins Zentrum stellen, jede heroisierende,

orthodoxe kann nichts Klügeres tun, als sie so nichtig wie möglich zeigen" (Every dialectical consideration of George's poetry will have Romanticism at its center; every lionizing and orthodox consideration [of George's poetry] can do nothing more clever than present it as nugatory as possible). Walter Benjamin, "Wider ein Meisterwerk," in *Gesammelte Schriften*, ed. Hella Tiedemann-Bartels, vol. 3 (Frankfurt: Suhrkamp, 1972), 254.

35. Max Horkheimer and Theodor Adorno, *Dialektik der Aufklärung: Philosophische Fragmente* (Frankfurt: Fischer, 2019); Ernst Cassirer, *The Myth of the State* (New Haven, CT: Yale University Press, 1946).

Chapter One Discovering Dante and Theorizing Myth

1. Voltaire, *Dictionnaire Philosophique*, part II, in *Œuvres Complètes de Voltaire*, vol. 18 (Paris: Garnier Frères, 1878), 312. Voltaire wrote of Dante's "oracles," a loaded term in the French Enlightenment. Bernard Fontenelle's *Histoires des Oracles* (1687) had demythologized the oracles of pagan antiquity as frauds and aimed thereby to demythologize the rites of Christian Europe. Voltaire's use of the term with respect to Dante suggests similar fraudulence. Israel writes of the controversy in Jonathan Israel, *Radical Enlightenment: Philosophy and the Making of Modernity 1650–1750* (Oxford: Oxford University Press, 2001), 359–374.

2. Nicolo Ciangulo published the first full translation of the *Inferno* into German in 1755. Leberecht Bachenschwanz translated the *Commedia* in its entirety for the first time into German prose between 1767 and 1769. Critics like Johann Nicolaus Meinhard and Johann Jakob Bodmer had translated portions of the poem in critical essays in the mid- to late eighteenth century.

3. Joseph Luzzi, *Romantic Europe and the Ghost of Italy* (New Haven, CT: Yale University Press, 2008), 104.

4. The Gottschedian poet and critic Daniel Wilhelm Triller, for example, dismissed Dante—together with Milton and Ariosto—as a poet of "fieberhaften Träumen" (feverish dreams). Daniel Wilhelm Triller, *Poetische Betrachtungen* (Hamburg: Herold, 1751). In a dedicatory poem to Heinrich Brockes, he mocked Dante's simplemindedness: "Zwar Dantes stellet uns des Ditis Hofstadt dar, / Und schreibt ein langes Werk von der Verdammten Plagen: / Alleine, wird man nur der Einfalt recht gewahr, / So müssen wir dabey mehr lachen, als verzagen" (Dante portrays the royal city of Dis / And writes a long work about the plagues of the damned: / But when one considers its simplicity / We must laugh more than we despair). Quoted in Emil Sulger-Gebing, "Dante in der deutschen Litteratur des XVIII. Jahrhunderts," *Zeitschrift für vergleichende Litteraturgeschichte* 9 (1896): 470. Meinhard marvels over the heights of Dante's genius, yet criticizes him for the "größten Ungereimtheiten" (greatest infelicities) and the "frostigsten und niedrigsten Einfällen" (frostiest and lowest ideas) to which he sinks. Johann Nicolaus Meinhard, *Versuche über den Charakter und die Werke der besten Italiänischen Dichter* (Braunschweig: Waysenhaus-Buchhandlung, 1774), 23.

5. Johann Jakob Bodmer, "Über das dreyfache Gedicht des Dante," in *Schriften zur Literatur*, ed. Volker Meid (Stuttgart: Reclam, 1980), 283–294.

6. Meinhard, *Versuche über den Charakter*, 23.

7. Percy Shelley, "A Defence of Poetry," in *Shelley's Poetry and Prose: A Norton Critical Edition*, ed. Donald H. Reiman and Sharon B. Powers (New York: Norton, 1977), 499.

8. Behler was correct that Schlegel's study of the *Commedia* had shifted interest "from the political, theological, and historical aspects of the work to its poetry and poetic structure," but only because he had argued in the first place for the contemporaneity of those facets. Ernst Behler, "Dante in Germany," in *Dante Encyclopedia*, ed. Richard Lansing (New York: Routledge, 2010), 266.

9. Goethe voiced similar concerns in *Unterhaltungen deutscher Ausgewanderten* (*Conversations of German Refugees*), published, incidentally, next to Schlegel's translations of and comments on Dante's *Inferno* in *Die Horen* (1795).

10. A. W. Schlegel's position toward the Revolution must be reconstructed from Friedrich Schlegel's letters to his brother. In a letter of August 26, 1791, Friedrich acknowledges that A. W. would like for him to read Edmund Burke, a stalwart opponent of the Revolution (KFSA 23:23). On November 24, 1793, amid the Reign of Terror, Friedrich writes to his brother, "Mit Rührung verehre ich Deine edle Menschlichkeit, die . . . Gewaltthätigkeit verabscheut, sie mag im Namen der Ordnung oder im Namen der Freyheit verübt werden; aber ungern sehe ich daß Dein Haß gegen die Franken Dich unbillig macht, daß alle Theilnahme, die Du einem großen Volke zu schenken hast, einige bittre Spöttereyen sind" (With emotion do I revere your noble humanity, which detests the least act of violence, be it exercised in the name of order or in the name of Freedom. Yet it is with displeasure that I see your hatred for the French makes you unreasonable; that all the energy you might give to a great people amounts to a few bitter bits of mockery) (KFSA 23:161).

11. In his Berlin lectures, Schlegel alters and idealizes the notion of the medieval feud. No longer does factionalism mark the Middle Ages as barbaric; instead, it concentrates itself in the form of the feud and finds expression in honorable, hand-to-hand combat (KAV 2/1:76). In fact, the rise of knightly culture became central to Schlegel's historiography of the Middle Ages. He enthused over Germans' knightly heritage and defended religious warfare (KAV 2/1:72–73).

12. The conception of Dante as a "great man" of literature worked against his popularity in the Enlightenment, Luzzi writes, when the principle of *humanité* militated against the celebration of individual genius. But it was the notion of solitary genius, cast into relief by the triumph of Dante's exile, that led to a turn in his fortune in Romantic Italy. Luzzi, *Romantic Europe*, 104–140.

13. Schlegel translated and commented on excerpts from the *Purgatorio* and *Paradiso* between 1795 and 1797. These publications included considerably reduced commentaries and appeared in *Beckers Taschenbuch zum geselligen Vergnügen* (AWSW 3).

14. Friedrich Schiller, *Schillers Werke: Nationalausgabe*, ed. Günter Schulz, vol. 35 (Weimar: Hermann Böhlaus Nachfolger, 1993), 175.

15. Friedrich Schiller, *Schillers Werke: Nationalausgabe*, ed. Günter Schulz, vol. 27 (Weimar: Hermann Böhlaus Nachfolger, 1989), 194.

16. Schiller, *Schillers Werke*, 35:250.

17. Friedrich Klopstock, *Werke und Briefe*, ed. Horst Gronemeyer et al., vol. 9/1 (Berlin: de Gruyter, 1993), 186. While Klopstock displays some knowledge of Dante, joking to Böttiger, for example, that Dante's Latin resembled Kant's German, he seems to have been thwarted by Dante's language, writing that he usually could not understand Dante. Decades earlier he had written to Bodmer that he wished fervently for a translation of Dante (51).

18. L. Mariotti, *Italy: General Views of its History and Literature*, vol. 1 (London: Saunders and Otley, 1841), 169.

19. Robert S. Haller, *Literary Criticism of Dante Alighieri* (Lincoln: University of Nebraska Press, 1973), 99. Schlegel insists on the authenticity of the letter (KAV 2/1, 150), but the matter has provoked debate. See especially Peter Dronke, *Dante and Medieval Latin Traditions* (Cambridge: Cambridge University Press, 1986), and Robert Hollander, *Dante's Epistle to Can Grande* (Ann Arbor: University of Michigan Press, 1993).

20. Schlegel again uses the term *Hieroglyph* to describe the verbal and visual signs of the *Commedia* in his 1799 essay "Ueber Zeichnungen zu Gedichten und John Flaxmans Umriße" (AWSW 9:114).

21. G.W.F. Hegel, *Vorlesungen über die Ästhetik I*, in *Werke*, ed. Eva Moldenhauer and Karl Markus Michel, vol. 13 (Frankfurt: Suhrkamp, 1970).

22. Erich Auerbach, "Figura," in *Time, History, and Literature: Selected Essays of Erich Auerbach*, trans. Jane Newman, ed. James Porter (Princeton, NJ: Princeton University Press, 2015), 65–113, 107.

23. Erich Auerbach, "Entdeckung Dantes in der Romantik," in *Gesammelte Aufsätze zur romanischen Philologie*, 2nd ed., ed. Matthias Bormuth and Martin Vialon (Tübingen: Narr Francke, 2018), 172–179, 178–179.

24. Jeremy Tamblin, *Allegory* (London: Routledge, 2010), 73.

25. William Blake, "A Vision of the Last Judgment," in *Complete Writings*, ed. Geoffrey Keynes (Oxford: Oxford University Press, 1966), 604–617.

26. Edwin Honig, *Dark Conceit: The Making of Allegory* (Evanston, IL: Northwestern University Press, 1959), 46.

27. Kathleen Wheeler, *German Aesthetic and Literary Criticism: The Romantic Ironists and Goethe* (New York: Cambridge University Press, 1984), 157.

28. Schlegel's fragment collections (*Athenäumsfragmente*, *Lyceumsfragmente*, and *Ideen*) are cited parenthetically by fragment collection and fragment number. All citations are from KFSA 2.

29. C. G. Heyne, "Inquiry into the Causes of Fables," in *The Rise of Modern Mythology 1680–1860*, ed. and trans. Burton Feldman and Robert D. Richardson (Bloomington: Indiana University Press, 1972), 218–220; Johann Gottfried Herder, "Vom neuern Gebrauch der Mythologie," in *Frühe Schriften 1764–1772*, ed. Ulrich Gaier, vol. 1 of *Werke in zehn Bänden* (Frankfurt: Deutscher Klassiker Verlag, 1985), 432–455.

30. By dint of his pantheism, Spinoza had been viewed by Romantics as "the man drunk on God," a philosopher whose interpretation of the cosmos had saved religion from the Enlightenment. Frederick Beiser, *The Romantic Imperative: The Concept of Early German Romanticism* (Cambridge, MA: Harvard University Press, 2003), 141–142.

31. Friedrich Daniel Ernst Schleiermacher, *Über die Religion: Reden an die Gebildeten unter ihren Verächtern*, in *Kritische Gesamtausgabe*, ed. Hans-Joachim Birkner, Gerhard Ebeling, Hermann Fischer, Heinz Kimmerle, and Kurt-Victor Selge, Erste Abteilung, vol. 2 (Berlin: de Gruyter, 1984), 185–326, 213.

32. Herder, *Vom neuern Gebrauch der Mythologie*; Karl Philipp Moritz, *Götterlehre: Oder mythologische Dichtungen der Alten* (Berlin: Unger, 1791).

33. See KFSA 16:256, 279, 307; also KFSA 2:318.

34. The new mythology dates at least to the *Systemprogramm*, but Schelling's interest in myth is even older, dating as far back as his 1793 paper "Über Mythen, historische Sagen und Philosopheme der ältesten Welt" (HkA 1/1).

35. G.W.F. Hegel, "Das älteste Systemprogramm des deutschen Idealismus," in *Frühe Schriften*, ed. Eva Moldenhauer and Karl Markus Michel, vol. 1 of *Werke* (Frankfurt: Suhrkamp, 1971), 234–237, 235.

36. Moritz, *Götterlehre*, 4.

37. The most extensive treatment of reflection as a central device of Romantic poetry is Benjamin's dissertation, *Der Begriff der Kunstkritik in der deutschen Romantik* (*The Concept of Criticism in German Romanticism*) (Frankfurt: Suhrkamp, 1973). Lacoue-Labarthe and Nancy took up that concept and applied it to the poetry of Schelling; see Phillippe Lacoue-Labarthe and Jean-Luc Nancy, *The Literary Absolute: The Theory of Literature in German Romanticism*, trans Philip Barnard (Albany: State University of New York Press, 1988). Whistler has argued convincingly, however, that reflection is a point where—even in his "Romantic" phase—Schelling's poetics is to be distinguished from that of Friedrich Schlegel; see Daniel Whistler, "Schelling's Poetry," *Clio* 43, no. 2 (2014): 143–175.

38. Luzzi, *Romantic Europe*, 125.

39. Xavier Tilliette, *Schelling: Une Philosophie en Devenir*, vol. 1 (Paris: Librairie Philosophique J. Vrin, 1970), 369n50, 392n48, 398n65.

40. The belated classicism the Romantics witnessed in Dante's absolutization of the medieval world convinced them of his status as the father of modern poetry. This was especially true of Schelling and Friedrich Schlegel (KFSA 16:171, 131, 272; KFSA 2:52; SW 5:152, 154).

41. Ernst Behler, *German Romantic Literary Theory* (Cambridge: Cambridge University Press, 1993), 154.

42. For the various generic references see KFSA 16:116 (epic); KFSA 16:157 (novel, drama, prophecy); KFSA 16:375 (didactic and lyric poetry); KFSA 16:493 (epic and didactic).

43. The same comparison is made in the essay on Flaxman, except there Dante is contrasted with Milton. Schlegel writes that Dante "stellt . . . eine vollständige Galerie aller menschlichen und göttlichen Charaktere auf" (displays a complete gallery of all human and divine characters) (AWSW 9:118). It is also worth consulting A. W. Schlegel's comments in *Athenäumsfragment* 193, where he discusses Dante with respect to the visual arts and Michelangelo.

44. Schlegel's notebooks in these years teem with such considerations; see KFSA 16:255, 264, 270, 280, 281, 286, 290, 302, 332, 356.

45. Wolfgang Herwig, ed., *Goethes Gespräche: Eine Sammlung zeitgenössischer Berichte aus seinem Umgang*, 3 vols. (Zürich: Artemis Verlag, 1965–1972), 3/1:590.

46. George S. Williamson, *The Longing for Myth in Germany: Religion and Aesthetic Culture from Romanticism to Nietzsche* (Chicago: University of Chicago Press, 2004), 121–150.

47. For discussions of Tieck and Eichendorff with respect to Dante, see Annette Budzinski-Luftig, "The Divine Comedy of Education: Curious German Encounters with Dante" (PhD diss., Johns Hopkins University, 2010); Irmgard Osols-Wehden, *Pilgerfahrt und Narrenreise: Der Einfluss der Dichtungen Dantes und Ariosts auf den frühromantischen Roman in Deutschland* (Hildesheim: Weidmann, 1998); and Thomas Riley, "Die Allegorie in *Ahnung und Gegenwart*," *Aurora: Jahrbuch der Eichendorff-Gesellschaft* 44 (1984): 23–31. Dante appears in the novella *Die Hochzeit des Mönchs* (*The Monk's Wedding*) by the Swiss

writer Conrad Ferdinand Meyer. He likewise appears later in Gerhart Hauptmann's *Der große Traum* (see chapter four).

Chapter Two *Schelling, Novalis, and the Legitimation of a Dantean Mythology*

1. Josef Körner, ed., *August Wilhelm und Friedrich Schlegel im Briefwechsel mit Schiller und Goethe* (Leipzig: Insel-Verlag, 1926), 57.

2. Friedrich Schiller, *Schillers Werke: Nationalausgabe*, ed. Lieselotte Blumenthal, vol. 30 (Weimar: Hermann Böhlaus Nachfolger, 1961), 417.

3. Wolfgang Herwig, ed., *Goethes Gespräche: Eine Sammlung zeitgenössischer Berichte aus seinem Umgang*, 3 vols. (Zürich: Artemis Verlag, 1965–1972), 1:845.

4. Herwig, *Goethes Gespräche*, 714.

5. Reproductions of the caricatures and commentary are available in Rainer Schmitz, ed., *Die ästhetische Prügeley: Streitschriften der antiromantischen Bewegung* (Göttingen: Wallstein, 1992), 423–455.

6. Ernst Behler, *German Romantic Literary Theory* (Cambridge: Cambridge University Press, 1993), 164.

7. Emphasis added.

8. Emphasis added.

9. Jeremy Adler, "The Aesthetics of Magnetism: Science, Philosophy and Poetry in the Dialogue between Goethe and Schelling," in *The Third Culture: Literature and Science*, ed. Elinor S. Shaffer (Berlin: de Gruyter, 1998), 66–102; Hans Kunz, *Schellings Gedichte und dichterische Pläne* (Zürich: Juris-Verlag, 1955); H. B. Nisbet, "Lucretius in Eighteenth-Century Germany: With a Commentary on Goethe's 'Metamorphose der Tiere,'" *Modern Language Review* 100 (2005): 115–133; Margarete Plath, "Der Goethe-Schellingsche Plan eines philosophischen Naturgedichts: Eine Studie zu Goethes 'Gott und Welt,'" *Preußische Jahrbücher* 106 (1901): 44–74; Daniel Whistler, "Schelling's Poetry," *Clio* 43, no. 2 (2014): 143–175.

10. Caroline Schelling, *Briefe aus der Frühromantik*, ed. Erich Schmidt, 2 vols. (Leipzig: Insel, 1913), 2:6.

11. The poem is cited parenthetically by line number. The poem is printed in G. L. Plitt, *Aus Schellings Leben*, in *Briefen*, vol. 1 (Leipzig: Hirzel, 1869), 282–289. Lacoue-Labarthe and Nancy pair it with the *Nachtwachen von Bonaventura*, attributing both to Schelling on the basis of his pseudonym, Bonaventura. In actuality, as Haym pointed out, A. W. Schlegel had chosen the name as an alternative to the pseudonym of Schelling's youth, Venturus. Rudolf Haym, *Die romantische Schule* (Berlin: Gaertner, 1870), 635.

12. Whistler, "Schelling's Poetry," 150.

13. Whistler offers the single best contextualization of "Widerporst" and "Das himmlische Bild" as they relate to the system of Schelling's philosophy. His effort to rescue Schelling from the (mis)reading of Lacoue-Labarthe and Nancy results, however, in an overstatement of the distinctions between Schelling's poetic program and that of Early Romantics like the Schlegels, whose reading of the *Commedia* shaped Schelling's view of it. This is not to count Schelling among the Romantics' number, only to indicate that his reception and imitation of Dante are inextricable from those of the Schlegel brothers and the project of the new mythology.

14. The poem is cited parenthetically by line number. The editor of the *Sämmtliche Werke* errs in dating its composition between 1807 and 1811. We know from Friedrich Schlegel's letter to Schleiermacher on January 6, 1800, that it existed in its present form by

Christmas 1799. Furthermore, despite Schelling's intention to write in *terza rima*, he composed the poem in *ottava rima*. The forms have been confused on more than one occasion; see Liliane Weissberg, "Weimar and Jena: Goethe and the New Philosophy," in *Goethe und das Zeitalter der Romantik*, ed. Walter Hinderer (Würzburg: Königshausen & Neumann, 2002), 163–174, 173; and Whistler, "Schelling's Poetry," 175.

15. Whistler, "Schelling's Poetry," 169.

16. Schelling, *Briefe aus der Frühromantik*, 2:34.

17. Plitt, *Aus Schellings Leben*, 1:303–304.

18. The poem appeared in the *Musen-Almanach für das Jahr 1802*, ed. A. W. Schlegel and Ludwig Tieck (Tübingen: Cotta, 1802).

19. The poem is cited parenthetically by line number.

20. Wm. Arctander O'Brien, *Novalis: Signs of Revolution* (Durham, NC: Duke University Press, 1995), 11.

21. Karl Immermann, *Karl Immermann's Dramatische Schriften*, vol. 2 (Leipzig: Klemm, 1832).

22. Heinrich Heine, *Die Romantische Schule* (Hamburg: Hoffmann und Campe, 1836), 136.

23. The closest one comes to its possibility is a letter from Friedrich Schlegel to A. W. Schlegel: "Schiller hat sehr gut von dir geredet; vorzüglich Dein Dante hat ihm sehr gefallen, und nach dem was er von andern vom Dante gehört, glaubt er daß Du deßen Geist vortrefflich gefaßt hättest. Dies hat er Hardenberg gesagt, nicht *mir*" (Schiller spoke highly of you; your Dante pleased him especially, and judging by what he has heard of Dante from others, he believes you have captured his spirit excellently. He told this to Hardenberg [Novalis], not to *me*) (*Schriften* 4:573).

24. Silvio Vietta, "Dantes 'Matelda' und Novalis' 'Mathilde': Die säkularisierte Gestalt des irdischen Paradieses," in *Ästhetik, Religion, Säkularisierung: Von der Renaissance zur Romantik*, ed. Silvio Vietta and Herbert Uerlings (Paderborn: Fink, 2008), 111–131.

25. Albert Béguin, *L'âme romantique et le rêve: Essai sur le romantisme allemand et la poésie française* (Marseilles: Cahiers du Sud, 1937).

26. Edward Ahearn, *Visionary Fictions: Apocalyptic Writing from Blake to the Modern Age* (New Haven, CT: Yale University Press, 1996), 40.

27. Hans-Joachim Mähl, *Die Idee des goldenen Zeitalters im Werk des Novalis: Studien zur Wesensbestimmung der frühromantischen Utopie und zu ihren ideengeschichtlichen Voraussetzungen*, 2nd ed. (Tübingen: Niemeyer, 1994).

28. KFSA 2:283; HkA 9/1:329; *Schriften* 1:104.

29. Wilhelm Dilthey, *Das Erlebnis und die Dichtung: Lessing, Goethe, Novalis, Hölderlin* (Leipzig: Teubner, 1922).

30. Haym, *Die romantische Schule.*

31. Elisabeth Stopp, "'Übergang vom Roman zur Mythologie': Formal Aspects of the Opening Chapter of Hardenberg's *Heinrich von Ofterdingen, Part II*," *Deutsche Vierteljahrsschrift für Geistesgeschichte und Literaturwissenschaft* 48 (1974): 318–341.

32. Dennis Mahoney, "The Myth of Death and Resurrection in *Heinrich von Ofterdingen*," *South Atlantic Review* 48, no. 2 (1983): 52–66.

33. Haym, *Die romantische Schule*, 386–387.

34. The subjective idealism intrinsic to Haym's reading is neatly encapsulated in his observation that "Die Metaphysik des Menschenlebens, zusammenfallend mit der

Metaphysik des Universums, wird in geschichtlicher Form, in Form einer Erzählung von dem Lebenslauf eines Dichters mit der unbedingten Freiheit metaphysischer, transcendentaler Poesie vorgetragen" (The metaphysics of human life, coinciding with the metaphysics of the universe, is presented in historical form, in the form of a narrative of the life course of a poet with the unconditioned freedom of metaphysics, of transcendental poetry) (383).

35. Frederick Beiser, *German Idealism: The Struggle against Subjectivism, 1781–1801* (Cambridge, MA: Harvard University Press, 2002), 409; Dalia Nassar, *The Romantic Absolute: Being and Knowing in Early German Romantic Philosophy, 1795–1804* (Chicago: University of Chicago Press, 2014), 79.

36. Giovanni Boccaccio, *Life of Dante*, ed. and trans. G. R. Carpenter (New York: Grolier, 1900), 85.

37. Bruno Nardi, *Dante e la cultura medievale* (Bari: Laterza, 1984), 318; Charles Singleton, "The Irreducible Dove," *Comparative Literature* 9, no. 2 (1957): 129.

38. Teodolinda Barolini, *The Undivine* Comedy: *Detheologizing Dante* (Princeton, NJ: Princeton University Press, 1992).

39. Barolini, *The Undivine* Comedy, 144.

40. Statements like these were not uncommon before Novalis's death. Dorothea Schlegel, for example, wrote in 1799 that Novalis had the look of a "Geisterseher" (seer of spirits) (*Schriften* 4:647). His peers detected a mystical presence in him. The expression of these intuitions grew by leaps and bounds after his death.

41. Bruce Donehower, *The Birth of Novalis: Friedrich von Hardenberg's Journal of 1797, with Selected Letters and Documents* (Albany: State University of New York Press, 2015), 2–3.

42. O'Brien, *Novalis*, 2.

43. *Ofterdingen* and the *Rede* were both written in 1800. It is difficult to know whether Novalis's adaptation of Dante was a response to the comments on Dante in Schlegel's essay or vice versa. The Dante phenomenon was indeed a matter of Romantic *Symphilosophie*.

44. Judith Ryan, "Hybrid Forms in German Romanticism," in *Prosimetrum: Crosscultural Perspectives on Narrative in Prose and Verse*, ed. Karl Reichl and Joseph Harris (Suffolk, UK: Boydell and Brewer, 1997), 165–181, 169. Other commentators include Walter Strauss, *Descent and Return: The Orphic Theme in Modern Literature* (Cambridge, MA: Harvard University Press 1971), 26; Magdalena Boettcher, *Eine andere Ordnung der Dinge: Zur Ästhetik des Schönen und ihrer poetologischen Rezeption um 1800* (Würzburg: Königshausen und Neumann, 1998), 209; and Donehower, *The Birth of Novalis*, 1. Wachtel triangulates Dante, Novalis, and Viacheslav Ivanov but does not observe a direct relationship between Novalis and Dante. Michael Wachtel, "Vyacheslav Ivanov: From Aesthetic Theory to Biographical Practice," in *Creating Life: The Aesthetic Utopia of Russian Modernism*, ed. Irina Paperno and Joan Grossman (Stanford, CA: Stanford University Press, 1994), 151–166, 164–165.

45. In Dante's Ptolomaic cosmology, the number three refers to the third sphere removed from the earth, Venus, and therefore also to the goddess of love. The number figures centrally in the *Commedia*, as well, where it points to the Trinity. Dante explains that Beatrice is intimately linked with the number nine and with its root, the number three. Dante, *Vita Nuova*, trans. Mark Musa (New York: Oxford University Press, 1992), 61.

46. Robert Hollander, "*Vita nuova*: Dante's Perceptions of Beatrice," *Dante Studies* 92 (1974): 1–18.

47. Heinz Ritter, *Der unbekannte Novalis: Friedrich von Hardenberg im Spiegel seiner Dichtung* (Göttingen: Sachse & Pohl, 1967), 74.

Chapter Three Goethe's Dantean Mythologies of the Self and of the World

1. Nicholas Boyle, *Goethe: The Poet and the Age* (Oxford: Oxford University Press, 2000), vii.

2. The scholarship on the *Commedia* and *Faust* is unsurprisingly vast, yet often unilluminating. A full century ago, this led Hugo Daffner to suggest that the juxtaposition of the poems was not worth pursuing. Those who sought a "goldenes Korn" (golden kernel) would dig in vain; see Hugo Daffner, "Goethe und Dante," *Dante-Jahrbuch* 5 (1920): 166. Heaps of unhelpful scholarship render Daffner's skepticism well founded. An endeavor like that of Sulger-Gebing, for example, reads like a wild-goose chase (esp. 69–111); see Emil Sulger-Gebing, *Goethe und Dante* (Berlin: Duncker, 1907). The apparent futility, though, is often more reflective of the quest than of its object. Scholarship tries so hard to justify the endeavor that it leads to an exposition of cases in "proof," a record of "influence." The result is a body of literature that often has little to say. Wais explained the negative consequence of these impulses: they have led to a dismissal of Goethe's engagement with Dante as something trivial. This is bizarre, he explains, because it strips Goethe of poetic agency, as if the Dantean bookends of *Faust* were an afterthought or accidental; see Kurt Wais, "Die *Divina Commedia* als dichterisches Vorbild im 19. und 20. Jahrhundert," in *Europäische Literatur im Vergleich: Gesammelte Aufsätze*, ed. Johannes Hösle, Dieter Janik, and Wolfgang Theile (Tübingen: M. Niemeyer, 1983), 27–47, 32. On the other hand, there continue to appear compelling juxtapositions of the poems. Some develop out of an intertextual-historical reading (e.g., Gaier), while others pursue broader questions of cultural meaning and poetics (e.g., Hösle). The present chapter aligns more nearly with the former venture—not in vain, I hope. Ulrich Gaier, *Johann Wolfgang von Goethe: Faust. Der Tragödie zweiter Teil* (Stuttgart: Reclam, 2004); Vittorio Hösle, *Dantes Commedia und Goethes Faust: Ein Vergleich der beiden wichtigsten philosophischen Dichtungen Europas* (Basel: Schwabe, 2014).

3. Augustine, *Confessions*, trans. Henry Chadwick (New York: Oxford University Press, 1991), 26–27, 163.

4. Friedrich Nietzsche, *Menschliches, Allzumenschliches*, ed. Giorgio Colli and Mazzino Montinari (Munich: DTV, 1988), 139.

5. Hans Blumenberg, *Work on Myth*, trans. Robert M. Wallace (Cambridge, MA: MIT Press, 1985).

6. Garry Wills, *Augustine's Confessions: A Biography* (Princeton, NJ: Princeton University Press, 2011), 142.

7. Blumenberg, *Work on Myth*, 67–68.

8. Paul de Man, *The Rhetoric of Romanticism* (New York: Columbia University Press, 1984), 67–71.

9. Rudolf Safranski, *Goethe: Kunstwerk des Lebens* (Munich: Hanser, 2013).

10. The spelling throughout the excerpt belongs to the letter.

11. Daniel DiMassa, "Varieties of Radical Enlightenment: Secularization as Translation in Goethe's Autobiography," *Religion & Literature* 48, no. 1 (2016): 51–69; Blumenberg, *Work on Myth*, part 4.

12. Kirk Wetters, *Demonic History: From Goethe to the Present* (Evanston, IL: Northwestern University Press, 2014).

13. Vittorio Hösle, "Religion of Art, Self-Mythicization and the Function of the Church Year in Goethe's *Italienische Reise*," *Religion & Literature* 38, no. 4 (2006): 1–25.

14. Hösle, "Religion of Art," 11–13.

15. Edward Said, *On Late Style* (New York: Random House, 2006), 6.

16. In the years just after 1820, "neues Leben" may well have been a motto of Goethe's poetry. It is invoked in his poetry as a balm for the soul, a panacea whose sources are many. It might be a gift of the gods, as he suggests in a prayer to Brahma: "Uns, die tief herabgesetzten, / Alle hast du neu geboren" (Those of us laid low, / You have born anew) (MA 13/1:88). Or it could come from within, as he advised Princess Maria of Weimar on her twelfth birthday: if she summoned "inneres Erneuen" (inner renewal), she could overcome the "äußerlich[es] Zerstreuen" (external dissipation) of adolescence (MA 13/1:19). For his part, Goethe found new life in acquaintanceship with women, especially younger women. To the twenty-three-year-old Lili Parthey, he confessed, "Du hattest gleich mir's angetan, / Doch nun gewahr ich neues Leben" (You did it to me right away, / But now I sense new life) (MA 13/1:89). He recycled the same lines and dedicated them to the nineteen-year-old Ulrike von Levetzow just a few months later. Goethe, apparently, was reborn with some frequency.

17. Dante measured the middle of the walk of our life to be age thirty-five. It was a traditional computation based on Psalm 90:10.

18. The poem is in WA 1/2:141–147; I cite it by line number. My reading relies on and develops the observations of Steiner, in contrast to the skepticism of Hirdt; see Arpad Steiner, "A Trace of Dante in Goethe's 'Ilmenau,'" *Modern Language Notes* 48, no. 2 (1933): 86–87; and Willi Hirdt, "Goethe und Dante," *Deutsches Dante-Jahrbuch* 68/69 (1993/1994): 31–80.

19. Lines 10, 20, and 165. Admittedly, the first of these is not exactly "neues Leben," but rather "neues Eden."

20. The Dantean resonance is noted in Borchmeyer, Schulz, and Wellbery, who emphasize, in that connection, the significance of the poem as sonnet. Dieter Borchmeyer, *Weimarer Klassik: Portrait einer Epoche* (Weinheim: Beltz Athenäum, 2009), 508; Gerhard Schulz, "Mächtiges Überraschen," in *Goethe Handbuch*, ed. Bernd Witte and Regine Otto, vol. 1 (Stuttgart: Metzler, 2004), 334–336, 334; David Wellbery, "On the Logic of Change in Goethe's Work," *Goethe Yearbook* 21 (2014): 19. See also Andrew Piper, "Reading's Refrain: From Bibliography to Topology," *ELH* 80 (2013): 392.

21. This is not to reduce the complexity of the poem, debates over which Mülder-Bach has outlined; see Inka Mülder-Bach, "Mahomets Gesang," in *Goethe Handbuch*, ed. Bernd Witte and Regine Otto, vol. 1 (Stuttgart: Metzler, 2004), 99–107, 101. But as Wellbery notes, "every critic who has written on the poem has noted [the metaphor of the stream as 'the process of religious-historical foundation']"; see David Wellbery, *The Specular Moment: Goethe's Early Lyric and the Beginnings of Romanticism* (Stanford, CA: Stanford University Press, 1996), 136. Mülder-Bach, to cite one example, describes it as a metaphor of the "zivilisatorischen Prozesses" (civilizing process) (102).

22. Wellbery, *The Specular Moment*, 123.

23. Blumenberg, *Work on Myth*, 435.

24. Wellbery, *The Specular Moment*, 122.

25. The figure of the river coursing down the mountain alludes to Horace, ode IV, book 2. Pindar's voice is like a river rushing down the mountain. See Goethe's letter to Herder (WA 4/2:15–16).

26. See chapter two.

27. I quote the text of the drama by line number, here and subsequently, using Johann Wolfgang Goethe, *Faust: Texte*, ed. Albrecht Schöne (Frankfurt: Deutscher Klassiker Verlag, 2017).

28. On one other occasion, Goethe used *terza rima* to compose lines on the occasion of his contemplation of Schiller's skull. This poem, "Im ernsten Beinhaus" (In the Charnel House), was composed at the same time as the Faust monologue. In an interesting thesis, Paul Friedländer surmised that Goethe may have planned a cycle of poems in *terza rima*; see Paul Friedländer, *Rhythmen und Landschaften im zweiten Teil des Faust* (Weimar: Böhlaus Nachfolger, 1953). Most recently, Daniel Carranza has written about Goethe's use of the tercet; see Daniel Carranza, "The (Dis)Consolations of Form. On the Temporality of Rhyme in Goethe's *Im ernsten Beinhaus war's*," in *Goethes Spätwerk*, ed. Kai Sina and David Wellbery (Berlin: de Gruyter, 2020), 99–140. I have discussed it with respect to automythologization elsewhere; see Daniel DiMassa, "Der göttliche Poet: Romantische Selbstmythologisierung in Goethes Terzinen," *Goethe-Jahrbuch* 131 (2014): 59–70.

29. The griffin's two natures (lion and eagle) represent the two natures of Christ (human and divine).

30. I refer to *Faust II* in these terms since it contends less with dynamics of subjectivity than with forces of modernity, notably capitalism, imperialism, industry, and technology. Albrecht Schöne's textual analysis is particularly helpful in the assertion of this point. By his reckoning, Faust's speech accounts for 30 percent of the drama's first part, but only 13 percent of its second part; the collective speech of groups, however, rises from 7 percent of the text in the first part to 20 percent in the second part. The shifts are indicative, to use Schöne's words, of a drama that is concerned with "die großen Weltverhältnisse" (the great relations in the world). See Albrecht Schöne, *Faust: Kommentare* (Frankfurt: Deutscher Klassiker Verlag, 2017), 387–388.

31. The paper money scheme relies on the earth inasmuch as the value of paper is ostensibly vouchsafed by what the emperor may lay claim to in the ground (4937–4938).

32. William Clare Roberts, *Marx's Inferno*: *The Political Theory of Capital* (Princeton, NJ: Princeton University Press, 2018), 3.

33. Hans Cristoph Binswanger, *Money and Magic: A Critique of the Modern Economy in the Light of Goethe's* Faust (Chicago: University of Chicago Press, 1994); Heinz Schlaffer, *Faust: Zweiter Teil: Die Allegorie des 19. Jahrhunderts* (Stuttgart: Metzler, 1981).

34. Schöne, *Faust*, 426.

35. The topic of homosexuality in the *Commedia* is notably ambiguous. Dante refers to a notion of homosexuality as *Soddoma* (*Inf.* 11.48–50; *Purg.* 26.40), characterizing it as a sin against nature. But many of his descriptions are elliptical. There are signs in the text that read like shibboleths, which Durling accounts for by explaining that same-sex love was a sin that "dare not speak its name" (*Inferno*, 557). I retain the term *sodomite*, despite its barbarism, because it seems more barbaric yet to conflate it with a contemporary concept of homosexuality, onto which the term *sodomy* can then attach itself.

36. I take seriously Jane Brown's contention that Mephistopheles is "consistently tied to the natural world"; nevertheless, I find more instructive in understanding his relation to nature what Brown calls "his attitude toward it," which amounts to an impulse toward annihilation. Jane K. Brown, *Faust: Theater of the World* (New York: Twayne, 1992), 40–41.

37. Tobin points out several compelling examples of Mephistopheles's efforts to avert Faust's gaze from the feminine and to redirect it toward phallic objects. These examples

underscore the roots of what we find in "Grablegung": Mephistopheles's male–male fixation signals his impulse to thwart the *Menschengeist* from its pursuit of the feminine. Robert Tobin, *Warm Brothers: Queer Theory and the Age of Goethe* (Philadelphia: University of Pennsylvania Press, 2000), 141; W. Daniel Wilson, *Goethe Männer Knaben: Ansichten zur Homosexualität* (Berlin: Insel, 2012).

38. Harold Jantz, "The Place of the 'Eternal-Womanly' in Goethe's Faust Drama," *PMLA* 68, no. 4 (1953): 791–805.

39. Commentators usually regard the battle over Faust's soul as a parodic adaptation of a common motif in medieval art and drama. Schöne, for example, points to Goethe's possession of a copperplate reproduction of a fresco, *Il trionfo della morte* (*The Triumph of Death*) (Schöne, *Faust*, 764). The reproduction was ostensibly the work of Andrea Orgagna (Orcagna). Schöne does not note that it was Goethe's engagement with Dante, in the summer of 1826, that led him to seek out the artwork of Orcagna (MA 13/1:878).

40. Johann Peter Eckermann, *Gespräche mit Goethe in den letzten Jahren seines Lebens*, 3 vols. (Leipzig: Brockhaus, 1836–1848), 1:170.

41. Herwig, *Goethes Gespräche*, 3/1:590.

42. Steiner, "A Trace of Dante"; Hirdt, "Goethe und Dante."

43. An exemplary expression of this impulse is the introduction in Karl Vossler's 1907 two-volume study of Dante and his age: "Die Zusammenstellung des größten italienischen mit dem größten deutschen Gedicht ist uns seit den Tagen der Romantiker zur Gewohnheit geworden. Sie hat ihre gute Berechtigung. Aber nicht etwa in einer tatsächlichen und geschichtlichen, sondern in einer rein geistigen, inneren und eben darum tieferen Verwandtschaft der beiden Werke" (The juxtaposition of the greatest Italian and the greatest German poems has become a common practice since the days of Romanticism—and with good reason. The affinity of both works, however, is not to be taken in a positive, historical sense, but rather in a purely intellectual, spiritual, and—therefore—profounder sense.) Karl Vossler, *Die göttliche Komödie: Entwicklungsgeschichte und Erklärung*, 2 vols. (Heidelberg: Winter, 1907), 1:1.

44. Friedrich Gundolf, "Dante," *Castrum Peregrini* 91 (1970): 34.

Chapter Four   Trespassing the Sign

1. Johann Peter Eckermann, *Gespräche mit Goethe in den letzten Jahren seines Lebens*, 3 vols. (Leipzig: Brockhaus, 1836–1848), 2:92.

2. Sean Franzel, *Connected by the Ear: The Media, Pedagogy, and Politics of the Romantic Lecture* (Evanston, IL: Northwestern University Press, 2013).

3. G.W.F. Hegel, "Das älteste Systemprogramm des deutschen Idealismus," in *Frühe Schriften*, ed. Eva Moldenhauer and Karl Markus Michel, vol. 1 of *Werke* (Frankfurt: Suhrkamp, 1971), 235.

4. Schlegel's *Rede* and Schleiermacher's *Reden* were speeches in name alone. They were never "delivered" as such. The point suggests the degree to which Romantic rhetoric aspired to oratory.

5. Hugo von Hofmannsthal, "Das Schrifttum als geistiger Raum der Nation," in *Reden und Aufsätze III*, ed. Bernd Schoeller, vol. 10 of *Gesammelte Werke in zehn Einzelbänden* (Frankfurt: Fischer, 1980), 24–41, 30.

6. Hofmannsthal acknowledged the similarity of these figures to the Romantics, but he sought to distinguish the seekers by characterizing them as more manly, more deliberate,

and more patient. They were no longer subject to boyish whimsicality; they had been hardened in their spiritual quest. Hofmannsthal, "Das Schrifttum als geistiger Raum," 35–36.

7. Attendees noted that Borchardt screamed and gesticulated wildly while speaking. It was not a lecture so much as a sermon. Hans Carossa, *Tagebücher, 1925–1935*, ed. Eva Kampmann-Carossa (Frankfurt: Insel, 1993), 35.

8. Unless noted otherwise, citations of Borchardt in parentheses refer to individual volumes in his *Gesammelte Werke in Einzelbänden*, ed. Marie Luise Borchardt, 14 vols. (Stuttgart: Ernst Klett, 1955–).

9. It was the same love spoken of by Thomas Mann in his speech "Von deutscher Republik" (On the German Republic). That speech was delivered on Hauptmann's birthday, one year after Hauptmann had propounded the national ideal of love in his speech, "Deutsche Wiedergeburt" (German rebirth). I discuss Mann's speech in chapter six.

10. Hofmannsthal, "Das Schrifttum als geistiger Raum," 39.

11. Glenn Most, "Dante's Greeks," *Arion: A Journal of Humanities and the Classics* 13, no. 3 (2006): 41.

12. They are bound, too, in that each man has undertaken a journey to the underworld while still living (cf. *Odyssey*, book 9).

13. Hofmannsthal, in his mention of a conservative revolution, states that "Ihr[e] Ziel ist Form" (its goal is form); see Hofmannsthal, "Das Schrifttum als geistiger Raum," 40. The Neo-Romantic reforms of the German language were often conducted self-consciously in the light of Luther's Reformation. See Hauptmann (CA 6:888–889); Hofmannsthal, "Das Schrifttum als geistiger Raum," 40; and GW, *Prosa II*, 505–507.

14. Hofmannsthal, "Das Schrifttum als geistiger Raum," 23.

15. Most, "Dante's Greeks," 40.

16. Rolf Italiaander, "Gerhart Hauptmann in Dresden 1943," *Gerhart Hauptmann Jahrbuch* 1 (1948): 134.

17. The Bergpater sees German labor movements as an untapped reservoir with the utopian potential outlined by Dante (CA 10:877).

18. Leif Weatherby, *Transplanting the Metaphysical Organ: German Romanticism between Leibniz and Marx* (New York: Fordham University Press, 2016), 212.

19. Martin Heidegger, *Was heisst Denken?* (Tübingen: Niemeyer, 1954).

20. Karl Guthke, "Die Mythologie des späten Gerhart Hauptmann," *Monatshefte* 49, no. 6 (1957): 289–303.

21. Hitler, Adolf, *Mein Kampf* (Munich: Eher Verlag, 1943), 116. Hauptmann read and heavily annotated a copy of *Mein Kampf* in 1933. Othmar Plöckinger, *Geschichte eines Buches: Adolf Hitlers "Mein Kampf," 1922–1945* (Berlin: De Gruyter, 2011), 448.

22. Carl Friedrich Wilhelm Behl, *Zwiesprache mit Gerhart Hauptmann* (Munich: Desch, 1948), 103.

23. Peter Sprengel, *Gerhart Hauptmann: Bürgerlichkeit und großer Traum* (Munich: Beck, 2012), 590.

24. Guthke, "Die Mythologie des späten Gerhart Hauptmann."

25. The novelty of what Hauptmann shows Dante depends on our suspension of disbelief. It is difficult to find a poet, who, after all, is more critical of churchmen than Dante.

26. See, for example, Douglas Radcliff-Umstead, "Dante's Influence on *The Great Dream* of Gerhart Hauptmann," *Forum Italicum* 2, no. 1 (1968): 24.

27. For example: "Oh, diese Fahrt!" (Oh, this journey!) (1067); "Es war, als hockten wir in einem Boot / stocktaub und segelten mit schwarzen Föhnen" (It was as if we hunkered in a boat / stone-deaf and sailed with black winds) (1067); "Heil'gen Entsetzens voll blickt' ich umher, / indes uns abwärts fuhr der Mann am Steuer" (Full of holy horror I glanced around, / while the man at the helm led us down) (1069).

28. Heidegger, *Was heisst Denken?*, 7.

29. Frederick Beiser, *The Romantic Imperative: The Concept of Early German Romanticism* (Cambridge, MA: Harvard University Press, 2003), 63.

30. Max Horkheimer and Theodor W. Adorno, *Dialektik der Aufklärung: Philosophische Fragmente* (Frankfurt: Fischer, 2019).

31. Günter Scholdt, *Autoren über Hitler: Deutschsprachige Schriftsteller (1919–1945) und ihr Bild vom Führer* (Bonn: Bouvier, 1993), 33.

32. The latter is more true of Hauptmann than the early Romantics, though likely the case, as well, for Novalis (an important source of Hauptmann's Romanticism and possibly an important heir of Dantean political utopianism).

Chapter Five Abolishing History

1. Mircea Eliade, *Cosmos and History: The Myth of the Eternal Return*, trans. Willard Trask (New York: Harper, 1954).

2. Stefan George and Hugo von Hofmannsthal, *Briefwechsel zwischen George und Hofmannsthal* (Munich: Küpper, 1953), 150.

3. The notion became central to the George-Kreis at large. Among the clearest monuments to it was Max Kommerell's influential history *Der Dichter als Führer in der deutschen Klassik: Klopstock, Herder, Goethe, Schiller, Jean Paul, Hölderlin* (Berlin: Bondi, 1928).

4. Borchardt prescribed the adoption of *terza rima* and the *endecasillabo*. Goethe had taken the first steps in *Faust II* and "Im ernsten Beinhaus" (In the charnel house). Eichendorff, Platen, and Immermann, too, pointed in the right direction (GW, *Prosa II*, 364–365).

5. David Miles, *Hofmannsthal's Novel "Andreas": Memory and Self* (Princeton, NJ: Princeton University Press, 1972).

6. Karl Vossler, "Dante, Göttliche Komödie: Übertragen von Stefan George," *Deutsche Literaturzeitung* 36 (1912): 2288–2290.

7. Quoted in Karl-Heinz Barck and Martin Treml, *Erich Auerbach: Geschichte und Aktualität eines europäischen Philologen* (Berlin: Kadmos, 2007), 411–412.

8. Edith Landmann, *Gespräche mit Stefan George* (Düsseldorf: Helmut Küpper vormals Georg Bondi, 1963), 105.

9. Robert Boehringer, *Mein Bild von Stefan George* (Düsseldorf: Helmut Küpper vormals Georg Bondi, 1968), 38.

10. Ernst Morwitz, *Kommentar zu dem Werk Stefan Georges* (Düsseldorf: Helmut Küpper vormals Georg Bondi, 1969), 291. The passages are *Inferno* 7.1 and *Inferno* 31.67. These passages likely had broad significance for the Kreis. Friedrich Gundolf, for example, devoted one of his seven doctoral theses to defending the contention that Plutus's exclamation had no semantic meaning; see Stefan George and Friedrich Gundolf, *Stefan George–Friedrich Gundolf: Briefwechsel*, ed. Robert Boehringer and Georg Peter Landmann (Munich: Helmut Küpper, 1962), 134.

11. Maria Arrighetti, "Dante · *Die Göttliche Komödie: Übertragungen*," in *Stefan George und sein Kreis: Ein Handbuch*, ed. Achim Aurnhammer, Wolfgang Braungart, Stefan Breuer, and Ute Oelmann, 2nd ed., vol. 1 (Berlin: de Gruyter, 2016), 218–253, 219.

12. Landmann, *Gespräche mit Stefan George*, 42. The preface to the collected translations of 1909, in addition to the lines cited above, include the remark that Dante stands "am anfang aller Neuen Dichtung" (at the outset of all modern poetry) (SGSW 10/11:5).

13. Landmann, *Gespräche mit Stefan George*, 17, 37, 42, 65.

14. Peter Sprengel, *Gerhart Hauptmann: Bürgerlichkeit und großer Traum* (Munich: Beck, 2012), 70.

15. The letter is dated January 14, 1906, in Rudolf Borchardt, *Briefe 1895–1906* (Munich: Hanser, 1995). See also Borchardt's account of the episode in Rudolf Borchardt, *Aufzeichnung Stefan George betreffend*, ed. Ernst Osterkamp (Munich: Rudolf Borchardt-Gesellschaft, 1998), 31–32.

16. Borchardt, *Aufzeichnung Stefan George betreffend*, 179.

17. Sprengel, *Gerhart Hauptmann*, 141, 171.

18. Friedrich Gundolf, "Das Bild Georges," *Jahrbuch für die geistige Bewegung* 1 (1910): 33.

19. Kai Kaufmann, "Von Minne und Krieg: Drei Stationen in Rudolf Borchardts Auseinandersetzungen mit Stefan George," *George-Jahrbuch* 6 (2006–2007): 74.

20. "Italien [war] damals unter deutscher Herrschaft, Dante [war] ein Anhänger des Kaisers, und die ganze Grundlage seiner Bildung [war] eine deutsche; dem Geiste nach [war] die *Divina Commedia* durchaus mittelalterlich deutsch" (Back then Italy was under German rule, Dante was a subject of the Kaiser, and the whole foundation of his education was German; the *Divina Commedia*, according to its spirit, is medieval German through and through). Herman Riegel, *Peter Cornelius: Festschrift zu des grossen Künstlers hundertstem Geburtstage, 23. September 1883* (Berlin: R. v. Decker, 1883), 103.

21. Borchardt remained sanguine about Hofmannsthal, but the *ästhetische Bewegung* had failed to develop a "süßen neuen Stil" (sweet new style). Its successes were illusory (GW, *Reden* 111–112).

22. Henry Wadsworth Longfellow, *The Divine Comedy of Dante Alighieri*, vol. 9 of *The Works of Henry Wadsworth Longfellow*, ed. Charles Welsh (New York: Davos Press, 1909), 104. I have chosen to cite the translation of Longfellow for its archaicizing tendencies, but this is admittedly a (very) imperfect way of rendering Borchardt's translation. The reader of English might imagine a modernist who translates Dante into an English that he imagines approximates the language of Langland or Chaucer. This, too, is an imperfect analogy, but closer to the endeavor Borchardt was attempting.

23. Karl Vossler, *Dante als religiöser Dichter* (Bern: Seldwyla, 1921), 15.

24. Ernst Robert Curtius, "Neue Dante-Studien I," *Romanische Forschungen* 60, no. 2 (1947): 241.

25. George Caffrey, "Rudolf Borchardt," *The Criterion* 5, no. 1 (1927): 81–87.

26. George Steiner, *After Babel: Aspects of Language and Translation*, 3rd ed. (New York: Oxford University Press, 1998), 356.

27. Wolfgang Schieder, *Mythos Mussolini* (Munich: Oldenbourg, 2013), 271.

28. Marie von Bunsen, *Die Welt in der ich Lebte* (Leipzig: Koehler & Amelang, 1929), 153.

29. Boehringer, *Mein Bild von Stefan George*, 12.

30. Georg Bondi, *Erinnerungen an Stefan George* (Düsseldorf: Küpper, 1965), 12.

31. Friedrich Gundolf, *Goethe* (Berlin: Bondi, 1916); Friedrich Gundolf, *George* (Berlin: Bondi, 1920).

32. George and Gundolf, *Stefan George–Friedrich Gundolf*, 77.

33. Landmann, *Gespräche mit Stefan George*, 105.

34. A facsimile edition was produced in 1909. The first widely published volume of his translations appeared in 1912.

35. This requirement is recorded in the so-called Index zur Bibliothek eines jungen Menschen (Index for the library of a young man), a curricular device used for pedagogical purposes within the Kreis. A copy of the list is available in Carola Groppe, *Die Macht der Bildung: Das deutsche Bürgertum und der George-Kreis 1890–1933* (Cologne: Böhlau, 1997), 482.

36. Karl Wolfskehl and Hannah Wolfskehl, *Briefwechsel mit Friedrich Gundolf, 1899–1931*, vol. 1 (Amsterdam: Castrum Peregrini, 1977), 204.

37. Eva Hölter, *Der Dichter der Hölle und des Exils: Historische und systematische Profile der deutschsprachigen Dante-Rezeption* (Würzburg: Königshausen & Neumann, 2002), 136–137.

38. Poems from the volume are cited by page number, unless noted otherwise.

39. Boehringer, *Mein Bild von Stefan George*, 12–13.

40. The image repeats itself in "Das Sechste" (The sixth) (SGSW 6/7:104).

41. Robert Norton, *Secret Germany: Stefan George and His Circle* (Ithaca, NY: Cornell University Press, 2002), 331.

42. Norton, *Secret Germany*, 333; Thomas Karlauf, *Die Entdeckung des Charisma* (Munich: Blessing, 2007), 345.

43. Norton, *Secret Germany*, 326.

44. Morwitz, *Kommentar zu dem Werk Stefan Georges* , 215–216.

45. Morwitz, *Kommentar zu dem Werk Stefan Georges*, 268; Norton, *Secret Germany*, 326.

46. Morwitz, *Kommentar zu dem Werk Stefan Georges*, 268. Morwitz's attempt to desexualize "Maximin" seems congruent with what Adrian Daub has described as a postwar phenomenon among George's adherents: "Even when they presented evidence of the imbrication of homoeroticism and esotericism, George's postwar propagandists took to eliding that imbrication, often denying both elements in one fell swoop." Adrian Daub, "From Maximin to Stonewall: Sexuality and the Afterlives of the George Circle," *The Germanic Review* 87, no. 1 (2012): 22.

47. Ernst Glöckner, *Begegnung mit Stefan George*, ed. Friedrich Adam (Heidelberg: Stiehm, 1972), 25.

48. Armin Schäfer, *Die Intensität der Form: Stefan Georges Lyrik* (Cologne: Böhlau, 2005), 225.

49. *Der Stern des Bundes* was released in a few copies in 1913 and widely in 1914.

50. Schäfer, *Die Intensität der Form*, 223.

51. Lorenzo Bianchi, *Stefan George und Dante: Einführung in ein Problem* (Bologna: N. Zanichelli, 1936), 9; Claude David, *Stefan George: Sein dichterisches Werk*, trans. Alexa Remmen and Karl Thiemer (Munich: Hanser, 1967), 202.

52. Friedrich Gundolf, "Gefolgschaft und Jüngertum," *Blätter für die Kunst* 8 (1908–1909): 110.

53. Other departures from Dante's text suggest a proclivity to code Latini's gestures as more unequivocally sexual. One of these is the inclusion of the word *begehrte* (from *begehren* = to desire, covet), which lacks an equivalent in Dante's text.

54. Bertram Schefold has argued this formulation derives from Dante's Saint Bernard of Clairveaux; see Bertram Schefold, "Stefan George als Übersetzer Dantes," *Deutsches Dante-Jahrbuch* 83, no. 1 (2008): 235.

55. The translation is my own. For reference, compare George's translation of Cacciaguida's speech to that of Borchardt (above).

56. Friedrich Gundolf and Elisabeth Salomon, *Friedrich Gundolf–Elisabeth Salomon: Briefwechsel (1914–1931)*, ed. Gunilla Eschenbach, Helmuth Mojem, and Michael Matthiesen (Berlin: de Gruyter, 2015), 510.

57. Friedrich Gundolf, "Dante," *Castrum Peregrini* 91 (1970): 30–31.

58. Bernhard Zeller, ed., *Stefan George, 1868–1968: Der Dichter und sein Kreis: Eine Ausstellung des Deutschen Literaturarchivs im Schiller-Nationalmuseum Marbach am Neckar* (Munich: Kosel, 1968), 80.

59. See especially note 11 in Curtius, "Neue Dante-Studien I," 249–250.

60. Kurt Hildebrandt, *Erinnerungen an Stefan George und Seinen Kreis* (Bonn: Bouvier, 1965), 280–281.

61. Zeller, *Stefan George, 1868–1968*, 132.

62. Hildebrandt, *Erinnerungen an Stefan George*, 280.

Chapter Six Thomas Mann and the Demythologization of Dante

1. Whitman's collection *Calamus* is linked by name to the ancient Greek myth of Kalamos, a youth who drowned himself after his male lover had drowned in a swimming contest. Kalamos was said to be transformed into the reed whose rustling now connotes grieving.

2. Ernst Glöckner was long a disciple of George, while his partner, Ernst Bertram, knew George but maintained a critical distance.

3. Ironically, Mann first conceived the novel as a smaller project that would complement *Der Tod in Venedig* (*Death in Venice*), a novella that had offended George for its unabashed homoeroticism; see Ernst Glöckner, *Begegnung mit Stefan George*, ed. Friedrich Adam (Heidelberg: Stiehm, 1972), 25. In a further irony, that novella's protagonist, Aschenbach, hounds younger men much like George had done (e.g., Hugo von Hofmannsthal, Maximilian Kronberger, among others).

4. See chapter five.

5. Stephen Dowden, "Mann's Ethical Style," in *A Companion to Thomas Mann's* The Magic Mountain, ed. Stephen Dowden (Columbia, SC: Camden House, 1999), 14–40, 30.

6. As Michael Naumann, the commentator of the novel in the *Große kommentierte Frankfurter Ausgabe*, points out, George's disciple, Ernst Bertram, had led Mann to Adalbert Stifter and the snowstorm in *Bergkristall* (*Rock Crystal*), which forms another intertext of this scene (GkFA 5.2:304–305).

7. Oskar Seidlin, "The Lofty Game of Numbers: The Mynheer Peeperkorn Episode in Thomas Mann's *Der Zauberberg*," *PMLA* 86, no. 5 (1971): 929.

8. The chapter is a doubly incisive barb at George. Its depiction of Peeperkorn's French sympathies (a French card game, his dissatisfaction with sausages, his pleasure over omelets, his choice of French and Swiss wines) calls into question the Germanness of George's secret Germany. After all, the Meister had studied under Mallarmé and spent the War in Switzerland.

9. The appearance of the ouroborous in Peeperkorn's death is likewise noted by Michael Minden; see Michael Minden, "Mann's Literary Techniques," in *The Cambridge Companion to Thomas Mann*, ed. Ritchie Roberson (Cambridge: Cambridge University Press, 2002), 43–63, 55. It is worth noting, too, that Peeperkorn has long been recognized as a satirization of Hauptmann; see Hans Rudolf Vaget, "The Making of *The Magic Mountain*," in *Thomas Mann's* The Magic Mountain: *A Casebook*, ed. Hans Rudolf Vaget (New York: Oxford University Press, 2008), 13–30. Inasmuch as the figure, by the present reading, merges Hauptmann and George, it is an especially economical mockery of *Mystifikation*.

10. Gunilla Bergsten, *Thomas Mann's* Doctor Faustus*: Sources and Structure of the Novel* (Chicago: University of Chicago Press, 1969), 31.

11. Mann wrote that the model for Daniel zur Höhe was Ludwig Derleth, a poet who published in George's *Blätter für die Kunst*. He was also parodied in Mann's short story *Beim Propheten* (*At the Prophet's*). Georg Vogler is a fairly transparent imitation of Josef Nadler, a Germanist whose *Literaturgeschichte der deutschen Stämme und Landschaften* (Literary history of the German tribes and landscapes, 1912–1928) had won the approbation of Rudolf Borchardt. On these, and other models in the Kridwiss-Kreis, see Bergsten, *Thomas Mann's* Doctor Faustus, 28–34.

12. Notice, as well, that the inspiration is French. As he had in the case of Peeperkorn, as well as in the speech "Von deutscher Republik," Mann needles the secret Germany for its French heritage.

13. Bergsten, *Thomas Mann's* Doctor Faustus, 94.

14. These include Ascanio Condivi, Giorgio Vasari, Donato Giannotti, and Benedetto Varchi. On this see Bernadine Barnes, "Metaphorical Painting: Michelangelo, Dante, and the *Last Judgment*," *The Art Bulletin* 77, no. 1 (1995): 64–81.

15. Barnes, "Metaphorical Painting," 64.

Conclusion

1. Thomas Taterka, *Dante Deutsch: Studien zur Lagerliteratur* (Berlin: Erich Schmidt, 1999).

2. Arno Widmann, "Dante: Die Guten ins Töpfchen, die Schlechten ins Kröpfchen," *Frankfurter Rundschau*, March 26, 2021, https://www.fr.de/kultur/literatur/dante-die-guten-ins-toepfchen-die-schlechten-ins-kroepfchen-90259881.html.

3. Manfred Frank, *Der kommende Gott: Vorlesungen über die neue Mythologie* (Frankfurt: Suhrkamp, 1982); Manfred Frank, *Gott im Exil* (Frankfurt: Suhrkamp, 1988); George S. Williamson, *The Longing for Myth in Germany: Religion and Aesthetic Culture from Romanticism to Nietzsche* (Chicago: University of Chicago Press, 2004).

BIBLIOGRAPHY

Acocella, Joan. "Cloud Nine: A New Translation of the *Paradiso*." *New Yorker*, August 27, 2007. https://www.newyorker.com/magazine/2007/09/03/cloud-nine.

Adler, Jeremy. "The Aesthetics of Magnetism: Science, Philosophy and Poetry in the Dialogue between Goethe and Schelling." In *The Third Culture: Literature and Science*, edited by Elinor S. Shaffer, 66–102. Berlin: de Gruyter, 1998.

Ahearn, Edward. *Visionary Fictions: Apocalyptic Writing from Blake to the Modern Age*. New Haven, CT: Yale University Press, 1996.

Arrighetti, Anna Maria. "Dante · *Die Göttliche Komödie. Übertragungen*." In *Stefan George und sein Kreis: Ein Handbuch*, edited by Achim Aurnhammer, Wolfgang Braungart, Stefan Breuer, and Ute Oelmann, 2nd ed., vol. 1, 218–253. Berlin: de Gruyter, 2016.

Ascoli, Albert Russell. *Dante and the Making of a Modern Author*. Cambridge: Cambridge University Press, 2011.

Auer, Flavio. "Schelling über Dantes *Commedia* und Goethes *Faust* als neue Mythologien." *Scientia Poetica* 24, no. 1 (2020): 115–132.

Auerbach, Erich. *Dante als Dichter der irdischen Welt*. Berlin: de Gruyter, 1969.

Auerbach, Erich. "Dante's Addresses to the Reader." *Romance Philology* 7 (1953–1954): 268–278.

Auerbach, Erich. "Entdeckung Dantes in der Romantik." In *Gesammelte Aufsätze zur romanischen Philologie*, 2nd ed., edited by Matthias Bormuth and Martin Vialon, 172–179. Tübingen: Narr Francke, 2018.

Auerbach, Erich. "Figura." In *Time, History, and Literature: Selected Essays of Erich Auerbach*, translated by Jane Newman, edited by James Porter, 65–113. Princeton, NJ: Princeton University Press, 2015.

Augustine. *Confessions*. Translated by Henry Chadwick. New York: Oxford University Press, 1991.

Barck, Karl-Heinz, and Martin Treml. *Erich Auerbach: Geschichte und Aktualität eines europäischen Philologen*. Berlin: Kadmos, 2007.

Barnes, Bernadine. "Metaphorical Painting: Michelangelo, Dante, and the *Last Judgment*." *The Art Bulletin* 77, no. 1 (1995): 64–81.

Barolini, Teodolinda. *The Undivine* Comedy: *Detheologizing Dante*. Princeton, NJ: Princeton University Press, 1992.

Becker, Claudia. "'Im Allerheiligsten, wo Religion und Poesie verbündet'—F.W.J. Schellings Aufsatz 'Über Dante in philosophischer Beziehung' im Kontext der idealistischen Bemühungen um eine neue Mythologie." In *Poetische Autonomie? Zur Wechselwirkung von Dichtung und Philosophie in der Epoche Goethes und Hölderlins*, edited by Helmut Bachmaier and Thomas Rentsch, 308–328. Stuttgart: Klett-Cotta, 1987.

Béguin, Albert. *L'âme romantique et le rêve: Essai sur le romantisme allemand et la poésie française*. Marseilles: Cahiers du Sud, 1937.

Behl, Carl Friedrich Wilhelm. *Zwiesprache mit Gerhart Hauptmann*. Munich: Desch, 1948.

Behler, Ernst. "Dante in Germany." In *Dante Encyclopedia*, edited by Richard Lansing, 262–269. New York: Routledge, 2010.

Behler, Ernst. *German Romantic Literary Theory*. Cambridge: Cambridge University Press, 1993.

Beiser, Frederick. *German Idealism: The Struggle against Subjectivism, 1781–1801*. Cambridge, MA: Harvard University Press, 2002.

Beiser, Frederick. *The Romantic Imperative: The Concept of Early German Romanticism*. Cambridge, MA: Harvard University Press, 2003.

Benjamin, Walter. *Der Begriff der Kunstkritik in der deutschen Romantik*. Frankfurt: Suhrkamp, 1973.

Benjamin, Walter. "Wider ein Meisterwerk." In *Gesammelte Schriften*, edited by Hella Tiedemann-Bartels, vol. 3. Frankfurt: Suhrkamp, 1972.

Bergsten, Gunilla. *Thomas Mann's* Doctor Faustus: *Sources and Structure of the Novel*. Chicago: University of Chicago Press, 1969.

Bianchi, Lorenzo. *Stefan George und Dante: Einführung in ein Problem*. Bologna: N. Zanichelli, 1936.

Binswanger, Hans Christoph. *Money and Magic: A Critique of the Modern Economy in the Light of Goethe's* Faust. Chicago: University of Chicago Press, 1994.

Blake, William. "A Vision of the Last Judgment." In *Complete Writings*, edited by Geoffrey Keynes, 604–617. Oxford: Oxford University Press, 1966.

Blumenberg, Hans. *Work on Myth*. Translated by Robert M. Wallace. Cambridge, MA: MIT Press, 1985.

Boccaccio, Giovanni. *Life of Dante*. Edited and translated by G. R. Carpenter. New York: Grolier, 1900.

Bodmer, Johann Jakob. "Über das dreyfache Gedicht des Dante." In *Schriften zur Literatur*, edited by Volker Meid, 283–294. Stuttgart: Reclam, 1980.

Boehringer, Robert. *Mein Bild von Stefan George*. Düsseldorf: Helmut Küpper vormals Georg Bondi, 1968.

Boettcher, Magdalena. *Eine andere Ordnung der Dinge: Zur Ästhetik des Schönen und ihrer poetologischen Rezeption um 1800*. Würzburg: Königshausen und Neumann, 1998.

Bohrer, Karl Heinz. "Friedrich Schlegels Rede über die Mythologie." In *Mythos und Moderne*, edited by Karl Heinz Bohrer, 52–82. Frankfurt: Suhrkamp, 1983.

Bondi, Georg. *Erinnerungen an Stefan George*. Düsseldorf: Küpper, 1965.

Borchardt, Rudolf. *Aufzeichnung Stefan George betreffend*. Edited by Ernst Osterkamp. Munich: Rudolf Borchardt-Gesellschaft, 1998.

Borchardt, Rudolf. *Briefe 1895–1906*. Munich: Hanser, 1995.

Borchardt, Rudolf. *Gesammelte Werke in Einzelbänden*. Edited by Marie Luise Borchardt. 14 vols. Stuttgart: Ernst Klett, 1955–.

Borchmeyer, Dieter. *Weimarer Klassik: Portrait einer Epoche*. Weinheim: Beltz Athenäum, 2009.

Boyle, Nicholas. *Goethe: The Poet and the Age*. Oxford: Oxford University Press, 2000.

Broch, Hermann. *Der Tod des Vergil*. Zürich: Rhein, 1945.

Brown, Jane. *Faust: Theater of the World*. New York: Twayne, 1992.

Budzinski-Luftig, Annette. "The Divine Comedy of Education: Curious German Encounters with Dante." PhD diss., Johns Hopkins University, 2010.

Bunsen, Marie von. *Die Welt in der ich Lebte*. Leipzig: Koehler & Amelang, 1929.

Büttner, Frank. *Peter Cornelius: Fresken und Freskenprojekte*. 2 vols. Wiesbaden: Steiner, 1980–1999.

Caesar, Michael. *Dante: The Critical Heritage, 1314(?)–1870*. London: Routledge, 1989.

Caffrey, George. "Rudolf Borchardt." *The Criterion* 5, no. 1 (1927): 81–87.

Camilletti, Fabio, Manuele Gragnolati, and Fabian Lampart, eds. *Metamorphosing Dante: Appropriations, Manipulations, and Rewritings in the Twentieth and Twenty-First Centuries*. Vienna: Turia + Kant, 2011.

Carolsfeld, Julius Schnorr von. *Briefe aus Italien geschrieben in den Jahren 1817 bis 1827*. Gotha: Perthes, 1886.

Carossa, Hans. *Tagebücher, 1925–1935*. Edited by Eva Kampmann-Carossa. Frankfurt: Insel, 1993.

Carranza, Daniel. "The (Dis)Consolations of Form. On the Temporality of Rhyme in Goethe's *Im ernsten Beinhaus war's*." In *Goethes Spätwerk*, edited by Kai Sina and David Wellbery, 99–140. Berlin: de Gruyter, 2020.

Cassirer, Ernst. *The Myth of the State*. New Haven, CT: Yale University Press, 1946.

Croce, Benedetto. *La Poesia di Dante*. Bari: Laterza & Figli, 1921.

Curtius, Ernst Robert. "Neue Dante-Studien I." *Romanische Forschungen* 60, no. 2 (1947): 237–289.

Daffner, Hugo. "Goethe und Dante." *Dante-Jahrbuch* 5 (1920): 166–172.

Dante. *Vita Nuova*. Translated by Mark Musa. New York: Oxford University Press, 1992.

Daub, Adrian. "From Maximin to Stonewall: Sexuality and the Afterlives of the George Circle." *The Germanic Review* 87, no. 1 (2012): 19–34.

David, Claude. *Stefan George: Sein dichterisches Werk*. Translated by Alexa Remmen and Karl Thiemer. Munich: Hanser, 1967.

de Man, Paul. *The Rhetoric of Romanticism*. New York: Columbia University Press, 1984.

Dilthey, Wilhelm. *Das Erlebnis und die Dichtung: Lessing, Goethe, Novalis, Hölderlin*. Leipzig: Teubner, 1922.

DiMassa, Daniel. "Der göttliche Poet: Romantische Selbstmythologisierung in Goethes Terzinen." *Goethe-Jahrbuch* 131 (2014): 59–70.

DiMassa, Daniel. "Stefan George, Thomas Mann, and the Politics of Homoeroticism." *The German Quarterly* 86, no. 3 (2013): 311–333.

DiMassa, Daniel. "Varieties of Radical Enlightenment: Secularization as Translation in Goethe's Autobiography." *Religion & Literature* 48, no. 1 (2016): 51–69.

Donehower, Bruce. *The Birth of Novalis: Friedrich von Hardenberg's Journal of 1797, with Selected Letters and Documents*. Albany: State University of New York Press, 2015.

Dowden, Stephen. "Mann's Ethical Style." In *A Companion to Thomas Mann's* The Magic Mountain, edited by Stephen Dowden, 14–40. Columbia, SC: Camden House, 1999.

Dronke, Peter. *Dante and Medieval Latin Traditions*. Cambridge: Cambridge University Press, 1986.

Eckermann, Johann Peter. *Gespräche mit Goethe in den letzten Jahren seines Lebens*. 3 vols. Leipzig: Brockhaus, 1836–1848.

Eliade, Mircea. *Cosmos and History: The Myth of the Eternal Return*. Translated by Willard Trask. New York: Harper, 1954.

Ensenzberger, Hans Magnus. *Der Untergang der Titanic: Eine Komödie*. Frankfurt: Suhrkamp, 2016.

Farinelli, Arturo. *Dante in Spagna–Francia–Inghilterra–Germania (Dante e Goethe)*. Turin: Fratelli Bocca, 1922.

Frank, Manfred. *Der kommende Gott: Vorlesungen über die neue Mythologie*. Frankfurt: Suhrkamp, 1982.

Frank, Manfred. *Gott im Exil*. Frankfurt: Suhrkamp, 1988.

Frank, Manfred. "Wie reaktionär war eigentlich die Frühromantik?" *Athenäum: Jahrbuch für Romantik* 7 (1997): 141–166.

Franzel, Sean. *Connected by the Ear: The Media, Pedagogy, and Politics of the Romantic Lecture*. Evanston, IL: Northwestern University Press, 2013.

Friederich, Werner P. *Dante's Fame Abroad, 1350–1850: The Influence of Dante Alighieri on the Poets and Scholars of Spain, France, England, Germany, Switzerland and the United States: A Survey of the Present State of Scholarship*. Rome: Edizioni di Storia e letteratura, 1950.

Friedländer, Paul. *Rhythmen und Landschaften im zweiten Teil des Faust*. Weimar: Böhlaus Nachfolger, 1953.

Fuchs, Clara Charlotte. "Dante in der deutschen Romantik." *Deutsches Dante-Jahrbuch* 15 (1933): 61–131.

Gaier, Ulrich. *Johann Wolfgang von Goethe: Faust. Der Tragödie zweiter Teil*. Stuttgart: Reclam, 2004.

George, Stefan. *Der Siebente Ring*. Berlin: Blätter für die Kunst, 1907.

George, Stefan, and Friedrich Gundolf. *Stefan George—Friedrich Gundolf: Briefwechsel*. Edited by Robert Boehringer and Georg Peter Landmann. Munich: Helmut Küpper, 1962.

George, Stefan, and Hugo von Hofmannsthal. *Briefwechsel zwischen George und Hofmannsthal*. Munich: Helmut Küpper, 1953.

Gerstenberg, Kurt, and Paul Rave. *Die Wändgemälde der deutschen Romantiker im Casino Massimo zu Rom*. Berlin: DVFK, 1934.

Glöckner, Ernst. *Begegnung mit Stefan George*. Edited by Friedrich Adam. Heidelberg: Stiehm, 1972.

Goethe, Johann Wolfgang. *Faust: Texte*. Edited by Albrecht Schöne. Frankfurt: Deutscher Klassiker Verlag, 2017.

Groppe, Carola. *Die Macht der Bildung: Das deutsche Bürgertum und der George-Kreis 1890–1933*. Cologne: Böhlau, 1997.

Gundolf, Friedrich. "Dante." *Castrum Peregrini* 91 (1970): 30–39.

Gundolf, Friedrich. "Das Bild Georges." *Jahrbuch für die geistige Bewegung* 1 (1910): 19–48.

Gundolf, Friedrich. "Gefolgschaft und Jüngertum." *Blätter für die Kunst* 8 (1908–1909): 106–112.

Gundolf, Friedrich. *George*. Berlin: Bondi, 1920.

Gundolf, Friedrich. *Goethe*. Berlin: Bondi, 1916.

Gundolf, Friedrich, and Elisabeth Salomon. *Friedrich Gundolf–Elisabeth Salomon: Briefwechsel (1914–1931)*. Edited by Gunilla Eschenbach, Helmuth Mojem, and Michael Matthiesen. Berlin: de Gruyter, 2015.

Guthke, Karl. "Die Mythologie des späten Gerhart Hauptmann." *Monatshefte* 49, no. 6 (1957): 289–303.

Hadot, Pierre. *The Veil of Isis: An Essay on the History of the Idea of Nature*. Cambridge, MA: Belknap Press of Harvard University Press, 2008.

Haller, Robert S. *Literary Criticism of Dante Alighieri*. Lincoln: University of Nebraska Press, 1973.

Halmi, Nicholas. *The Genealogy of the Romantic Symbol*. New York: Oxford University Press, 2011.

Hausmann, Frank-Rutger. *"Italien in Germanien": Deutsche Italien-Rezeption von 1750–1850*. Tübingen: Gunter Narr, 1996.

Haym, Rudolf. *Die romantische Schule*. Berlin: Gaertner, 1870.

Hegel, G.W.F. "Das älteste Systemprogramm des deutschen Idealismus." In *Frühe Schriften*, edited by Eva Moldenhauer and Karl Markus Michel, 234–237. Vol. 1 of *Werke*. Frankfurt: Suhrkamp, 1971.

Hegel, G.W.F. *Vorlesungen über die Ästhetik I*. In *Werke*, edited by Eva Moldenhauer and Karl Markus Michel, vol. 13. Frankfurt: Suhrkamp, 1970.

Heidegger, Martin. *Was heisst Denken?* Tübingen: Niemeyer, 1954.

Heine, Heinrich. *Die Romantische Schule*. Hamburg: Hoffmann und Campe, 1836.

Herder, Johann Gottfried. "Vom neuern Gebrauch der Mythologie." In *Frühe Schriften 1764–1772*, edited by Ulrich Gaier, 432–455. Vol. 1 of *Werke in zehn Bänden*. Frankfurt: Deutscher Klassiker Verlag, 1985.

Herwig, Wolfgang, ed. *Goethes Gespräche: Eine Sammlung zeitgenössischer Berichte aus seinem Umgang*. 3 vols. Zürich: Artemis Verlag, 1965–1972.

Heyne, C. G. "Inquiry into the Causes of Fables." In *The Rise of Modern Mythology 1680–1860*, edited and translated by Burton Feldman and Robert D. Richardson, 218–220. Bloomington: Indiana University Press, 1972.

Hildebrandt, Kurt. *Erinnerungen an Stefan George und Seinen Kreis*. Bonn: Bouvier, 1965.

Hirdt, Willi. "Goethe und Dante." *Deutsches Dante-Jahrbuch* 68/69 (1993/1994): 31–80.

Hitler, Adolf. *Mein Kampf*. Munich: Eher Verlag, 1943.

Hofmannsthal, Hugo von. "Das Schrifttum als geistiger Raum der Nation." In *Reden und Aufsätze III*, edited by Bernd Schoeller, 24–41. Vol. 10 of *Gesammelte Werke in zehn Einzelbänden*. Frankfurt: Fischer, 1980.

Hogrebe, Wolfram. "Schelling und Dante." *Deutsches Dante-Jahrbuch* 62 (1987): 7–31.

Hollander, Robert. "Dante and His Commentators." In *The Cambridge Companion to Dante*, edited by Rachel Jacoff, 226–236. New York: Cambridge University Press, 1993.

Hollander, Robert. *Dante's Epistle to Can Grande*. Ann Arbor: University of Michigan Press, 1993.

Hollander, Robert. "*Vita nuova*: Dante's Perceptions of Beatrice." *Dante Studies* 92 (1974): 1–18.

Höltenschmidt, Edith. *Die Mittelalter-Rezeption der Brüder Schlegel*. Paderborn: Schöningh, 2000.

Hölter, Achim. "Zur Rezeption der italienischen Literatur in der deutschen Frühromantik." In *Deutsche und italienische Romantik: Referate des Bad Homburger Colloquiums in der Werner-Reimers-Stiftung*, edited by Enrico de Angelis, 49–86. Pisa: Jacques e i suoi Quaderni, 1989.

Hölter, Eva. "Dante's Long Road to the German Library: Literary Reception from Early Romanticism until the Late Nineteenth Century." In *Dante in the Long Nineteenth Century*, edited by Aida Audeh and Nick Havely, 225–247. Oxford: Oxford University Press, 2012.

Hölter, Eva. *Der Dichter der Hölle und des Exils: Historische und systematische Profile der deutschsprachigen Dante-Rezeption*. Würzburg: Königshausen & Neumann, 2002.

Honig, Edwin. *Dark Conceit: The Making of Allegory*. Evanston, IL: Northwestern University Press, 1959.

Horkheimer, Max, and Theodor W. Adorno. *Dialektik der Aufklärung: Philosophische Fragmente*. Frankfurt: Fischer, 2019.

Hösle, Vittorio. *Dantes Commedia und Goethes Faust: Ein Vergleich der beiden wichtigsten philosophischen Dichtungen Europas*. Basel: Schwabe, 2014.

Hösle, Vittorio. "Religion of Art, Self-Mythicization and the Function of the Church Year in Goethe's *Italienische Reise*." *Religion & Literature* 38, no. 4 (2006): 1–25.

Howitt, Margaret. *Friedrich Overbeck: Sein Leben und Schaffen*. Edited by Margaret Howitt. Vol. 1. Freiburg: Herder'sche Verlagshandlung, 1886.

Immermann, Karl. *Karl Immermann's Dramatische Schriften*. Vol. 2. Leipzig: Klemm, 1832.

Israel, Jonathan. *Radical Enlightenment: Philosophy and the Making of Modernity 1650–1750*. Oxford: Oxford University Press, 2001.

Italiaander, Rolf. "Gerhart Hauptmann in Dresden 1943." *Gerhart Hauptmann Jahrbuch* 1 (1948): 121–140.

Jantz, Harold. "The Place of the 'Eternal-Womanly' in Goethe's Faust Drama." *PMLA* 68, no. 4 (1953): 791–805.

Jauss, Hans Robert. *Toward an Aesthetic of Reception*. Translated by Timothy Bahti. Minneapolis: University of Minnesota Press, 1982.

Karlauf, Thomas. *Die Entdeckung des Charisma*. Munich: Blessing, 2007.

Kaufmann, Kai. "Von Minne und Krieg: Drei Stationen in Rudolf Borchardts Auseinandersetzungen mit Stefan George." *George-Jahrbuch* 6 (2006–2007): 55–79.

Klopstock, Friedrich. *Werke und Briefe*. Edited by Horst Gronemeyer et al. 40 vols. Berlin: de Gruyter, 1974–.

Kommerell, Max. *Der Dichter als Führer in der deutschen Klassik: Klopstock, Herder, Goethe, Schiller, Jean Paul, Hölderlin*. Berlin: Bondi, 1928.

Körner, Josef, ed. *August Wilhelm und Friedrich Schlegel im Briefwechsel mit Schiller und Goethe*. Leipzig: Insel-Verlag, 1926.

Kunz, Hans. *Schellings Gedichte und dichterische Pläne*. Zürich: Juris-Verlag, 1955.

Lacoue-Labarthe, Phillippe, and Jean-Luc Nancy. *The Literary Absolute: The Theory of Literature in German Romanticism*. Translated by Philip Barnard. Albany: State University of New York Press, 1988.

Landmann, Edith. *Gespräche mit Stefan George*. Düsseldorf: Helmut Küpper vormals Georg Bondi, 1963.

Lange, Wolfgang, and Norbert Schnitzler. *Deutsche Italomanie in Kunst, Wissenschaft und Politik*. Munich: Wilhelm Fink, 2000.

Longfellow, Henry Wadsworth. *The Divine Comedy of Dante Alighieri*. Vol. 9 of *The Works of Henry Wadsworth Longfellow*, edited by Charles Welsh. New York: Davos Press, 1909.

Lukács, György. *Die Zerstörung der Vernunft: Der Weg des Irrationalismus von Schelling zu Hitler*. Berlin: Aufbau Verlag, 1954.

Luzzi, Joseph. *Romantic Europe and the Ghost of Italy*. New Haven, CT: Yale University Press, 2008.

Luzzi, Joseph. "This Could Be 'Heaven,' or This Could Be 'Hell.'" *New York Times*, April 19, 2013. https://www.nytimes.com/2013/04/21/books/review/dantes-divine-comedy-translated-by-clive-james.html.

Mähl, Hans-Joachim. *Die Idee des goldenen Zeitalters im Werk des Novalis: Studien zur Wesensbestimmung der frühromantischen Utopie und zu ihren ideengeschichtlichen Voraussetzungen*. 2nd ed. Tübingen: Niemeyer, 1994.

Mahoney, Dennis. "The Myth of Death and Resurrection in *Heinrich von Ofterdingen*." *South Atlantic Review* 48, no. 2 (1983): 52–66.

Mansen, Mirjam. *"Denn auch Dante ist unser!" Die deutsche Dante-Rezeption 1900–1950*. Tübingen: Niemeyer, 2003.

Mariotti, L. *Italy: General Views of Its History and Literature*. Vol. 1. London: Saunders and Otley, 1841.

Matuschek, Stefan. "Was heißt 'Mythologisieren'? Oder: Warum und wie sich die romantische Neue Mythologie der Aufklärung verdankt." In *Romantik und Revolution: Zum Reformpotential einer unpolitischen Bewegung*, edited by Klaus Ries, 71–82. Heidelberg: Universitätsverlag, 2012.

Meinhard, Johann Nicolaus. *Versuche über den Charakter und die Werke der besten Italiänischen Dichter*. Braunschweig: Waysenhaus-Buchhandlung, 1774.

Miles, David. *Hofmannsthal's Novel "Andreas": Memory and Self*. Princeton, NJ: Princeton University Press, 1972.

Minden, Michael. "Mann's Literary Techniques." In *The Cambridge Companion to Thomas Mann*, edited by Ritchie Roberson, 43–63. Cambridge: Cambridge University Press, 2002.

Moritz, Karl Philipp. *Götterlehre: Oder mythologische Dichtungen der Alten*. Berlin: Unger, 1791.

Morwitz, Ernst. *Kommentar zu dem Werk Stefan Georges*. Düsseldorf: Helmut Küpper vormals Georg Bondi, 1969.

Most, Glenn. "Dante's Greeks." *Arion: A Journal of Humanities and the Classics* 13, no. 3 (2006): 15–48.

Mülder-Bach, Inka. "Mahomets Gesang." In *Goethe Handbuch*, edited by Bernd Witte and Regine Otto, 99–107, vol 1. Stuttgart: Metzler, 2004.

Nardi, Bruno. *Dante e la cultura medievale*. Bari: Laterza, 1984.

Nassar, Dalia. *The Romantic Absolute: Being and Knowing in Early German Romantic Philosophy, 1795–1804*. Chicago: University of Chicago Press, 2014.

Nietzsche, Friedrich. *Menschliches, Allzumenschliches*. Edited by Giorgio Colli and Mazzino Montinari. Munich: DTV, 1988.

Nisbet, H. B. "Lucretius in Eighteenth-Century Germany: With a Commentary on Goethe's 'Metamorphose der Tiere.'" *Modern Language Review* 100 (2005): 115–133.

Norton, Robert. *Secret Germany: Stefan George and His Circle*. Ithaca, NY: Cornell University Press, 2002.

O'Brien, Wm. Arctander. *Novalis: Signs of Revolution*. Durham, NC: Duke University Press, 1995.

Osols-Wehden, Irmgard. *Pilgerfahrt und Narrenreise: Der Einfluss der Dichtungen Dantes und Ariosts auf den frühromantischen Roman in Deutschland*. Hildesheim: Weidmann, 1998.

Piper, Andrew. "Reading's Refrain: From Bibliography to Topology." *ELH* 80 (2013): 373–399.

Plath, Margarete. "Der Goethe-Schellingsche Plan eines philosophischen Naturgedichts: Eine Studie zu Goethes 'Gott und Welt.'" *Preußische Jahrbücher* 106 (1901): 44–74.

Plitt, G. L. *Aus Schellings Leben*. In *Briefen*, vol. 1. Leipzig: Hirzel, 1869.

Plöckinger, Othmar. *Geschichte eines Buches: Adolf Hitlers "Mein Kampf," 1922–1945*. Berlin: De Gruyter, 2011.

Radcliff-Umstead, Douglas. "Dante's Influence on *The Great Dream* of Gerhart Hauptmann." *Forum Italicum* 2, no. 1 (1968): 23–33.

Riegel, Herman. *Peter Cornelius: Festschrift zu des grossen Künstlers hundertstem Geburtstage, 23. September 1883*. Berlin: R. v. Decker, 1883.

Riley, Thomas. "Die Allegorie in *Ahnung und Gegenwart*." *Aurora: Jahrbuch der Eichendorff-Gesellschaft* 44 (1984): 23–31.

Ritter, Heinz. *Der unbekannte Novalis: Friedrich von Hardenberg im Spiegel seiner Dichtung*. Göttingen: Sachse & Pohl, 1967.

Roberts, William Clare. *Marx's Inferno: The Political Theory of Capital*. Princeton, NJ: Princeton University Press, 2018.

Ryan, Judith. "Hybrid Forms in German Romanticism." In *Prosimetrum: Crosscultural Perspectives on Narrative in Prose and Verse*, edited by Karl Reichl and Joseph Harris, 165–181. Suffolk, UK: Boydell and Brewer, 1997.

Safranski, Rudolf. *Goethe: Kunstwerk des Lebens*. Munich: Hanser, 2013.

Said, Edward. *On Late Style*. New York: Random House, 2006.

Schäfer, Armin. *Die Intensität der Form: Stefan Georges Lyrik*. Cologne: Böhlau, 2005.

Schefold, Bertram. "Stefan George als Übersetzer Dantes." *Deutsches Dante-Jahrbuch* 83, no. 1 (2008): 231–262.

Schelling, Caroline. *Briefe aus der Frühromantik*. Edited by Erich Schmidt. 2 vols. Leipzig: Insel, 1913.

Schieder, Wolfgang. *Mythos Mussolini*. Munich: Oldenbourg, 2013.

Schiller, Friedrich. *Schillers Werke: Nationalausgabe*. 43 vols. Weimar: Hermann Böhlaus Nachfolger, 1943–.

Schlaffer, Heinz. *Faust: Zweiter Teil: Die Allegorie des 19. Jahrhunderts*. Stuttgart: Metzler, 1981.

Schlegel, August Wilhelm, and Ludwig Tieck. *Musen-Almanach für das Jahr 1802*. Tübingen: Cotta, 1802.

Schleiermacher, Friedrich Daniel Ernst. *Über die Religion: Reden an die Gebildeten unter ihren Verächtern*. In *Kritische Gesamtausgabe*, edited by Hans-Joachim Birkner, Gerhard Ebeling, Hermann Fischer, Heinz Kimmerle, and Kurt-Victor Selge, 185–326. Erste Abteilung, vol. 2. Berlin: de Gruyter, 1984.

Schmitz, Rainer, ed. *Die ästhetische Prügeley: Streitschriften der antiromantischen Bewegung*. Göttingen: Wallstein, 1992.

Scholdt, Günter. *Autoren über Hitler: Deutschsprachige Schriftsteller (1919–1945) und ihr Bild vom Führer*. Bonn: Bouvier, 1993.

Schöne, Albrecht. *Faust: Kommentare*. Frankfurt: Deutscher Klassiker Verlag, 2017.

Schulz, Gerhard. "Mächtiges Überraschen." In *Goethe Handbuch*, edited by Bernd Witte and Regine Otto, 334–336, vol. 1. Stuttgart: Metzler, 2004.

Seidlin, Oskar. "The Lofty Game of Numbers: The Mynheer Peeperkorn Episode in Thomas Mann's *Der Zauberberg*." *PMLA* 86, no. 5 (1971): 924–939.

Shelley, Percy. "A Defence of Poetry." In *Shelley's Poetry and Prose: A Norton Critical Edition*, edited by Donald H. Reiman and Sharon B. Powers, 478–510. New York: Norton, 1977.

Singleton, Charles. "The Irreducible Dove." *Comparative Literature* 9, no. 2 (1957): 129–135.

Sprengel, Peter. *Gerhart Hauptmann: Bürgerlichkeit und großer Traum*. Munich: Beck, 2012.

Steiner, Arpad. "A Trace of Dante in Goethe's 'Ilmenau.'" *Modern Language Notes* 48, no. 2 (1933): 86–87.

Steiner, George. *After Babel: Aspects of Language and Translation*. 3rd ed. New York: Oxford University Press, 1998.

Stopp, Elisabeth. "'Übergang vom Roman zur Mythologie': Formal Aspects of the Opening Chapter of Hardenberg's *Heinrich von Ofterdingen, Part II*." *Deutsche Vierteljahrsschrift für Geistesgeschichte und Literaturwissenschaft* 48 (1974): 318–341.

Strauss, Walter. *Descent and Return: The Orphic Theme in Modern Literature*. Cambridge, MA: Harvard University Press, 1971.

Strich, Fritz. *Die Mythologie in der deutschen Literatur von Klopstock bis Wagner*. Bern: Francke, 1910.

Strobel, Jochen. "*Blumensträuße* für die Deutschen: August Wilhelm Schlegels produktive Rezeption der romanischen Poesie als Übersetzer und Literaturhistoriker." In *Der Europäer August Wilhelm Schlegel: Romantischer Kulturtransfer—romantische Wissenschaften*, edited by York-Gothart Mix and Jochen Strobel, 159–183. Berlin: De Gruyter, 2010.

Sulger-Gebing, Emil. "Dante in der deutschen Litteratur des XVIII. Jahrhunderts." *Zeitschrift für vergleichende Litteraturgeschichte* 9 (1896): 457–490.

Sulger-Gebing, Emil. *Goethe und Dante*. Berlin: Duncker, 1907.

Tamblin, Jeremy. *Allegory*. London: Routledge, 2010.

Taterka, Thomas. *Dante Deutsch: Studien zur Lagerliteratur*. Berlin: Erich Schmidt, 1999.

Tilliette, Xavier. *Schelling: Une Philosophie en Devenir*. Vol. 1. Paris: Librairie Philosophique J. Vrin, 1970.

Tobin, Robert. *Warm Brothers: Queer Theory and the Age of Goethe*. Philadelphia: University of Pennsylvania Press, 2000.

Triller, Daniel Wilhelm. *Poetische Betrachtungen*. Hamburg: Herold, 1751.

Vaget, Hans Rudolf. "The Making of *The Magic Mountain*." In *Thomas Mann's* The Magic Mountain: *A Casebook*, edited by Hans Rudolf Vaget, 13–30. New York: Oxford University Press, 2008.

Vietta, Silvio. "Dantes 'Matelda' und Novalis' 'Mathilde': Die säkularisierte Gestalt des irdischen Paradieses." In *Ästhetik, Religion, Säkularisierung: Von der Renaissance zur Romantik*, edited by Silvio Vietta and Herbert Uerlings, 111–131. Paderborn: Wilhelm Fink Verlag, 2008.

Voltaire. *Dictionnaire Philosophique*. Part II. In *Œuvres Complètes de Voltaire*, vol. 18. Paris: Garnier Frères, 1878.

Vossler, Karl. *Dante als religiöser Dichter*. Bern: Seldwyla, 1921.

Vossler, Karl. "Dante, Göttliche Komödie: Übertragen von Stefan George." *Deutsche Literaturzeitung* 36 (1912): 2288–2290.

Vossler, Karl. *Die göttliche Komödie: Entwicklungsgeschichte und Erklärung*. 2 vols. Heidelberg: Winter, 1907.

Wachtel, Michael. "Vyacheslav Ivanov: From Aesthetic Theory to Biographical Practice." In *Creating Life: The Aesthetic Utopia of Russian Modernism*, edited by Irina Paperno and Joan Grossman, 151–166. Stanford, CA: Stanford University Press, 1994.

Wais, Kurt. "Die *Divina Commedia* als dichterisches Vorbild im 19. und 20. Jahrhundert." In *Europäische Literatur im Vergleich: Gesammelte Aufsätze*, edited by Johannes Hösle, Dieter Janik, and Wolfgang Theile, 27–47. Tübingen: Niemeyer, 1983.

Weatherby, Leif. "The Risk of Theory: Romanticism, Science, Media." *German Quarterly* 89, no. 3 (2016): 352–354.

Weatherby, Leif. *Transplanting the Metaphysical Organ: German Romanticism between Leibniz and Marx*. New York: Fordham University Press, 2016.

Weiss, Peter. *Die Ermittlung*. Frankfurt: Suhrkamp, 1965.

Weissberg, Liliane. "Weimar and Jena: Goethe and the New Philosophy." In *Goethe und das Zeitalter der Romantik*, edited by Walter Hinderer, 163–174. Würzburg: Königshausen & Neumann, 2002.

Wellbery, David. "On the Logic of Change in Goethe's Work." *Goethe Yearbook* 21 (2014): 1–21.

Wellbery, David. *The Specular Moment: Goethe's Early Lyric and the Beginnings of Romanticism*. Stanford, CA: Stanford University Press, 1996.

Werfel, Franz. *Der Stern der Ungeborenen: Ein Reiseroman*. Stockholm: Bermann Fischer, 1946.

Wetters, Kirk. *Demonic History: From Goethe to the Present*. Evanston, IL: Northwestern University Press, 2014.

Wheeler, Kathleen. *German Aesthetic and Literary Criticism: The Romantic Ironists and Goethe*. New York: Cambridge University Press, 1984.

Whistler, Daniel. "Schelling's Poetry." *Clio* 43, no. 2 (2014): 143–175.

Widmann, Arno. "Dante: Die Guten ins Töpfchen, die Schlechten ins Kröpfchen." *Frankfurter Rundschau*, March 26, 2021. https://www.fr.de/kultur/literatur/dante-die-guten-ins-toepfchen-die-schlechten-ins-kroepfchen-90259881.html.

Williamson, George S. *The Longing for Myth in Germany: Religion and Aesthetic Culture from Romanticism to Nietzsche*. Chicago: University of Chicago Press, 2004.

Wills, Garry. *Augustine's Confessions: A Biography*. Princeton, NJ: Princeton University Press, 2011.

Wilson, W. Daniel. *Goethe Männer Knaben: Ansichten zur Homosexualität*. Berlin: Insel, 2012.

Wolfskehl, Karl, and Hannah Wolfskehl. *Briefwechsel mit Friedrich Gundolf, 1899–1931*. Vol. 1. Amsterdam: Castrum Peregrini, 1977.

Zeller, Bernhard, ed. *Stefan George, 1868–1968: Der Dichter und sein Kreis: Eine Ausstellung des Deutschen Literaturarchivs im Schiller-Nationalmuseum Marbach am Neckar*. Munich: Kosel, 1968.

INDEX

Note: Page numbers in *italics* indicate figures.

ABOUT THE AUTHOR

Daniel DiMassa is an assistant professor of German at Worcester Polytechnic Institute in Worcester, Massachusetts.